IMAGES
of America

LeSourdsville Lake Amusement Park

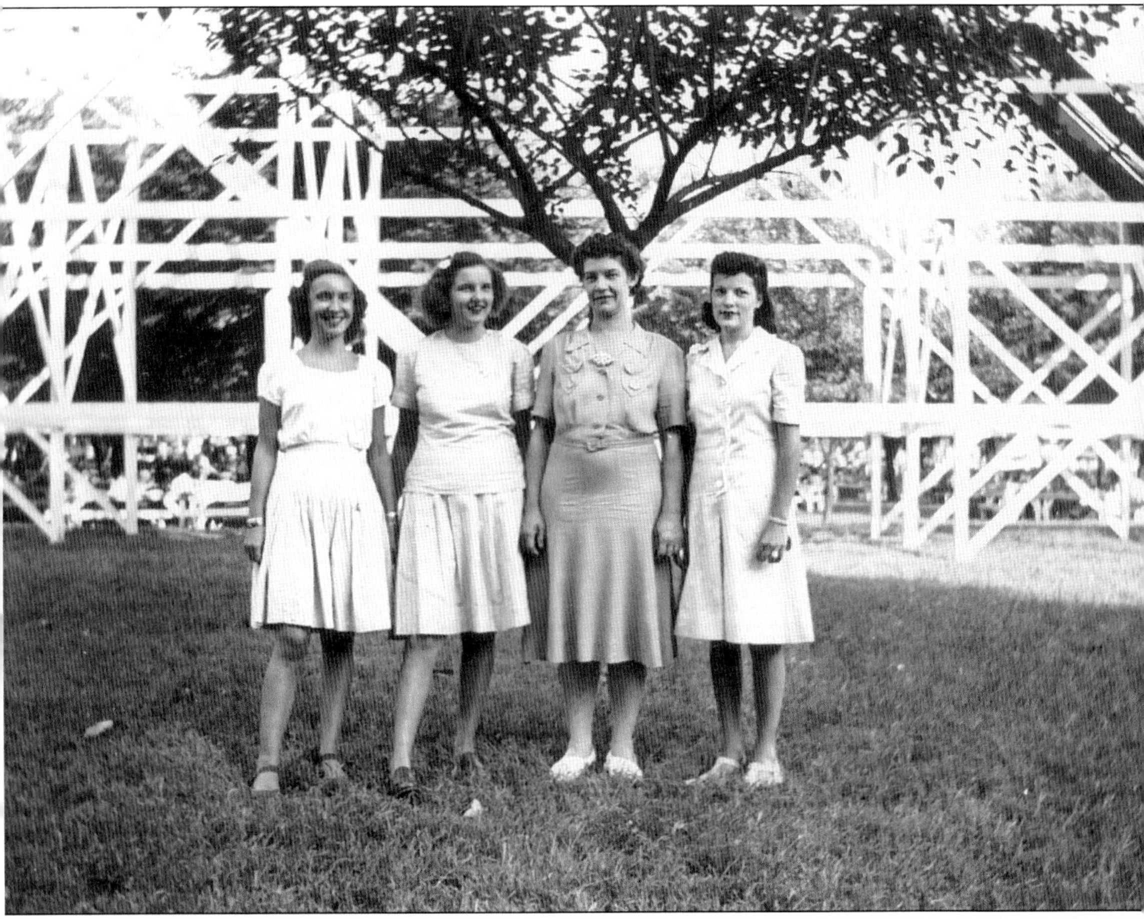

Pictured from left to right, Hamilton residents Elaine Simmons McMullen, Betty McMullen Fowler, Grace Thornley McMullen, and Janet Stumpf McMullen take a break in front of the legendary Cyclone roller coaster during a picnic in 1944. (Courtesy of Betty Fowler.)

On the Cover: The sandy beach at the park was a very popular place for all ages. This scene from the 1940s was captured by photographer Hayden Tobias from Middletown, Ohio. He was hired by the park to take all of the promotional photographs that were used for postcards and publicity material for several decades. Most of Mr. Tobias's work has "Tobias Photo" written in hand across the postcards. Hundreds of these postcards were printed and distributed throughout the area and can often be found for sale at antique stores and online auctions. (Courtesy of park archives.)

IMAGES
of America

LeSourdsville Lake Amusement Park

Scott Fowler

ARCADIA
PUBLISHING

ISBN 978-0-7385-8314-3

Published by Arcadia Publishing
Charleston, South Carolina

Printed in the United States of America

Library of Congress Control Number: 2010941411

For all general information, please contact Arcadia Publishing:
Telephone 843-853-2070
Fax 843-853-0044
E-mail sales@arcadiapublishing.com
For customer service and orders:
Toll-Free 1-888-313-2665

Visit us on the Internet at www.arcadiapublishing.com

To Betty and Jack Fowler, my mom and dad, who took me on those Sunday afternoon drives around southwest Ohio and enabled me to discover the rich history that this area affords.

Contents

Acknowledgments		6
Introduction		7
1.	The Rise of an Amusement Park	11
2.	New Challenges, New Direction	21
3.	The Little Giant Awakens	57
4.	Disasters Take Their Toll	115

ACKNOWLEDGMENTS

LeSourdsville Lake has served as a regional icon over five generations. Numerous newspaper articles have been written about the park since its inception in 1922. The park's founder, Edgar Streifthau, has made headlines of his own with a variety of lawsuits through the years. This book captures a small portion of information obtained from a variety of sources, including articles from the *Hamilton Journal-News*, the *Middletown Journal*, the *Hamilton Daily Republican*, and the *Hamilton Examiner*. Unless otherwise noted, all images were taken from park archives.

In addition, interviews have taken place over the years with Edgar Streifthau, former owners Howard and Mary Ann Berni, former park vice president William "Bill" Robinson, former partner Bill Barr, former vice president Ron Berni and his wife, Vicki, and former sales manager Debbie Berni Robison. We gratefully acknowledge their efforts in sharing their stories about the park.

Since 1997, I have maintained a website dedicated to LeSourdsville Lake (www.americanaamusementpark.com) featuring historical photographs, ride information, and letters from park patrons. We appreciate the many letters that describe the experiences of an employee's first job at the park, the couple that met and eventually got engaged on the midway, and the former manager who realized that LeSourdsville Lake was the best place he had ever worked.

Thanks go goes out to Wade Back, Ronny Salerno, George Siessel, Mac Tobias, Jerry Couch of Couch's Camper Sales, David Hahner, Rod Williams of WING-AM, Dianne Robinson, Dan Finfrock, Todd Shiverdecker, and Kevin Miller for their contributions of pictures. Many of the photographs in this book have never been published before or featured on the park's website. Thanks also to Arcadia editor Melissa Basilone for her patience and great editing skills.

Finally, I must acknowledge the LeSourdsville Lake fans on Facebook (facebook.com/lesourdsville.lake), the online social network. It is a great advantage to utilize traditional resources such as old newspapers and face-to-face interviews, but the fans on Facebook have been great to interact with as they share their experiences at the park. Many pictures submitted from these fans were considered for publication, but space did not permit us to use them.

Introduction

Today's amusement parks are reflections of our past—simple times when people just wanted a nice place to take the family and have enough change for an ice cream cone or a souvenir on the way home. LeSourdsville Lake in Middletown, Ohio, was reminiscent of amusement parks that dotted cities of all sizes across the country. LeSourdsville Lake, also known as Americana Amusement Park by a generation of visitors, managed to grow and bring in the thrill rides over the years despite being located within 12 miles of Kings Island, one of premier theme parks in the country. In the park's infancy, the rise of the automobile permitted people to not only go to LeSourdsville Lake but also Chester Park and Coney Island in Cincinnati, Lakeside and Frankie's Forest Park in Dayton, and Sandy Beach and Playland Park in Russell's Springs.

LeSourdsville Lake survived for decades by retaining yesteryear's carnival atmosphere that was prevalent at such renowned parks as Coney Island in New York, Riverview in Chicago, and Palisades in New Jersey. Each summer, companies, schools, hospitals, and churches converged on LeSourdsville Lake to celebrate time with their groups. Families visited the park as religiously as they drove the same route to work every day. The park hosted annual company picnics for some of the area's largest employers, including Ford, Champion Papers, Cinergy (Cincinnati Gas & Electric Company), AK Steel (Armco), and numerous hospitals, high school proms, and family reunions. The concept began in the mid-1930s and continued until the late 1990s. During that time, the park's infamous fried chicken was the highlight of every picnic.

However, it was a childhood memory of blocks of ice going down the Miami-Erie Canal that helped launch LeSourdsville Lake into becoming a nationally known amusement park.

Between 1600 and 1750, the LeSourdsville Lake area served as the battleground for Indian tribes from northern and southern Ohio. The northern Indians eventually were victorious and later settled in the area as far south as the Ohio River. The Miami Indians, who migrated from the Indiana Territory, also were settlers in the area. Because of the profitable trading activities between the Miami Indians and English and French traders, a rivalry developed between the English and the French. By 1763, the Miami were forced to leave the area, but other tribes from the New York region soon took their place.

In 1787, Chief Justice John Cleves Symmes of New Jersey purchased a million-acre tract of land in the southwestern Ohio area. In December of that year, the land that now encompasses LeSourdsville Lake was formed by a large group of Pennsylvania and New Jersey settlers. Four years later, one of the pioneers, Dr. Clarkson Freeman, purchased 631 acres of the Symmes Purchase at $5 per acre. Dr. Abraham Freeman then built the first home and sawmill on the property, and the village of LeSourdsville was born.

The area did not prosper until after the Miami-Erie Canal was routed through the property in 1828. Dr. Freeman's property was subdivided and sold in 1834 to four buyers at $30 per acre. One of those buyers was former French Army general Benjamin LeSourd. His ambition was to create a "great city." For a while, his dream almost came true. The village consisted of a blacksmith shop, packinghouse, sawmill, warehouse, a wagon wheel spoke manufacturing company, a post office, general store, two taverns, and 15 homes. The village was a major resting point for travelers riding stagecoaches or the canal boats between Dayton and Cincinnati. The canal stop also provided a point where local farmers could load their livestock and grain onto the boats for shipment to Cincinnati meat houses.

In 1855, LeSourd sold part of his property to the A.H. Knorr Company of Cincinnati. A dirt levee was built on 19 acres of farmland next to the canal to create a lake. The company erected 12 icehouses that measured 50 feet wide by 120 feet long by 28 feet high. The houses stored ice as it was cut from the lake during the winter. The ice was then shipped by boat to the company's office at Elm and Henry Streets in Cincinnati. From there, it was delivered by 74 ice wagons throughout the Cincinnati area. With the advent of ice manufacturing, the company found themselves a victim of late-1800s technology. The company sold the land to a Mr. Bender in 1892, and he used the land as a chicken farm. That business later failed, and the land was sold to Kentucky judge W.C. Taylor, who filled in the lake and farmed the property.

In 1920, Edgar Streifthau contacted Dan Hill, who owned a popular dance platform called Willow Grove on the Great Miami River, and offered him a deal. Hill rented tents from Streifthau's motorcycle and hardware store in Middletown, and Streifthau established a beach for swimming and camping facilities. Unfortunately, Mother Nature intervened and caused the beach to become a muddy and debris-ridden mess after heavy rains. Streifthau quickly gave up on Willow Grove location as a beach resort and continued to search for a more suitable location.

Streifthau then remembered his childhood home near the old A.H. Knorr Company lake in the village of LeSourdsville. He relived his memories of fishing and swimming in the lake. Streifthau attempted to convince his brother Ernest that the old lake could be rebuilt and used as a swimming area. Ernest was unimpressed with his brother's farfetched idea. Undaunted, Streifthau approached Judge Taylor and negotiated a deal. Streifthau arranged to lease the land for $600 annually for 10 years with a purchase option for $10,000 at the end of the lease. Local resident Bill Rothfuss was recruited to become Streifthau's partner.

Edgar Streifthau's first obstacle was to clear the cornfield and remove the numerous concrete foundations of the old icehouses. He rounded up some local help and spent three months digging up the old lake pit. Teams of horses fitted with slip scoops restored the south levee of the lake that bordered the Great Miami River. Other workers transformed part of the lake's perimeter into a resort area consisting of a dance hall, a bathhouse to serve 250 swimmers, a restaurant, and picnic area.

Streifthau used the old canal water to fill the lake. To provide a safe place to swim, Streifthau poured a concrete bottom in the lake, in addition to constructing a primitive diving board. A park-naming contest was conducted, and an unidentified Middletown girl won a $10 gold piece for her effort.

Rothfuss left after the first season, and Streifthau's brother Ernest became a partner. The park was operated as a resort until 1934, when Don Dazey was hired to design and construct a new bathhouse to replace one that had burned down weeks prior to the park opening. Dazey impressed Streifthau enough that he was asked to take over as park manager and become a partner. Dazey instituted a variety of changes that enabled LeSourdsville Lake to become a full-fledged amusement park and, eventually, the 27th largest park in the country.

After Dazey died in 1959, Streifthau sold LeSourdsville Lake to Howard Berni and Frank Murru. That partnership lasted until 1964, when Murru left and Bill Barr accepted a partnership.

In 1963, Edgar Streifthau opened a competing amusement park directly next door to LeSourdsville Lake called Fantasy Farm. One of the provisions in the sales contract stipulated that Streifthau was not to own an amusement park within 100 miles of LeSourdsville Lake for 10 years. Streifthau claimed that he only owned the land that the park sat on and that other personnel actually managed the park. A lawsuit was filed, and a judge determined that Streifthau was not an owner and that Fantasy Farm was targeting a different audience than LeSourdsville Lake.

Between 1964 and 1975, over a dozen rides and attractions were added to LeSourdsville Lake's lineup. In 1968, Frank Silvani took over catering and foods. Barr retired in 1975 and longtime park employee William "Bill" Robinson took over managing daily operations and promotions. In 1976, with the assistance of Robinson and the Butler County Bicentennial Commission, the park was named as the country's only Bicentennial Amusement Park.

After a major expansion culminated in 1978, the name of the park was changed to Americana Amusement Park. Berni's son Ron and son-in-law Guy Sutton were added to the management team. During the 1980s, Silvani passed away and Robinson left to open his own marketing firm, leaving Sutton to join International Theme Park Services. In 1990, Ron Berni left to become the operations manager of Kentucky Kingdom Amusement Park in Louisville, Kentucky.

After a major fire in January 1990 that was partially covered by insurance and the loss of local unions holding their annual picnics at the park, Berni was forced to file bankruptcy. In 1991, a group of former park personnel consisting of Guy Sutton, Joe Faggionato, Lenny Gottstein, and Don Robison purchased the park under the name Leisure International. In 1996, the park was sold to Park River Corporation, owners of Cincinnati's Coney Island. Park River abruptly sold the park to local businessman Jerry Couch in 2000.

The park was closed between 2000 and 2002 until Couch opened it back up and hired a former carnival operator to run the park. That company went bankrupt, and Couch decided to turn his focus on expanding his camper sales business, which was located in the parking lot of the park. In 2006, a large auction took place that resulted in over half of the rides being sold. Couch also purchased the former Fantasy Farm amusement park property and cleared the land except for a couple picnic shelters, the restaurant facility, and the former park office.

In 2008, some of the rides in LeSourdsville Lake's Kid's World were moved to new concrete pads on the site of Fantasy Farm's former warehouse and manufacturing building. In 2010, LeSourdsville's former circus tent was moved to the Fantasy Farm site. According to Couch, the plan is to create a small, private amusement park catering to corporate and private picnics and achieve his ultimate dream of establishing the only camper sales outlet in the country with its own amusement park.

One

THE RISE OF AN AMUSEMENT PARK

Within two years of opening the park, Edgar Streifthau stopped hosting dances because of the fights that occurred on a regular basis. Morris "Steamer" Moffatt of Canada became the first celebrity to appear at the park. He successfully rode a motorcycle 70 miles per hour, leaping 100 feet into the lake during a Fourth of July celebration in 1923. At the time, Moffatt held the world's record for motorcycle broad jumping with a 210-foot leap from land into Lake Ontario.

Despite the interesting attraction, visitors came to enjoy the lake and the beach. Although the park was served by bus and rail, Streifthau was forced to purchase 100 acres of apple orchard located between the park and the village of LeSourdsville in 1929. The land was needed to accommodate the increasing number of people visiting the park.

Despite the onset of the Depression, Streifthau continued to expand the park's offerings. He expanded the bathhouse, built the park's first office building, and imported over 1,000 tons of white sand for the beach. "We were slipping gate passes into sweaty palms of people going swimming, just so they'd return again," said Streifthau in his 1985 autobiography, *Edgar Streifthau: His Story* by Irene Wright. Admissions, food prices, and employee wages were cut. "We survived. Our employees worked at low wages just to have jobs. We gave them $1 a day, meals and a place to sleep. A million more workers would have taken us up on the offer, if we'd had a few more dollars to spread around," said Streifthau.

Just before the park was to open for the 1934 season, an accidental fire destroyed the bathhouse. Streifthau went to the Middletown Lumber Company and solicited the assistance of a personable and talented draftsman, Don Dazey. On May 30, the park opened with a new bathhouse and a new manager. Throughout the rebuilding process, Streifthau became impressed with Dazey's sincerity and his talent dealing effectively with people. Ultimately, Dazey was offered the position of park manager and offered a one-third interest in the park with an option to purchase a one-half interest at a later date. The direction of the park would be forever changed thanks to Dazey's initiative.

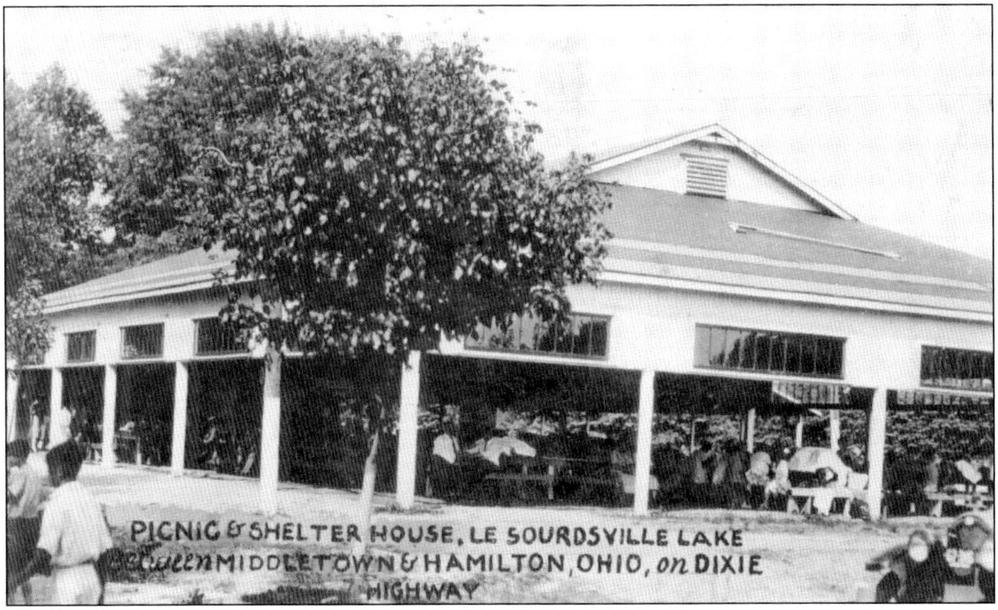

On June 10, 1922, LeSourdsville Lake opened for business as a resort featuring Ogle's Band, headed by local newspaper employee Ralph Olglsby. Additional shelters similar to the one here were quickly added to handle the crowds. Admission was 10¢ per person, 25¢ for swimming, and 10¢ per couple for a jitney dance.

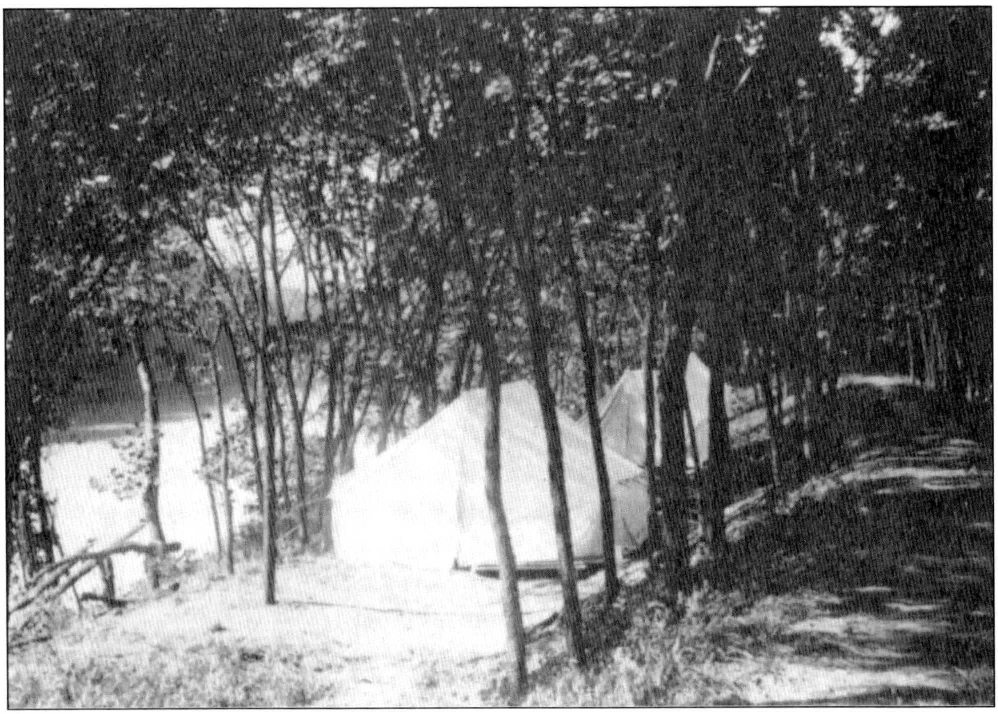

Tents were available for rent along the Great Miami River during the first season; the lake was located just to the right. LeSourdsville Lake survived its first season over $9,000 in debt.

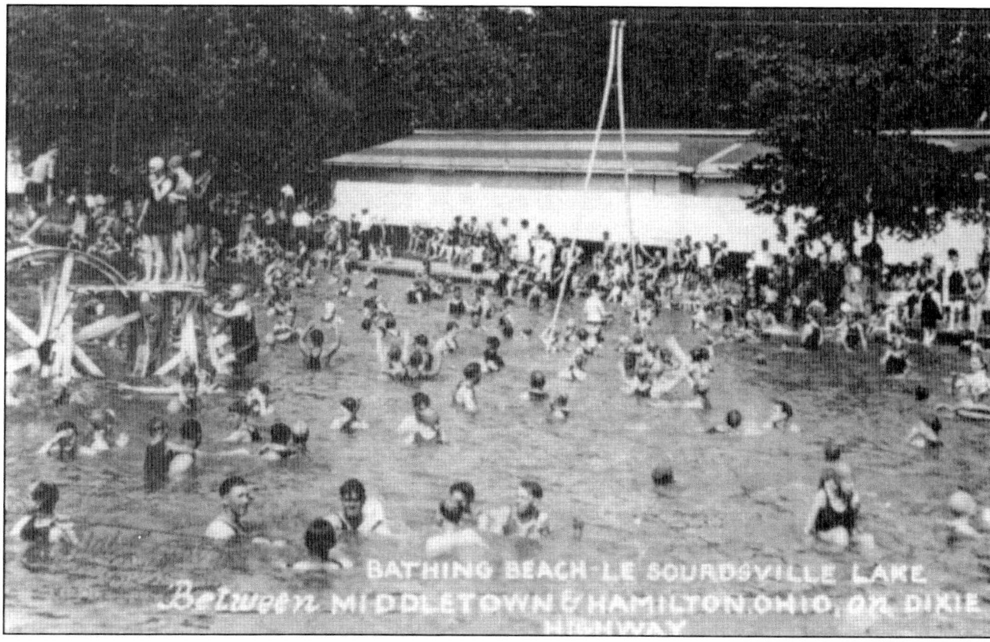

The park's original bathhouse was designed to handle 250 customers. The number of swimmers increased enough that by 1931 a 90-foot-by-190-foot bathhouse, located just inside the main entrance on the left, was built and designed to handle 4,000 swimmers daily.

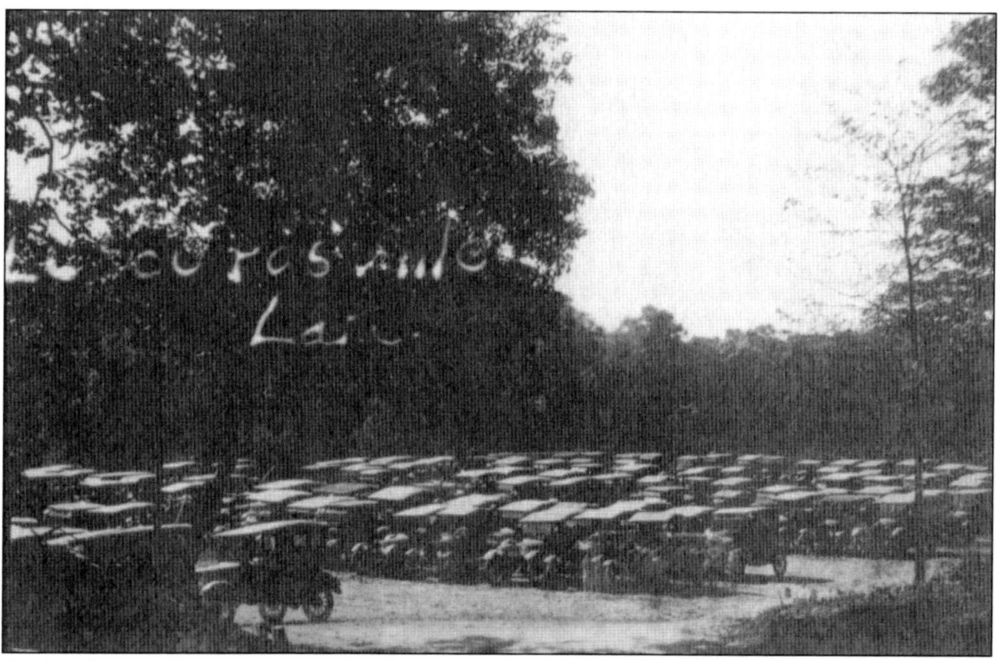

A *Hamilton Daily News* article dated August 11, 1922, stated, "It is surprising the number of states that are represented through auto license tags at LeSourdsville. During the past ten days tags have been noted from Oregon, Virginia, Florida, Massachusetts, New York and Oklahoma. LeSourdsville is bound to become a 'fixture' in the pleasure resorts of the Miami Valley."

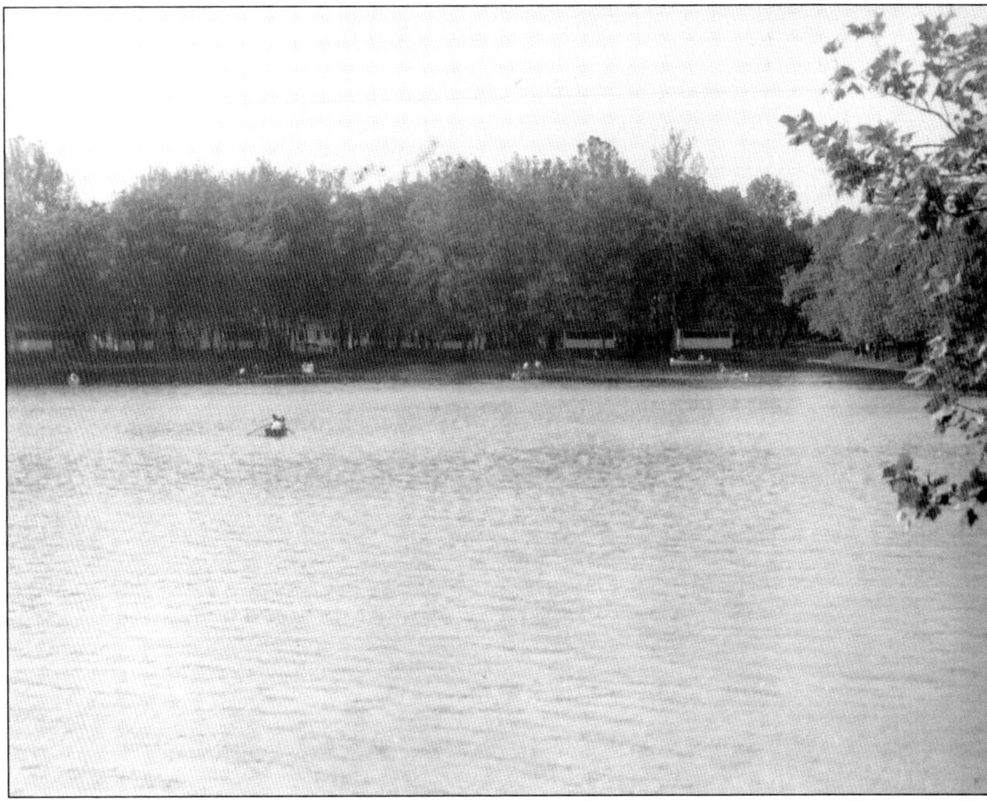

The 18-acre lake was the largest lake in southern Ohio, possessing a naturally controlled freshwater supply of deep well water. Two large pumps drew in 1.5 millions of gallons of water every 24 hours.

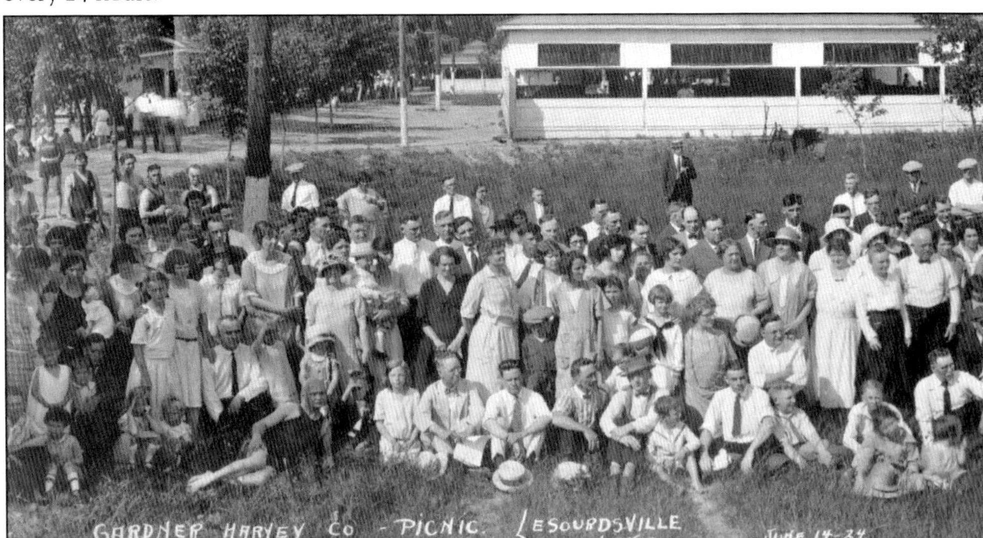

The Gardner Harvey Company was one of the first corporate picnics, documented in this 1924 photograph. The old Miami-Erie Canal bed is just to the right and the lake is on the left. The park featured boating, swimming, campsites, a dance hall, and a playground.

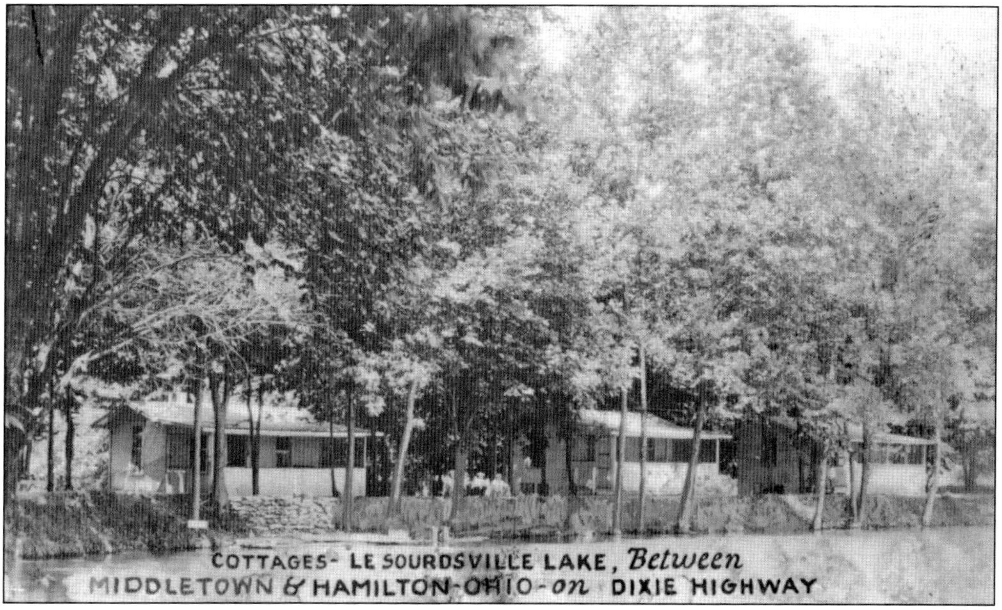

In 1924, five more cabins were built around the perimeter of the lake. Fishing was added and quickly became a popular attraction, especially for visitors staying in the cabins.

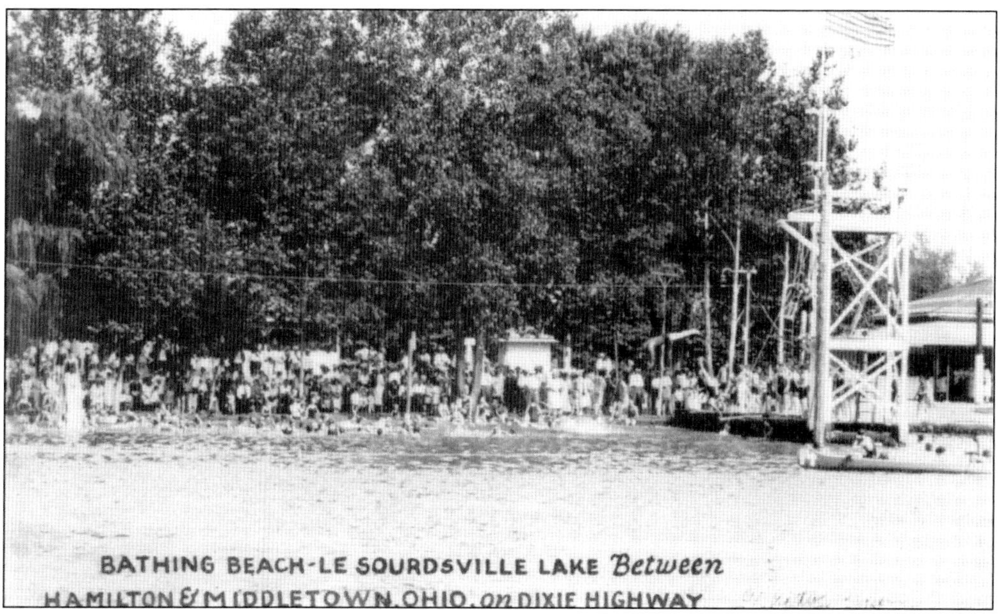

In 1926, new diving boards and a ladder swing were installed eight feet above the water. Two years later, a 50-foot-high toboggan slide was installed. In 1931, seven diving boards, two toboggan waterslides, a water wheel, and a 20-foot-high diving platform were added to the park, making it a water park of the future.

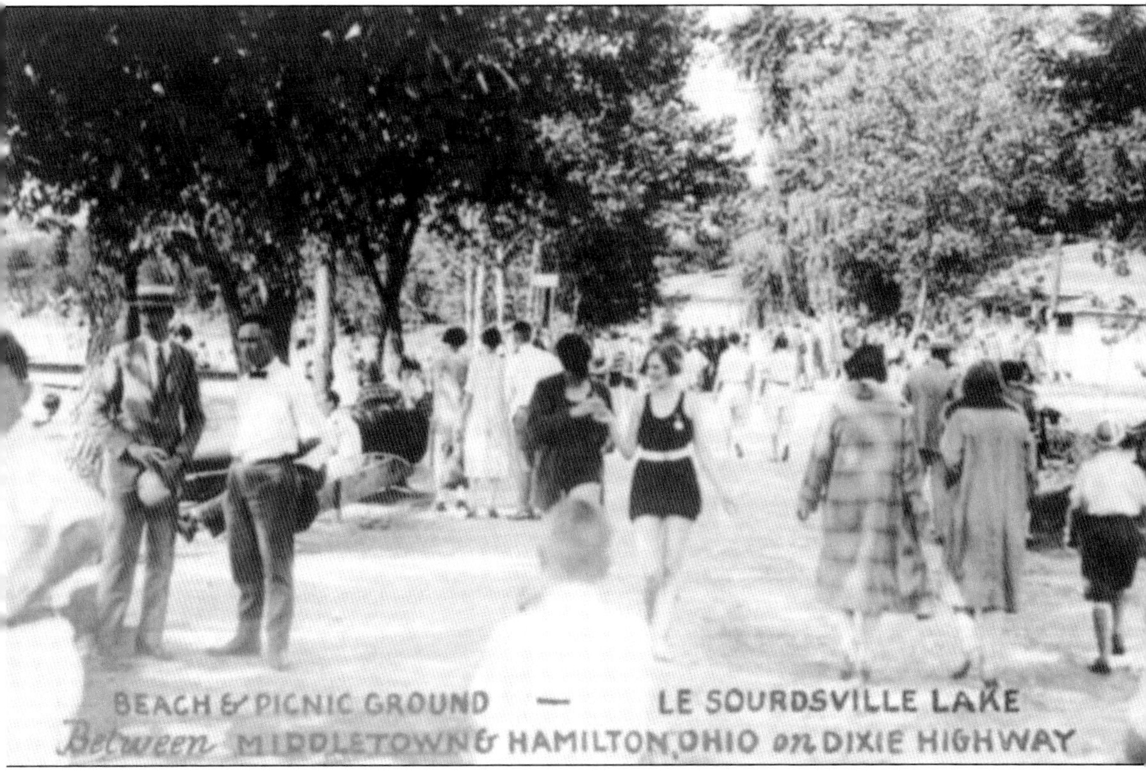

This 1930s postcard shows the variety of people that visited LeSourdsville Lake. The gentleman on the left is wearing a suit with a top hat. This was traditional wardrobe during the era, unless he was going swimming. In the center, a woman is walking down the midway in her swimming suit. The woman to the right of her, walking in the opposite direction, is wearing a full-length fur coat.

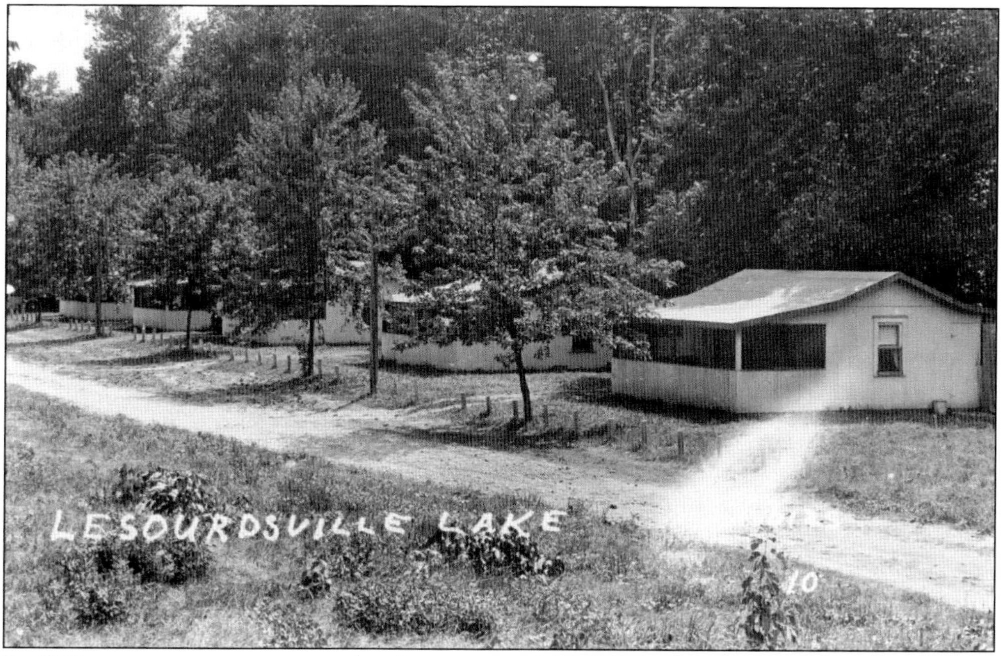

By 1930, twenty-two cottages outlined a portion of the lake. All cottages featured screened-in porches overlooking the lake and full-service bathrooms and kitchens. Rentals were available on a weekly basis throughout the season, yet many families lived in the cottages on an annual basis.

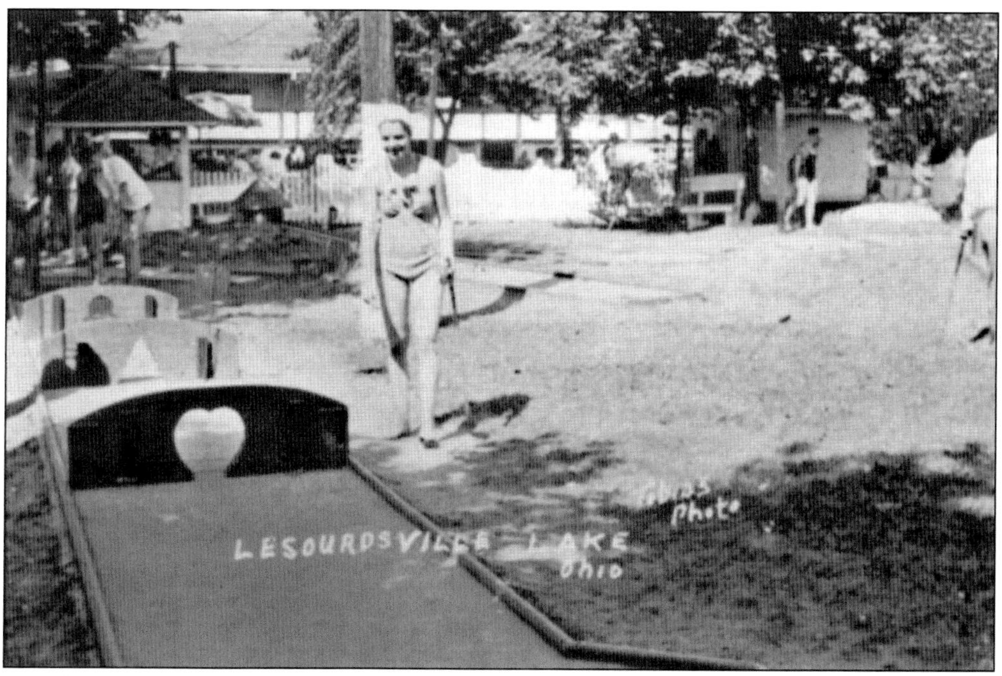

Hamilton, Ohio, resident Robert Kappel owned and managed the Tom Thumb 18-hole miniature golf course from 1930 to 1960. After Kappel left, ownership of the attraction reverted to the park. Eventually, the course was closed and used for the influx of new "thrill" rides. Miniature golf returned to the park in the late 1980s.

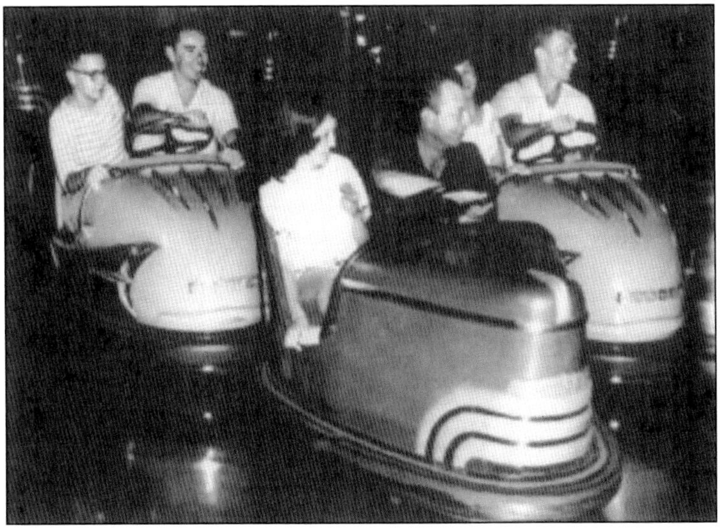

In 1930, the Dodgem ride was the first amusement ride added to the park. This picture from the early 1960s features WING-AM radio personalities, from left to right driving the cars, Rod Williams, Gene Barry, and Stan Scott. (Courtesy of Rod Williams/WING-AM.)

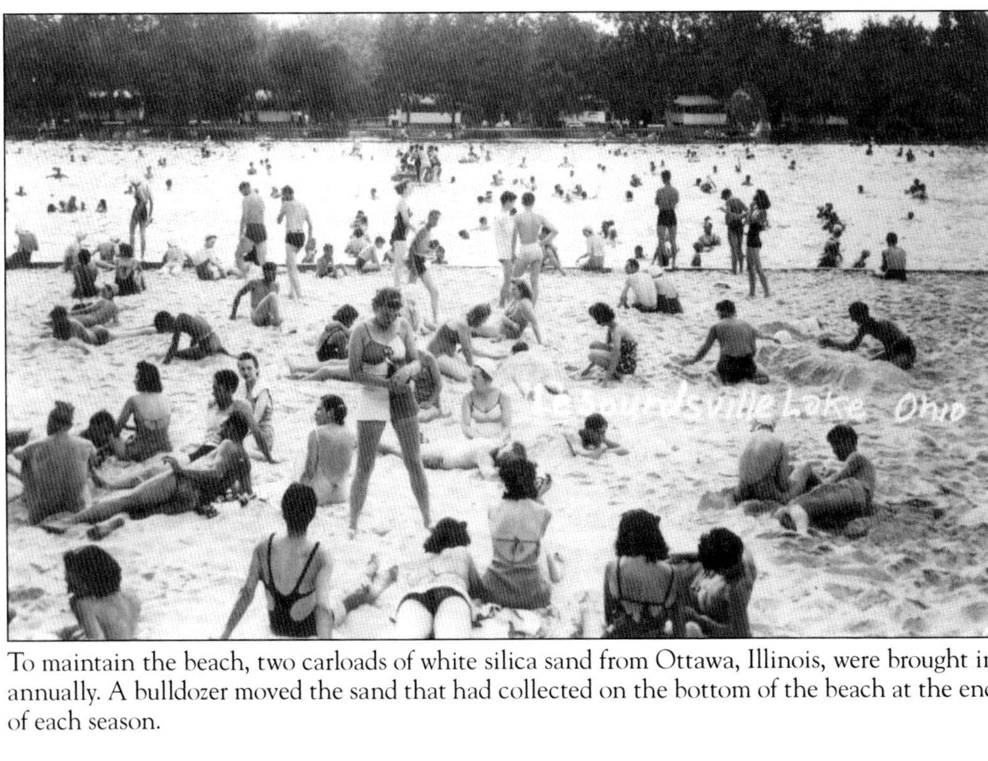

To maintain the beach, two carloads of white silica sand from Ottawa, Illinois, were brought in annually. A bulldozer moved the sand that had collected on the bottom of the beach at the end of each season.

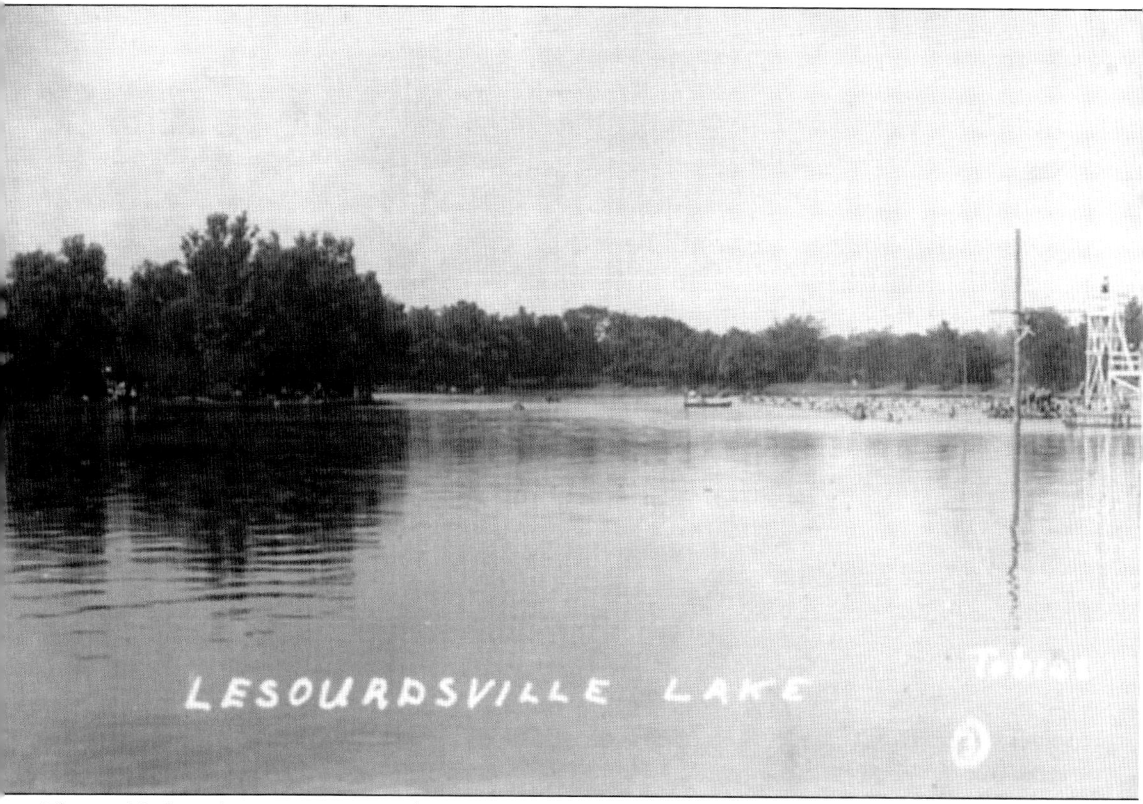

The park's first drowning occurred in 1930 when a 19-year-old northern Kentucky resident drowned after jumping in the lake from a canoe. It was speculated that he suffered stomach cramps and was unable to stay above the water. Park employee Olen Parsons rescued the person but was unable to revive him.

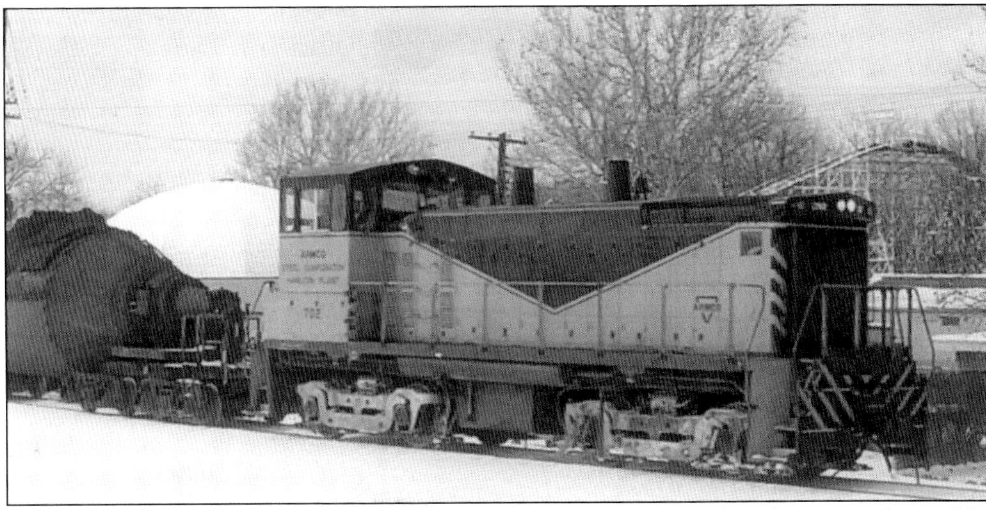

In the early 1930s, the Armco Steel Company began utilizing the rail line that ran in front of the park to haul molten steel from its nearby New Miami plant to its processing plant in Middletown. The regular train runs became an unofficial attraction, since visitors were frequently forced to wait for the trains to pass before crossing the track to enter the park. (Courtesy of Dan Frinfrock.)

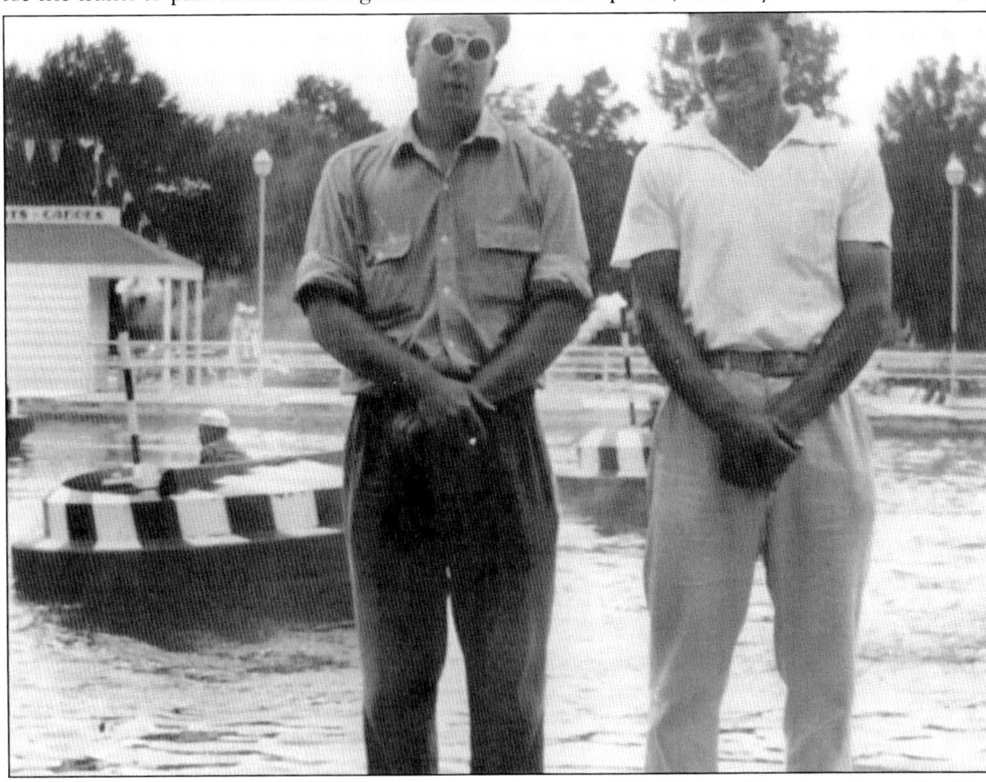

In March 1934, the bathhouse burned down, resulting in a $25,000 loss. Furniture from all of the cottages had been stored in the building over the winter and was lost, along with 20 canoes, 18 other boats, 2,500 swimming suits, and 15,000 towels. Edgar Streifthau (left) hired draftsman Don Dazey (right) of the Middletown Lumber Company to design and construct a new bathhouse to accommodate 5,000 swimmers. The bathhouse became reality on opening day, May 30, 1934.

Two

New Challenges, New Direction

As a businessman, Don Dazey realized the importance of a good public relations with local businesses' employees. He began offering deals to some of the area's largest companies, such as Armco, Sorg Paper, Champion Paper, Crystal Tissue, Beckett Paper, and smaller organizations to bring their employees to the park. The idea of offering corporate outings spread across the country to other parks. In 1935, the park broke its daily attendance record when 10,000 Armco employees and their families came to what would become an annual outing until the early 1990s. During the 1930s and 1940s, a special train that ran from Middletown to the park was provided by Armco. Champion Papers also provide their own train for their picnic outings.

Beginning in 1940, the popularity of the park encouraged it to employ the slogan, "Miami Valley's Chosen Playground," which continued into the late 1950s. National bands such as Eddie Kadle, Earl Holderman, Little Joe Hart, Eugene Jelesnick, Tommy Flynn, Jimmy Scriber, Emerson Gill, Carl Taylor, Lloyd Labrie, and Michael Mehas appeared regularly in the park's Stardust Gardens Ballroom.

In 1942, the park was the recipient of an award given by US Secretary of War Harry Stimson for the role the park played with providing Army and Navy personnel free admission and free use of the rides.

In 1945, a new one-day attendance record of 25,000 was achieved on the Fourth of July, thanks in part to the park's ongoing policy of allowing men and women of the armed forces free park admission.

Streifthau and Dazey realized that more had to be done to modernize LeSourdsville Lake. Disneyland opened in 1955 to such rave reviews from the public that they expected other parks to become just as modern and clean. At Cedar Point, a multimillion-dollar renovation was under way by 1957 in an attempt to become the Disneyland of the Midwest. Streifthau and Dazey took out a loan and initiated a multiyear improvement plan. The sudden death of Dazey in 1959 brought the plan to a halt, and Streifthau was forced to put up the park for sale in 1960.

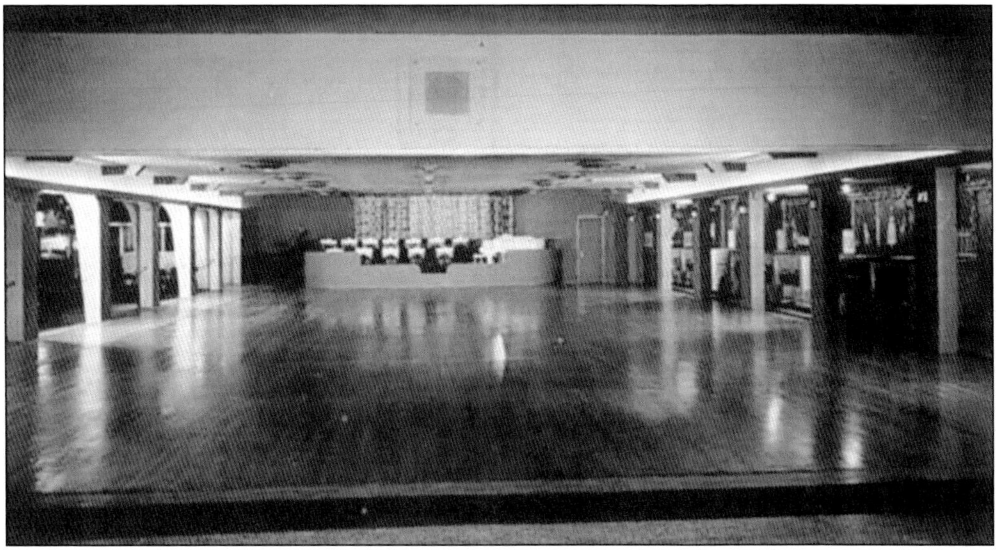

After Dazey was named park manager, he constructed the Stardust Gardens next door to the bathhouse. Bands such as Ray McKinley, Glenn Miller, the Dorsey Brothers, and Stan Kenton graced the rich Maplewood floor to thousands of delighted customers.

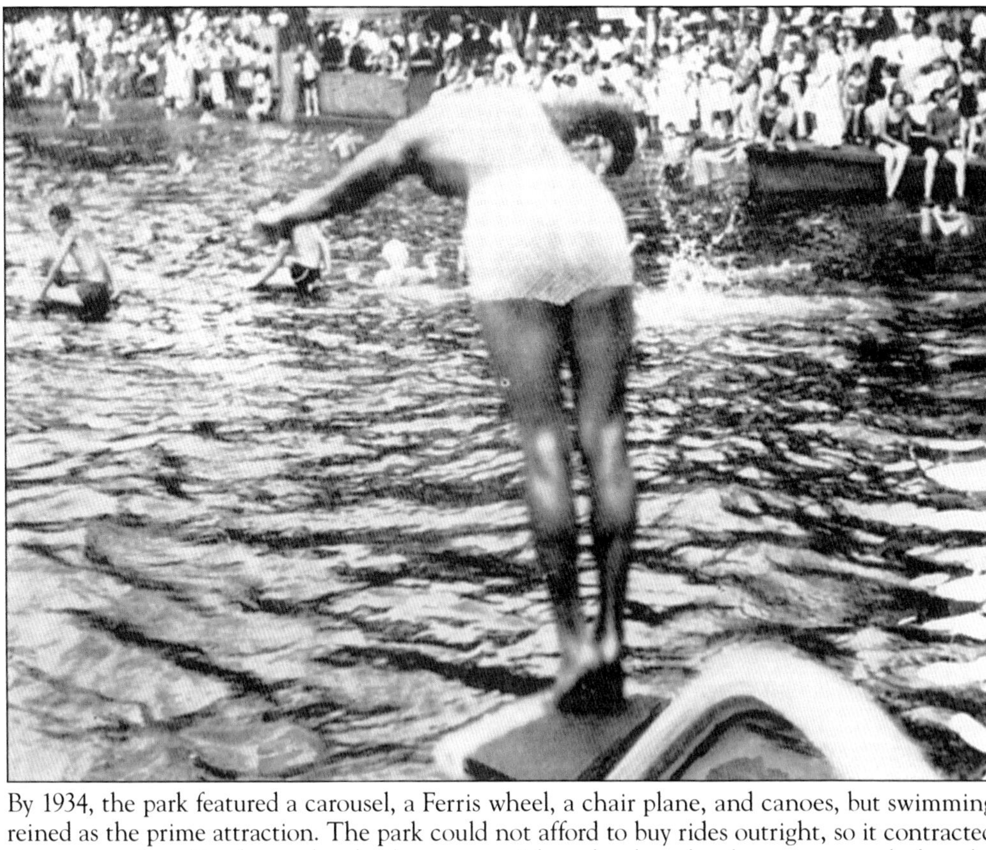

By 1934, the park featured a carousel, a Ferris wheel, a chair plane, and canoes, but swimming reined as the prime attraction. The park could not afford to buy rides outright, so it contracted them out to Ray Gooding, a local ride operator. That plan lasted only two seasons before the park began purchasing its own rides.

In 1936, Don Dazey instituted company picnics, a concept that was not a common practice in the amusement park industry. Dazey convinced local businessmen that providing annual picnics at LeSourdsville would enhance goodwill towards their employees.

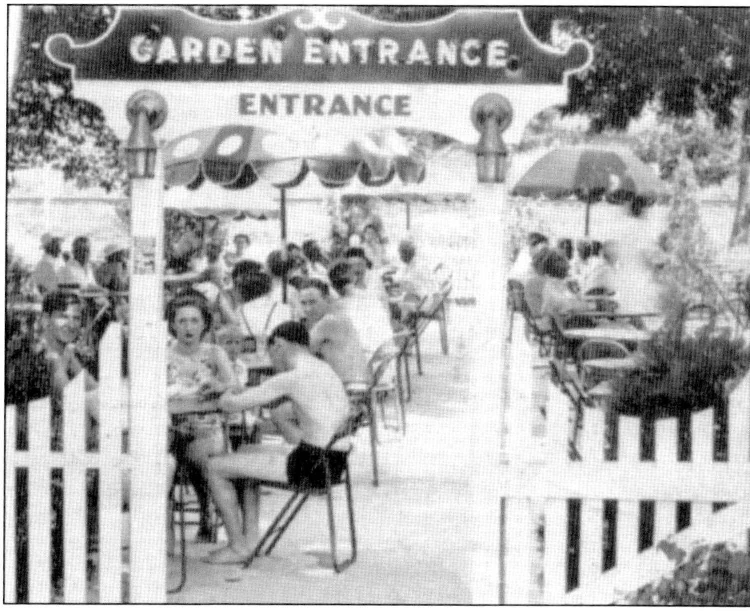

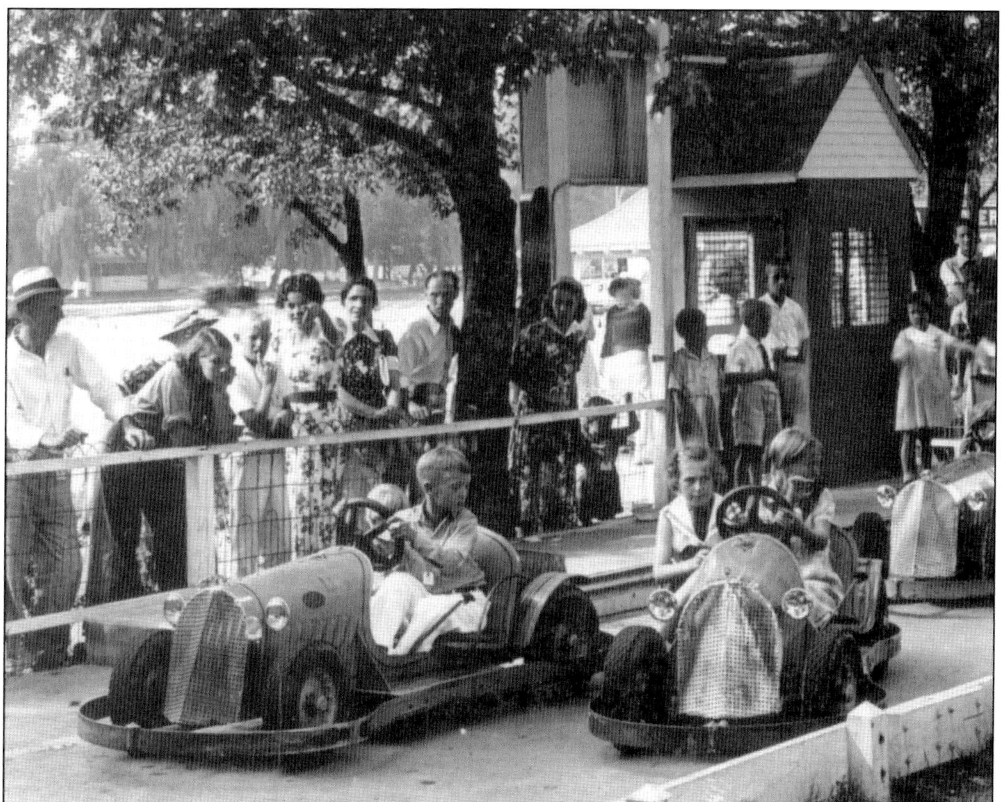

Custer Cars were produced in Dayton, Ohio, and did not need a track bar to operate; guards were installed to help protect the car body as well as the rider.

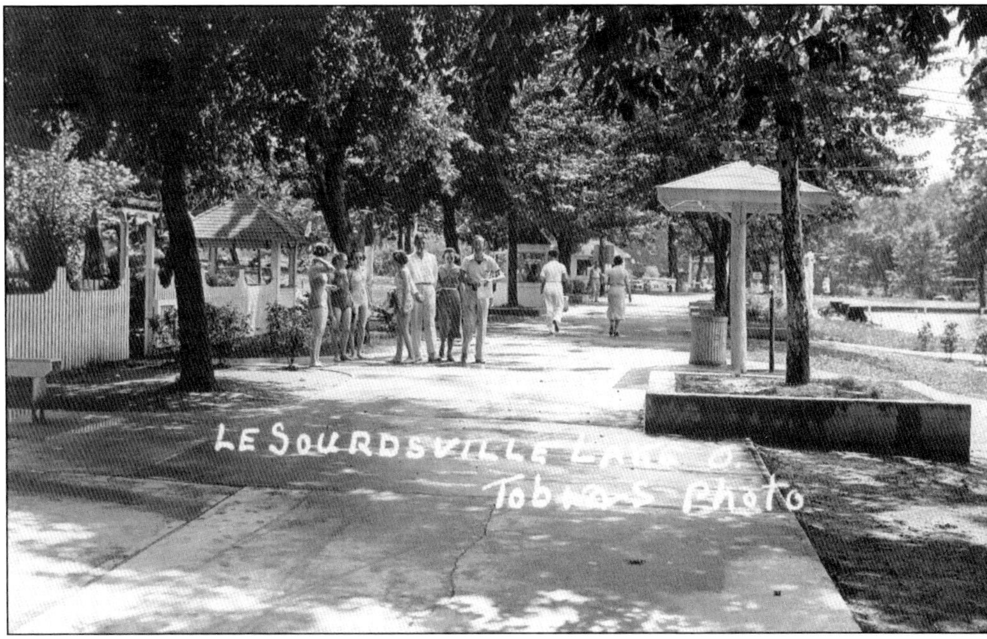

A multitude of trees along the midway provided lots of shade for thousands of weary guests. Over the years, many of them fell victim to Mother Nature, disease, or expansion. Today, only a handful of trees remain in this area.

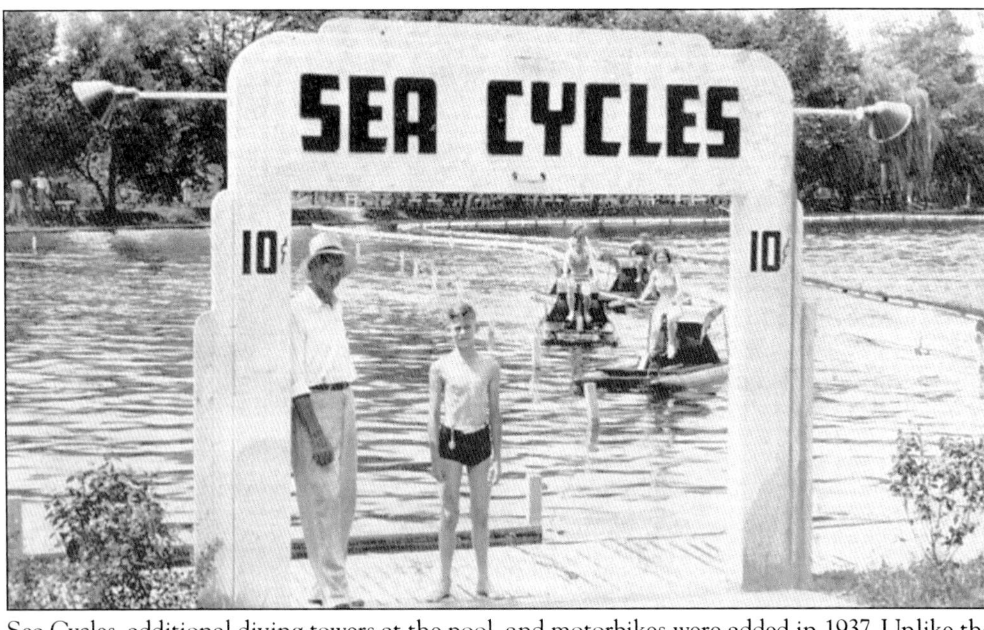

Sea Cycles, additional diving towers at the pool, and motorbikes were added in 1937. Unlike the traditional sea cycles seen today, riders were forced to go in the same direction similar to the pattern of a racetrack.

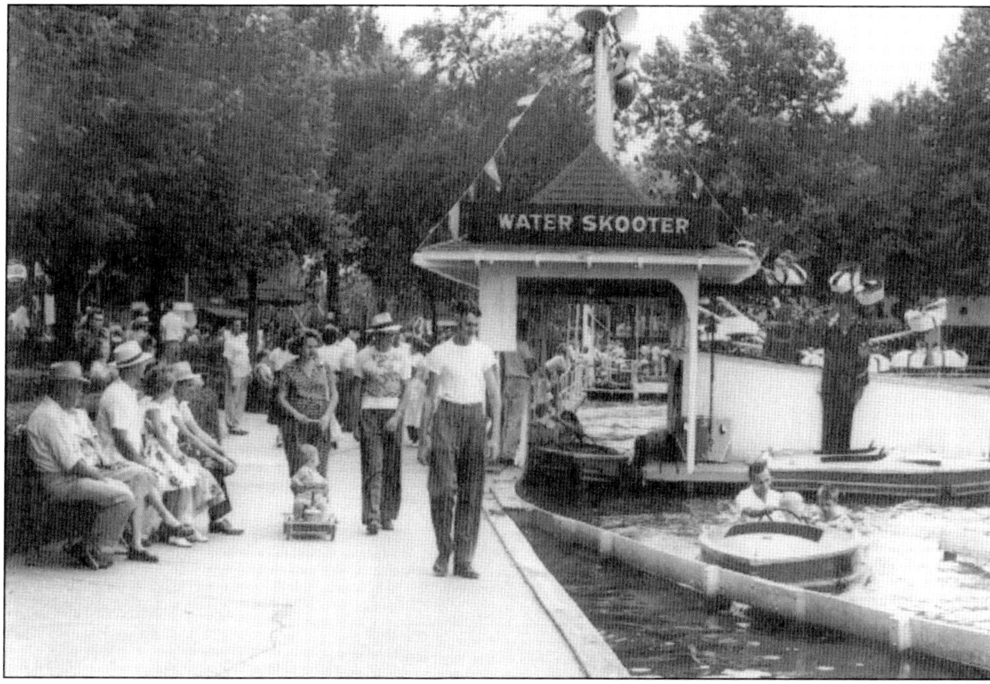

To assist in guiding the boats in one direction, track boards were added to the motorboat ride. The 1937 ride lineup included a carousel, Ferris wheel, chair plane, miniature train, a pony ride, Custer cars, scooter boats, motorbikes, sea cycles, bicycles, a water toboggan, boats, and canoes.

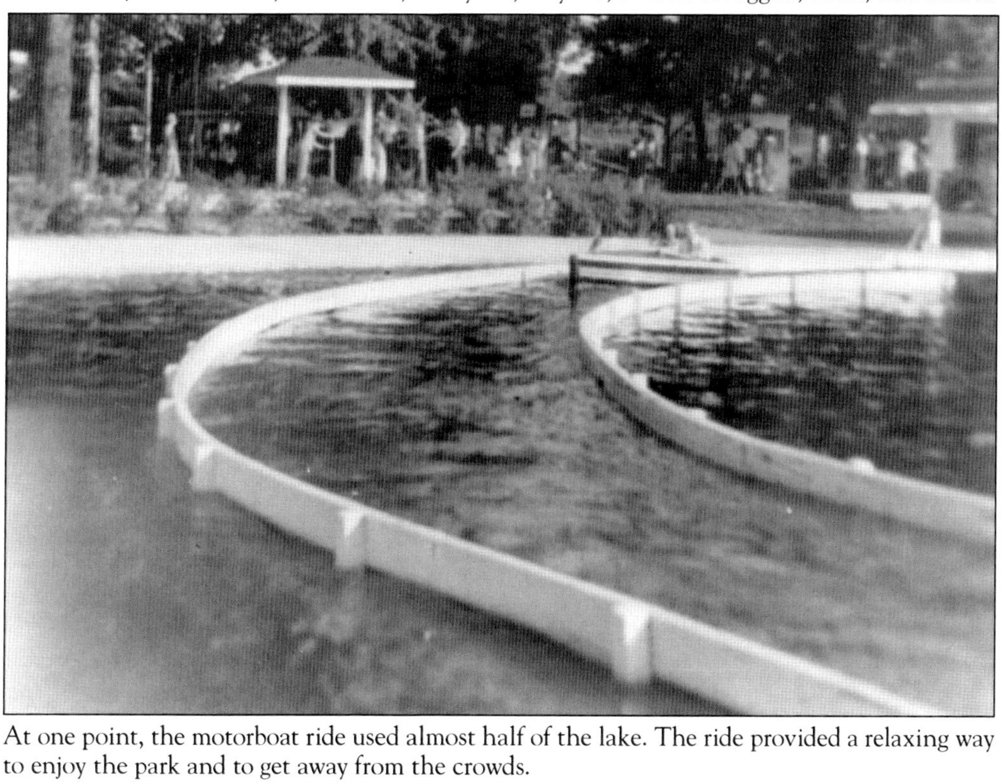

At one point, the motorboat ride used almost half of the lake. The ride provided a relaxing way to enjoy the park and to get away from the crowds.

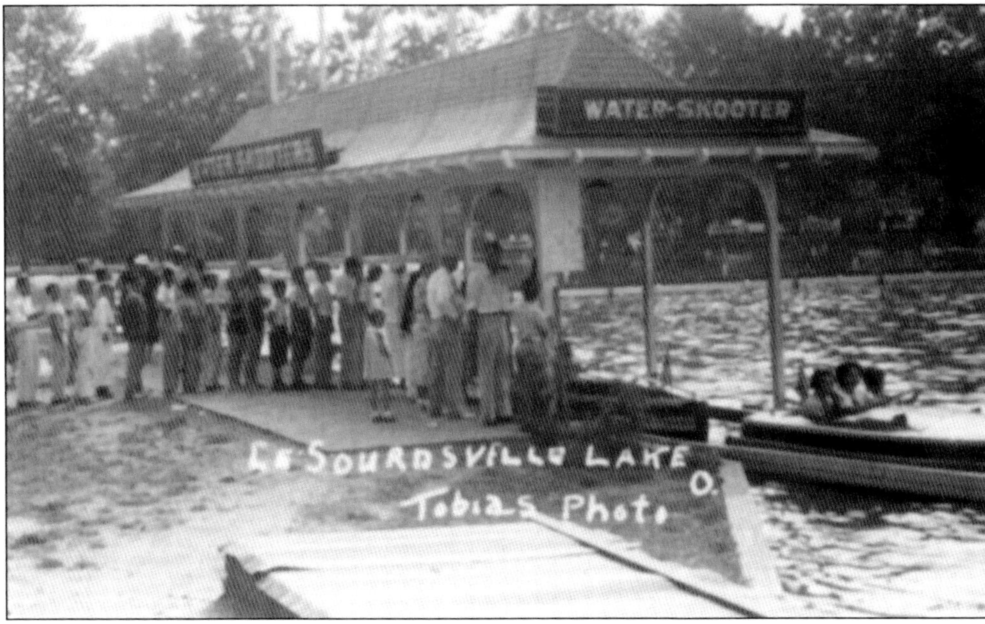

The waiting area for the attractions was constructed out of concrete. The main walkways were not as nice and consisted of compressed dirt, as the photograph above reveals. A few years later, concrete paths were installed to create a cleaner look for the park.

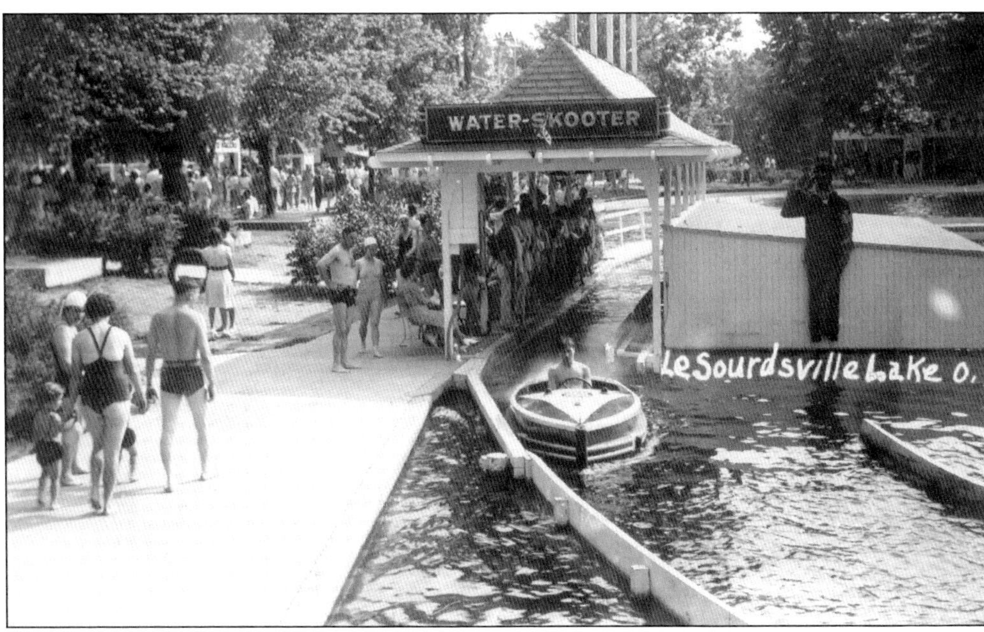

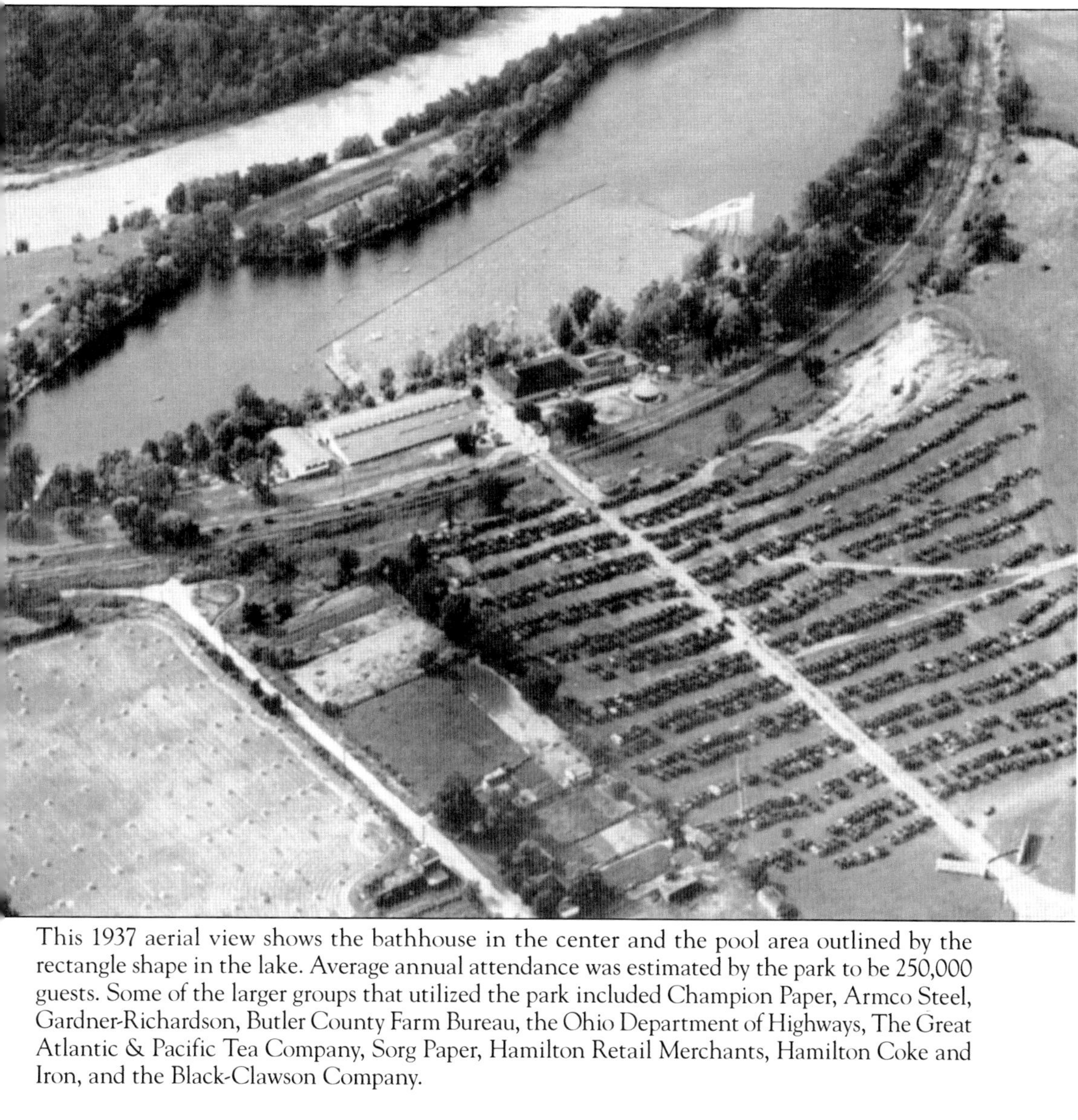

This 1937 aerial view shows the bathhouse in the center and the pool area outlined by the rectangle shape in the lake. Average annual attendance was estimated by the park to be 250,000 guests. Some of the larger groups that utilized the park included Champion Paper, Armco Steel, Gardner-Richardson, Butler County Farm Bureau, the Ohio Department of Highways, The Great Atlantic & Pacific Tea Company, Sorg Paper, Hamilton Retail Merchants, Hamilton Coke and Iron, and the Black-Clawson Company.

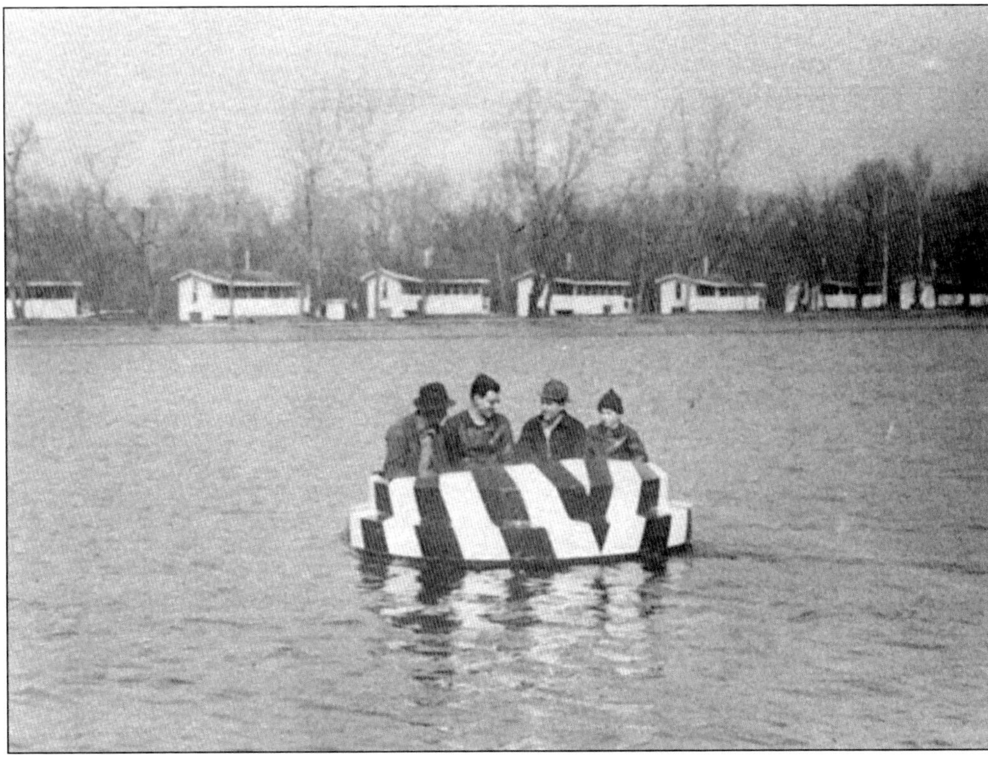

Edgar Streifthau developed his own ride in 1939 called the Krazy Bugs. It is not known how many years this ride lasted, but it was apparently never publicized in the local newspapers or in park brochures.

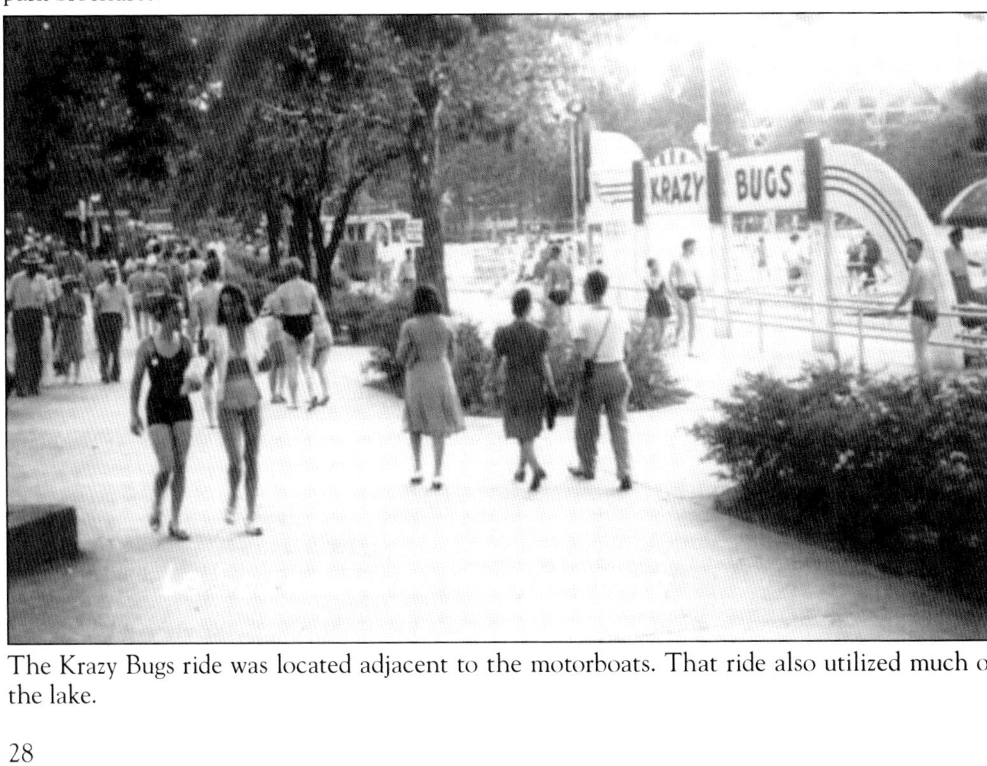

The Krazy Bugs ride was located adjacent to the motorboats. That ride also utilized much of the lake.

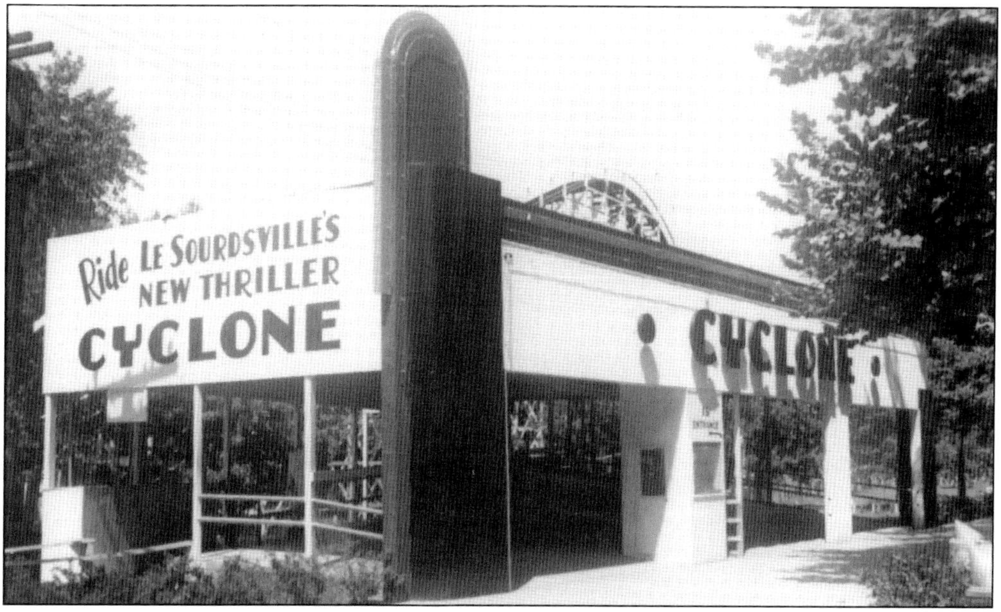

In the fall of 1939, a defunct John Miller roller coaster was dismantled at Moxahalia Amusement Park in Zanesville, Ohio, and moved to LeSourdsville Lake. Pictured is the loading station for the new coaster.

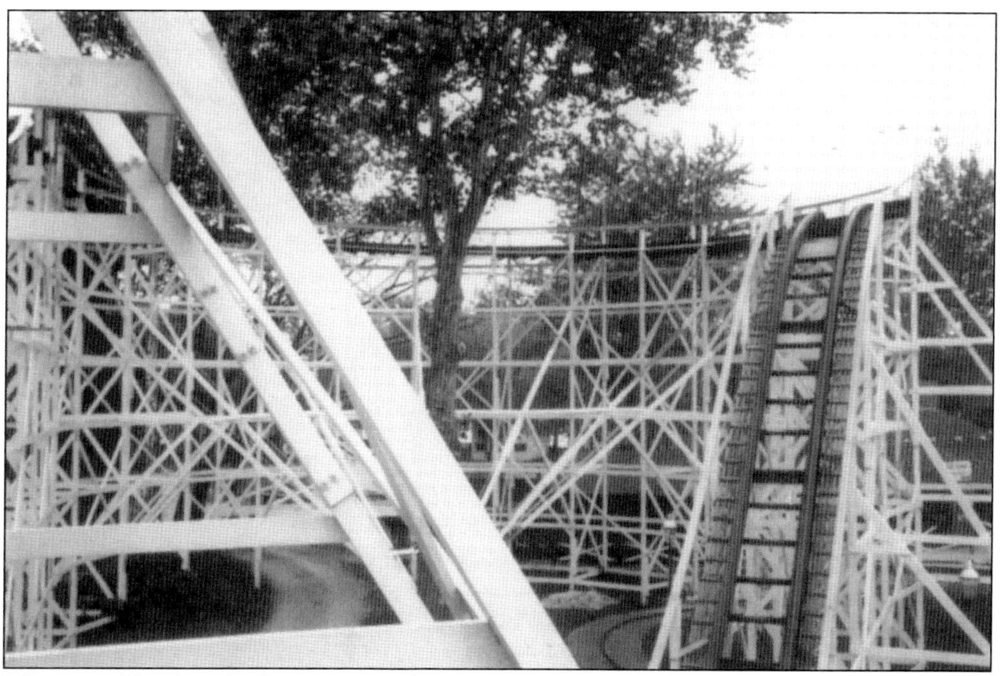
Edgar Streifthau bought the coaster for $35,000 and then rebuilt it in the northwest corner of the park near the carousel and named it the Cyclone. It opened in 1940 to rave reviews.

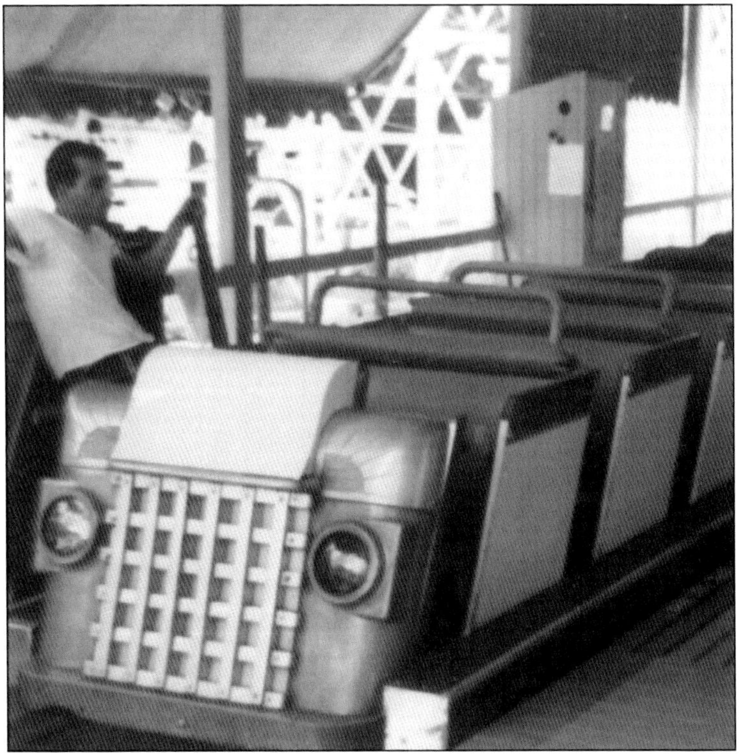

When the coaster was operating with two cars, the track had wires on the back turn that signaled to the operator where the other train was on the track. There was a lightbulb in the cabinet just to the right of the operator, pictured here, that signaled him when the train made the turn back towards the station. At that point, the car still in the station was sent on its way. There were three deaths from 1941 to 1973 due to people jumping from the cars while in motion. (Courtesy of Alex Freeman.)

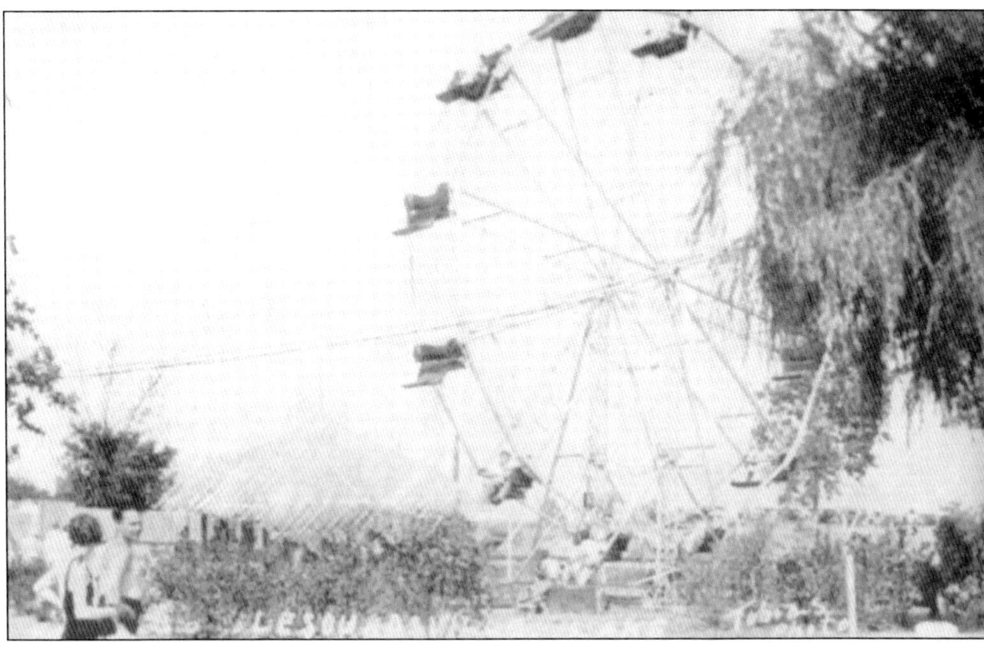

In 1941, the midway near the entrance to the Cyclone was extended to accommodate a giant Ferris wheel and the Whip. Bands appearing in the Stardust Gardens Ballroom included Eddie Kadle, Earl Holderman, Gene Roberts, Mary Marshall, Little Joe Hart, Eugene Jelesnick, Billy Snyder, Tommy Flynn, Billy Yates, Jimmy Scriber, and Emerson Gill. The following summer, Carl Taylor, Lloyd Labrie, and Michael Mehas joined the Stardust Gardens headliners.

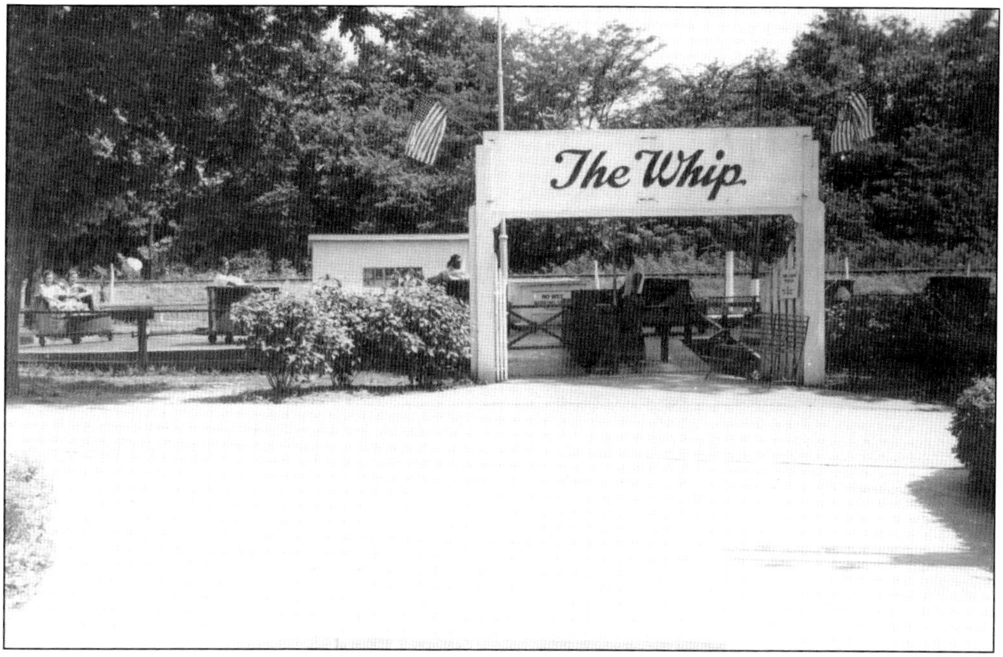

The Whip was one of the more popular rides across the country and was a prime attraction for years at LeSourdsville Lake.

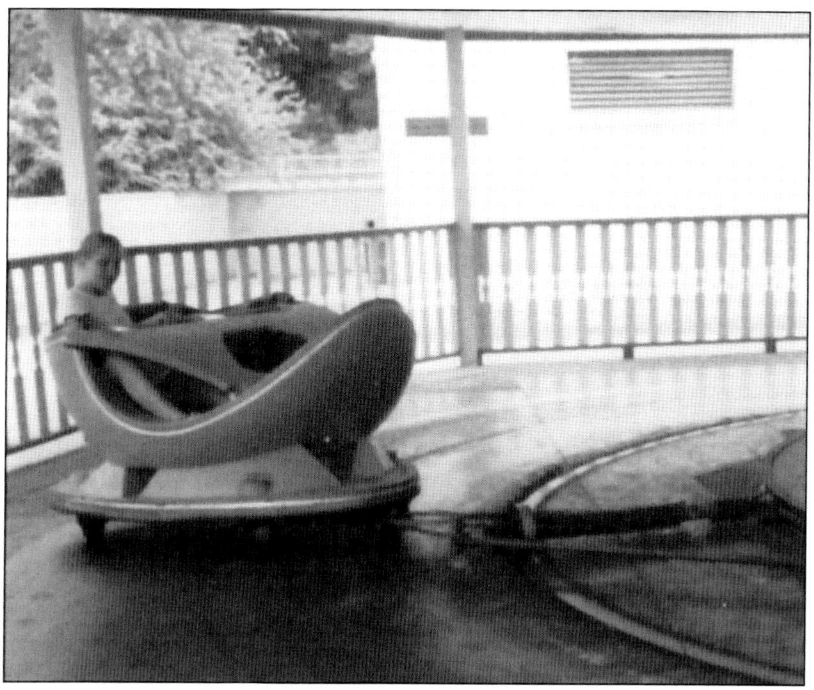

Shortly after the Whip was installed, a shelter was built over the ride to help protect it and the riders from the weather.

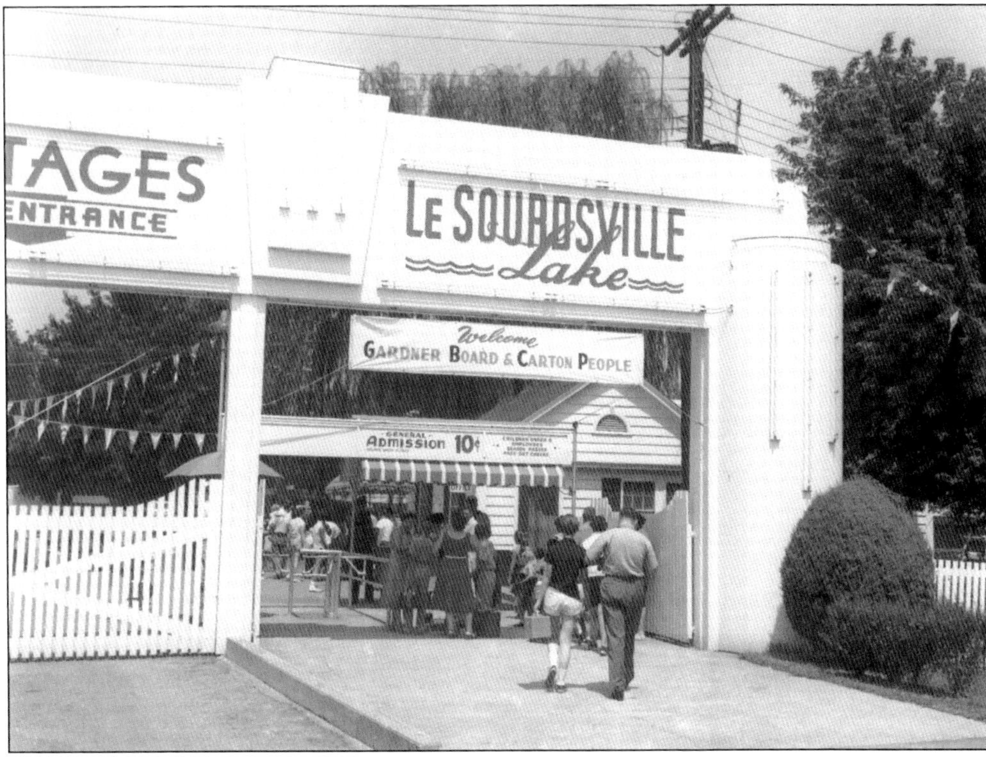

A new front entrance gate area was constructed in 1941. A removable canvas advertised names of groups meeting at the park.

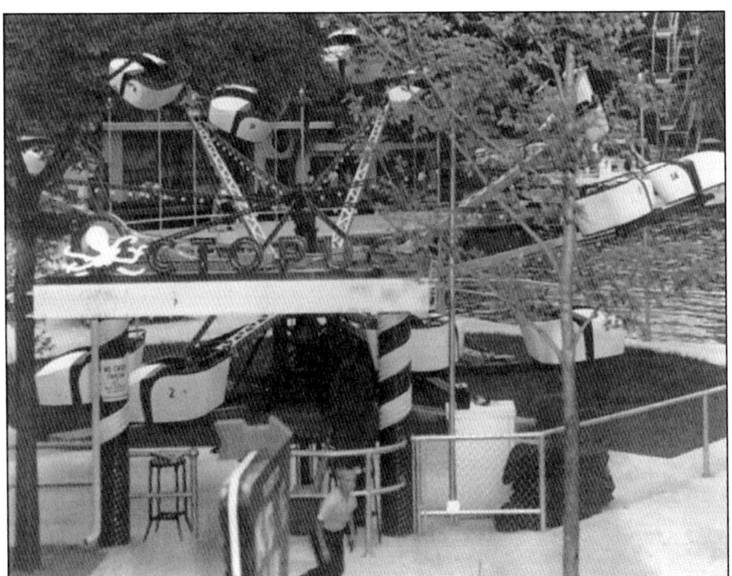

In 1944, the park boasted that the largest Octopus ride ever built was installed literally over the lake. By the end of World War II, LeSourdsville Lake was ranked 27th among the nation's amusement parks in attendance (although no attendance record was ever documented).

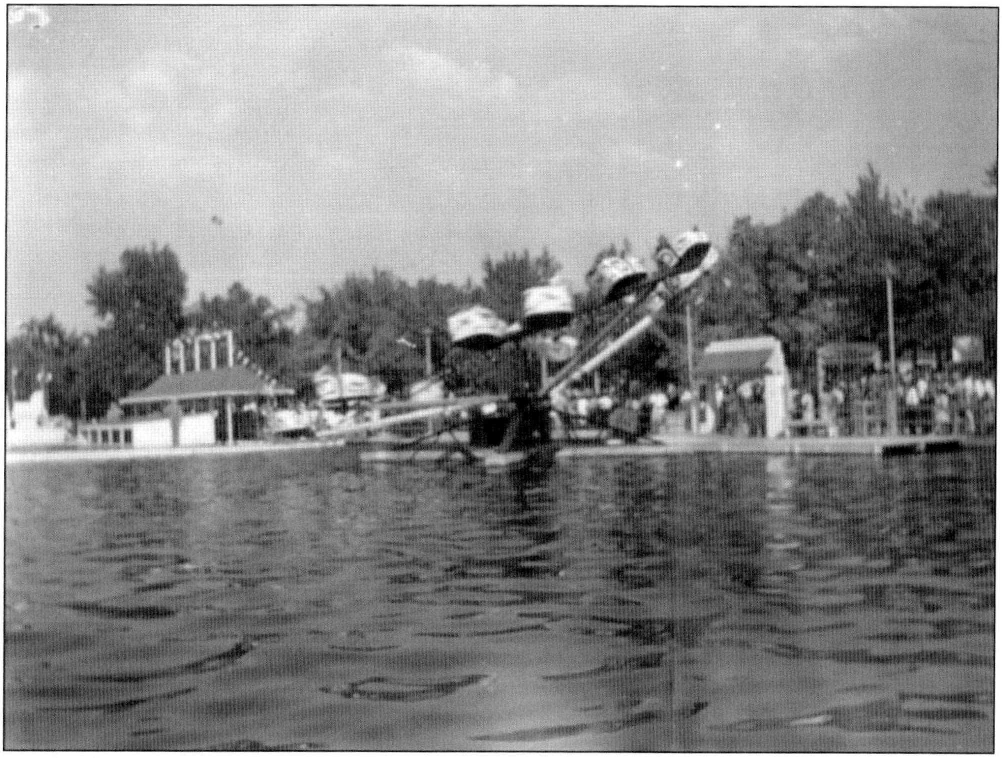

Besides the Octopus, the Airplane Swing made its debut in 1944. (Courtesy of Betty Fowler.)

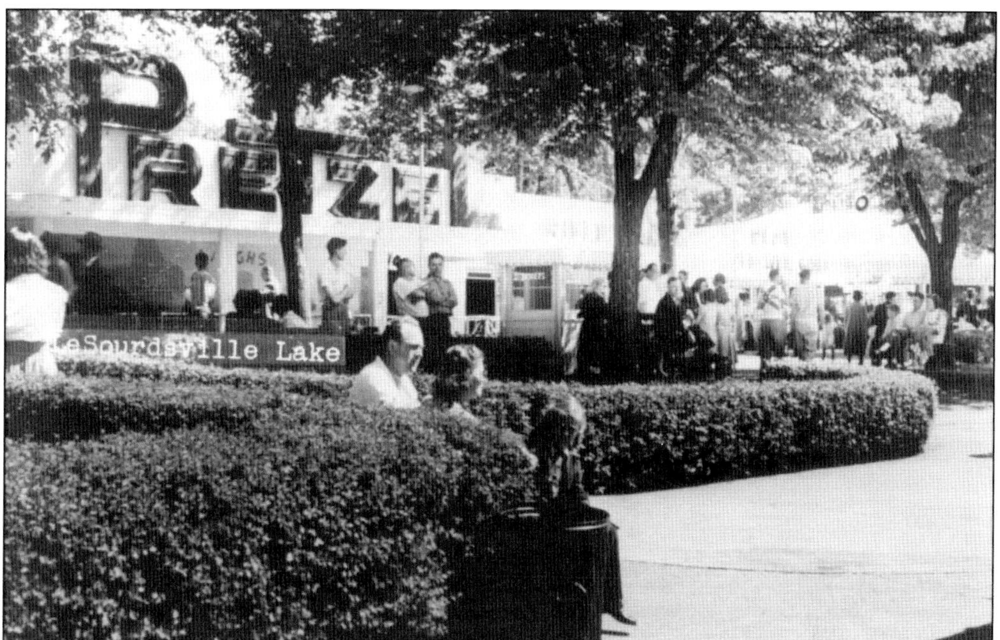

After the war was over, the park built a Pretzel attraction and added the Flying Scooters.

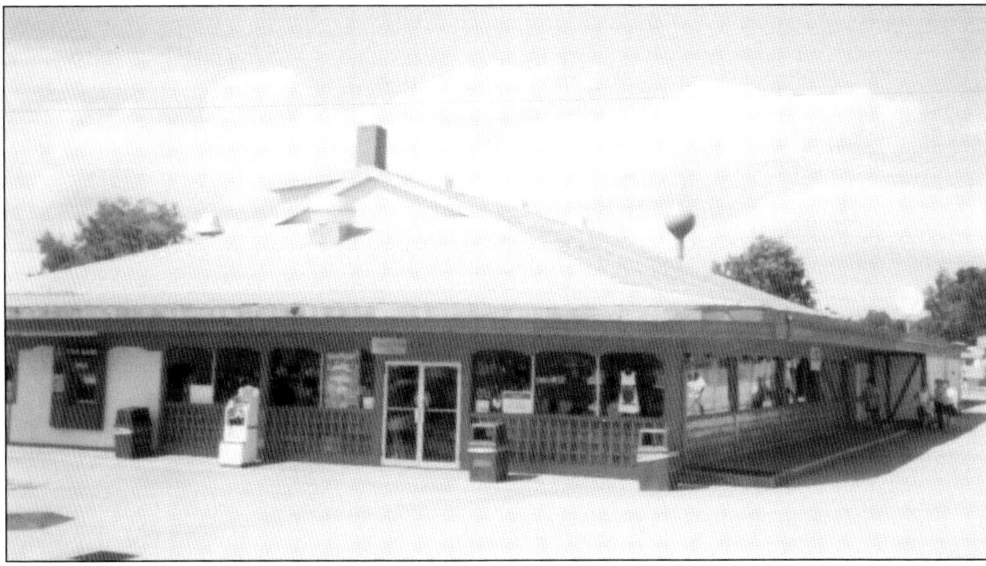

In 1946, a new dining room was built, and Stardust Gardens became the largest dance pavilion in southern Ohio. Dazey enlarged the facility to accommodate 2,500 people on a 100-foot-by-160-foot dance floor. The structure that housed the dining room pictured here also was home to a gift shop.

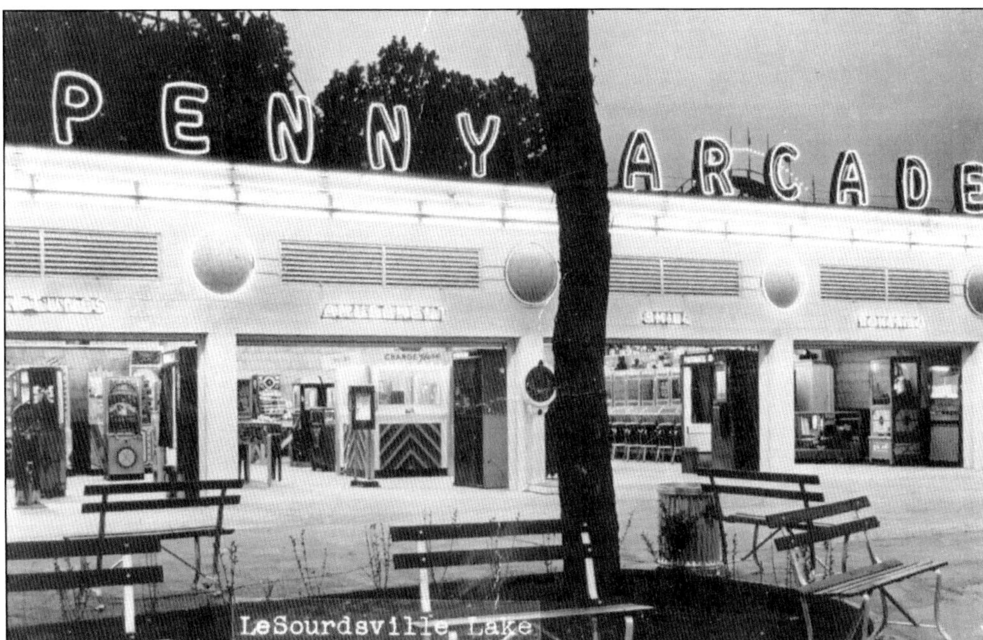

The midway was extended around the south end of the lake in 1949 with the double promenade bordered by new rides and a 116-foot-by-50-foot building to house the arcade and Parade of Fun. Neon lighting was added to the building to accent the reflection of the lights off the lake at night.

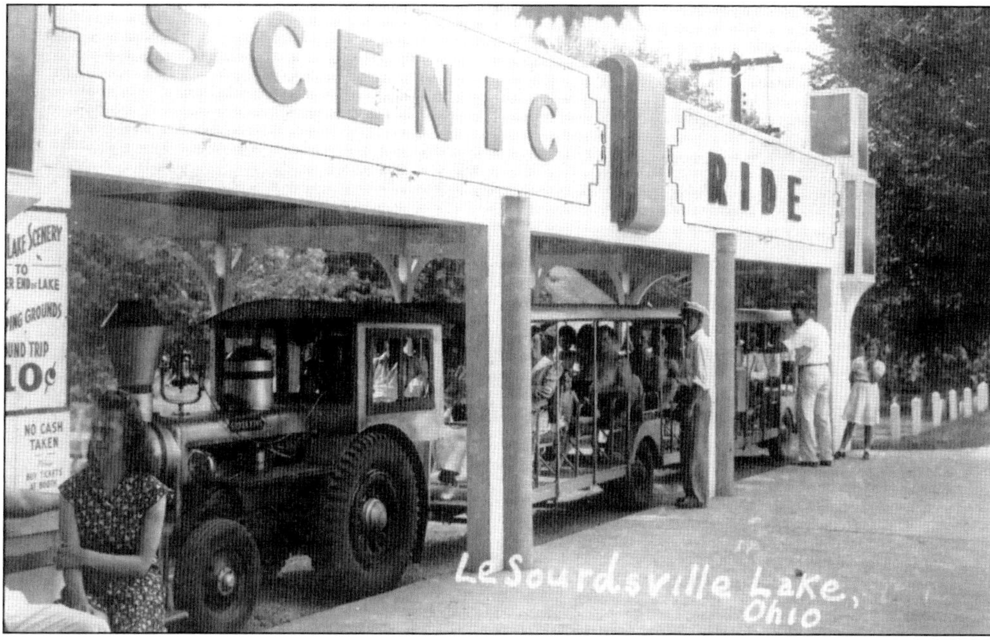

The Scenic Ride was relocated next to the Parade of Fun building. The ride was simply a tractor pulling two passenger cars on a concrete path running next to the roller coaster.

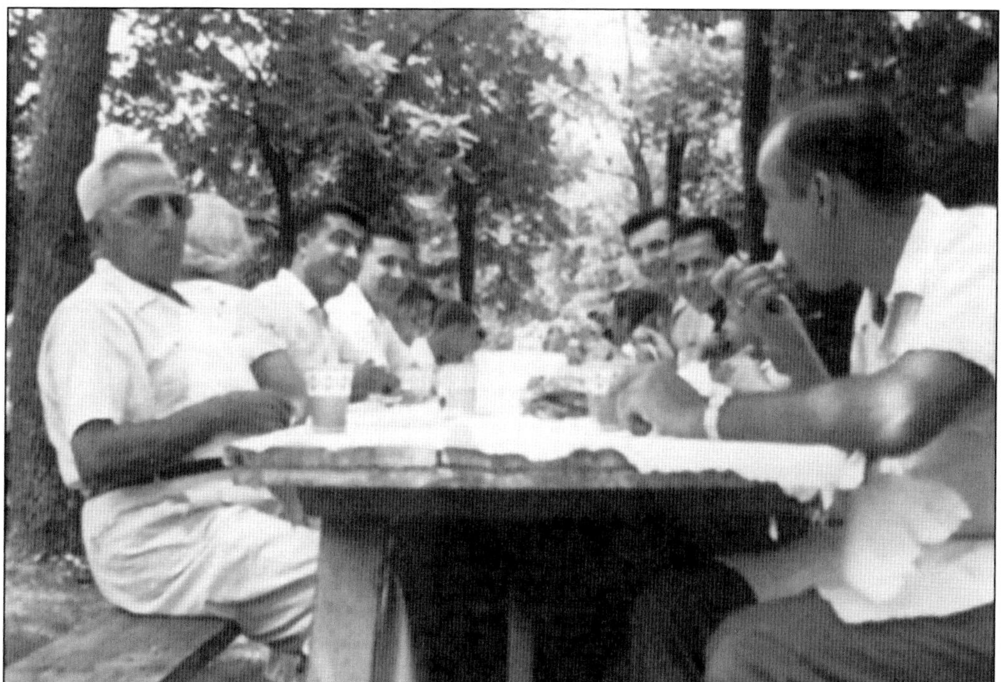

In 1949, the park purchased 500 additional picnic tables and improved the picnic grounds to accommodate the many groups using the park. The Middletown Greek Orthodox Church held their picnic here for several years. Taking advantage of the picnic grove is Stratis Petroglou (front left), Ourania Petroglou, Nick Georgopoulos, Costa Mathews (front right), Nick Ververis, George Comminos, and Fr. Steve Sarayiannis. (Courtesy of George Christy.)

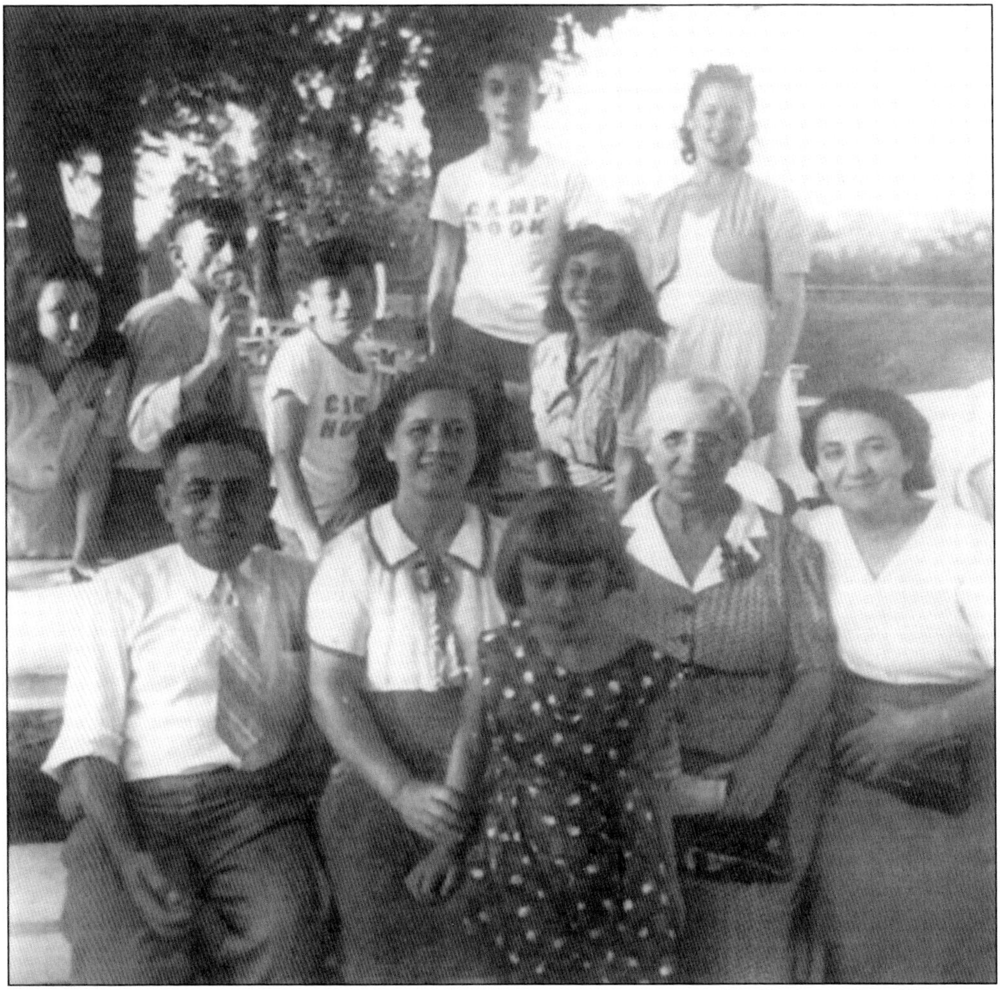

Several local area Greek organizations moved their picnics to LeSourdsville from the old Armco Park in Warren County during the 1940s and 1950s. Pictured here from left to right are (front row) James Demetrides, Antigone Demostenes, possibly her daughter Rebecca, Ourania Petroglou, and Sophia Demetrion; (back row) Kalliope Demetrides, Steve Demetrion, Jim Demetrion, unidentified, Catherine Demostenes, and Ruby ? . (Courtesy of George Christy.)

The Rock-o-Plane was added in 1949. The ride was the first of its kind east of the Mississippi River. The ride was eventually sold to Cincinnati's Coney Island in 2006, where it continues to thrill guests.

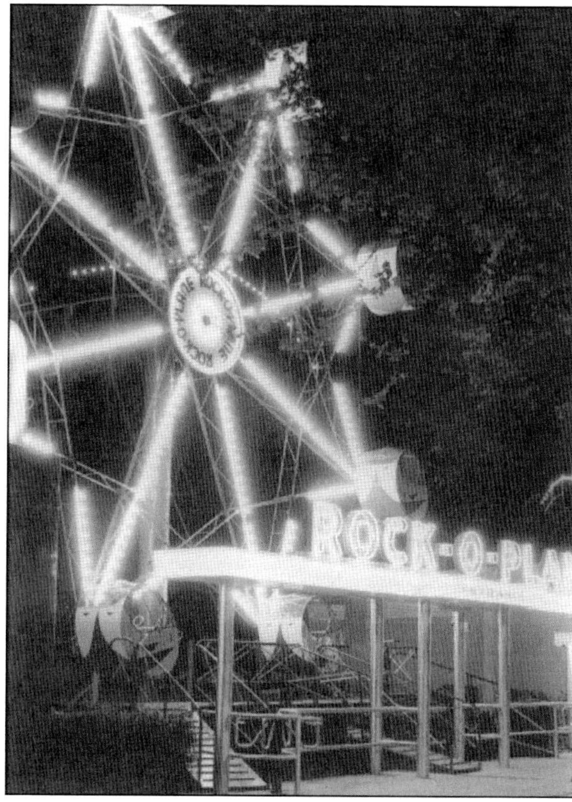

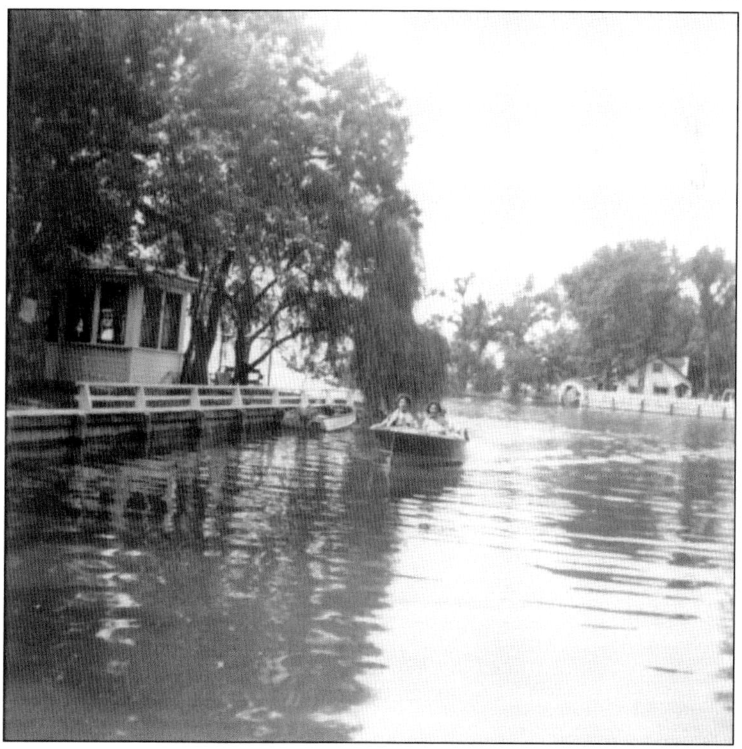

The park continued to emphasize water attractions such as the canoes, the beach, and water scooters. Lifeguard Merle Williams was recognized in 1949 for 21 years of continued service without a drowning by the Middletown Safety Council. Williams worked full-time as a basketball coach and teacher at Middletown's McKinley Junior High School. (Courtesy of Betty Fowler.)

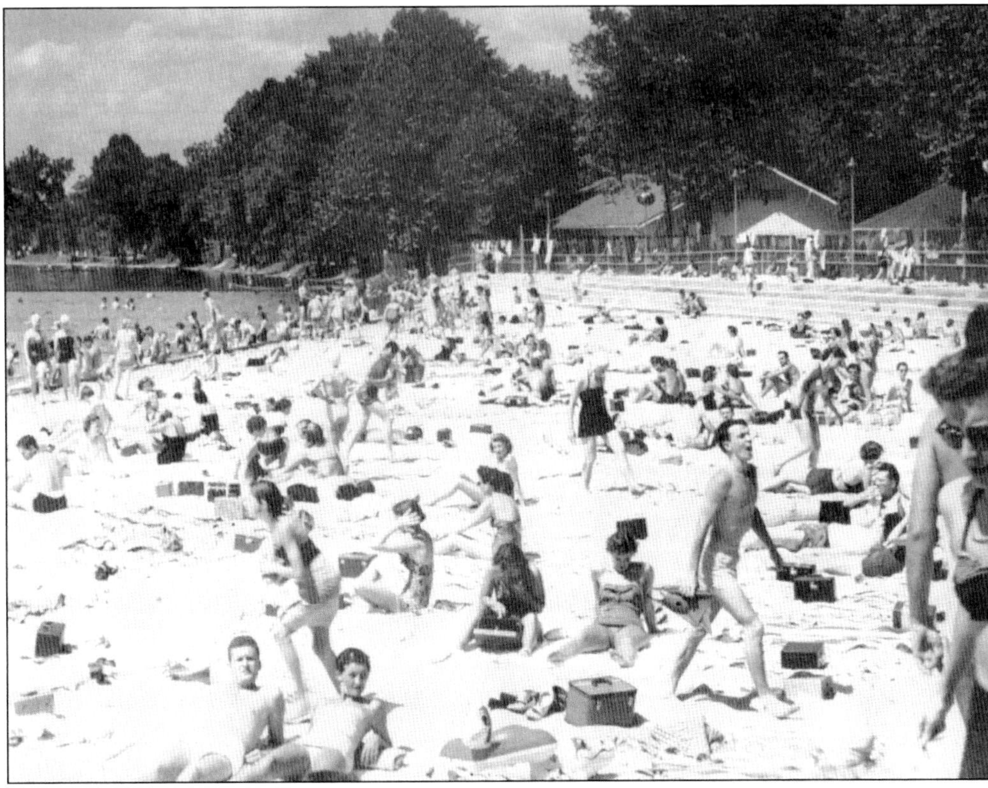

Guests enjoy the sandy beach in this picture from 1950. Sand was imported annually from Lake Michigan for several years.

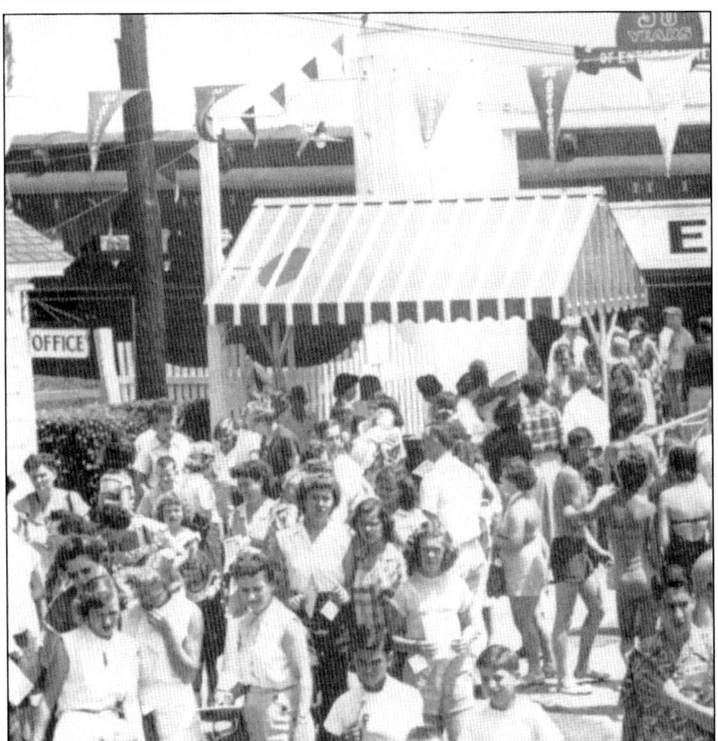

Champion Paper and Fiber Company employees flood through the main gate in this 1950 photograph. The park estimated that 28,000 people made their way into the park to enjoy their annual picnic and watch the Champion Parade of Beauties pageant. (Courtesy of Champion Paper and Fiber Company.)

A special passenger train ran between the park and Champion's headquarters in Hamilton so employees and their families could enjoy the park. A similar train was used to bring in Armco employees during their designated day each year.

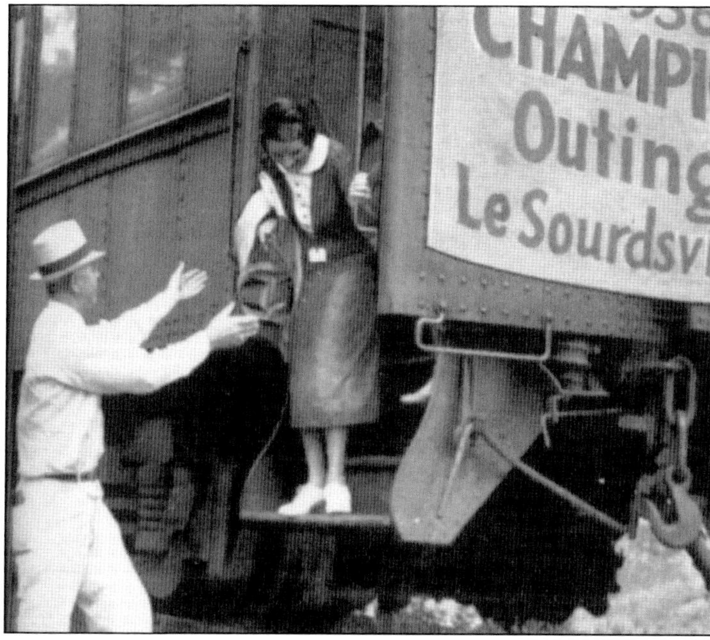

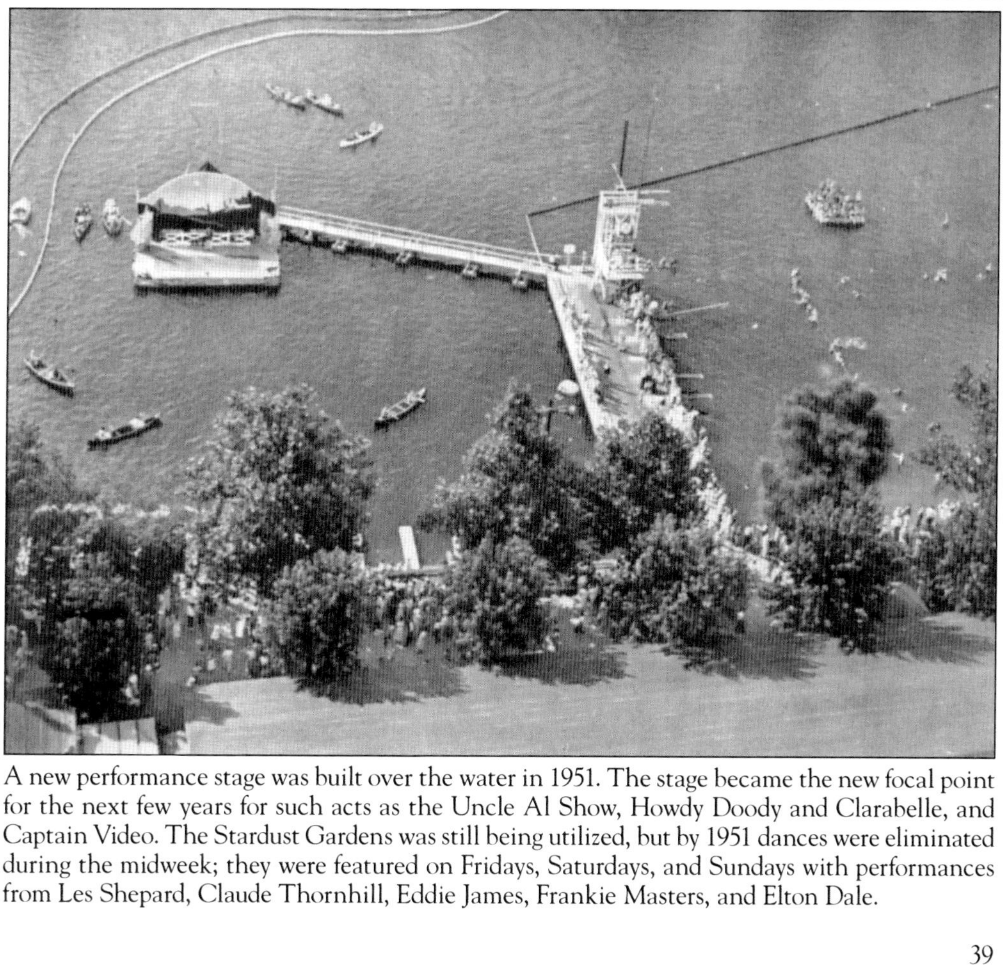

A new performance stage was built over the water in 1951. The stage became the new focal point for the next few years for such acts as the Uncle Al Show, Howdy Doody and Clarabelle, and Captain Video. The Stardust Gardens was still being utilized, but by 1951 dances were eliminated during the midweek; they were featured on Fridays, Saturdays, and Sundays with performances from Les Shepard, Claude Thornhill, Eddie James, Frankie Masters, and Elton Dale.

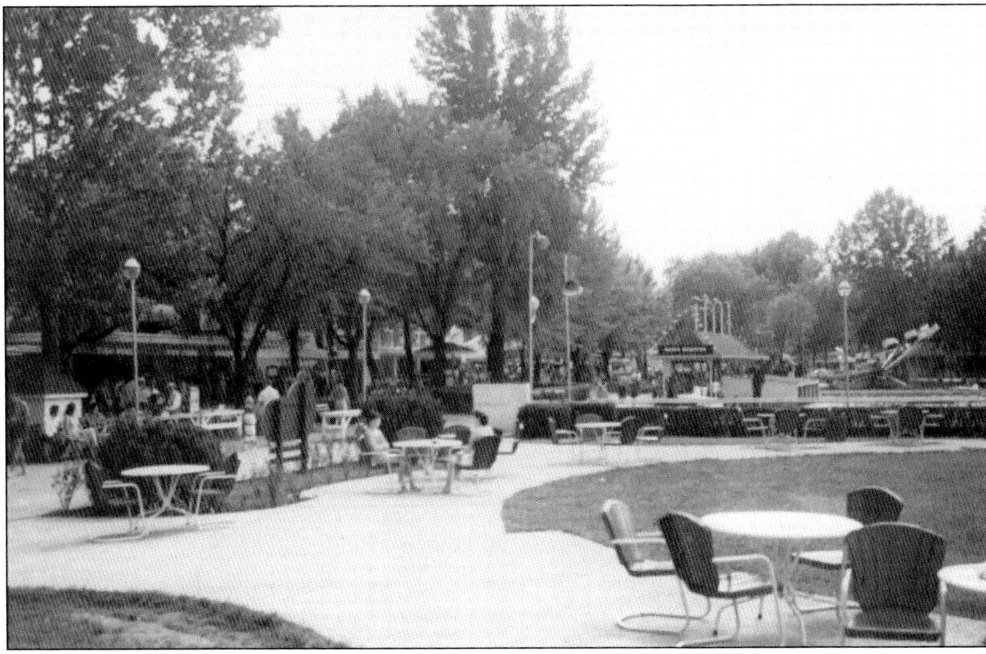

A promenade area was added in 1951, providing a rest area in the middle of the midway. In addition, boulevard-style lighting was added along the midway from the entrance to the Scenic Ride.

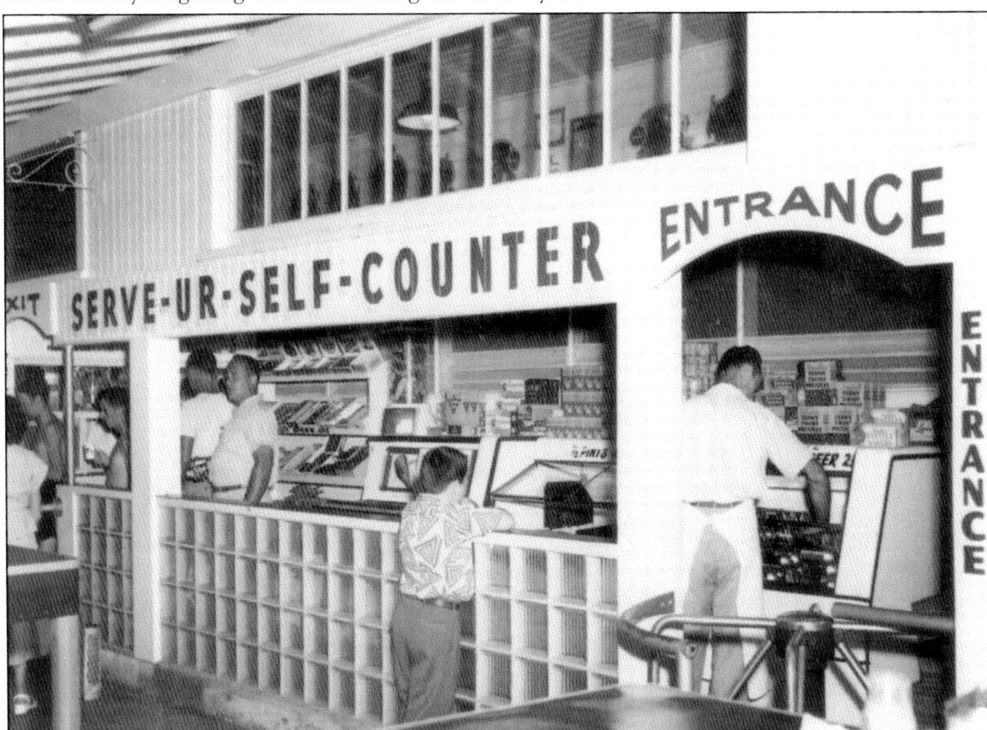

Edgar Streifthau conceived the idea of adding self-service lunch counters on the midway to help cut down on payroll. The self-service concept was reportedly the first of that type of lunch counter operating at an amusement park, but it did not catch on with other parks.

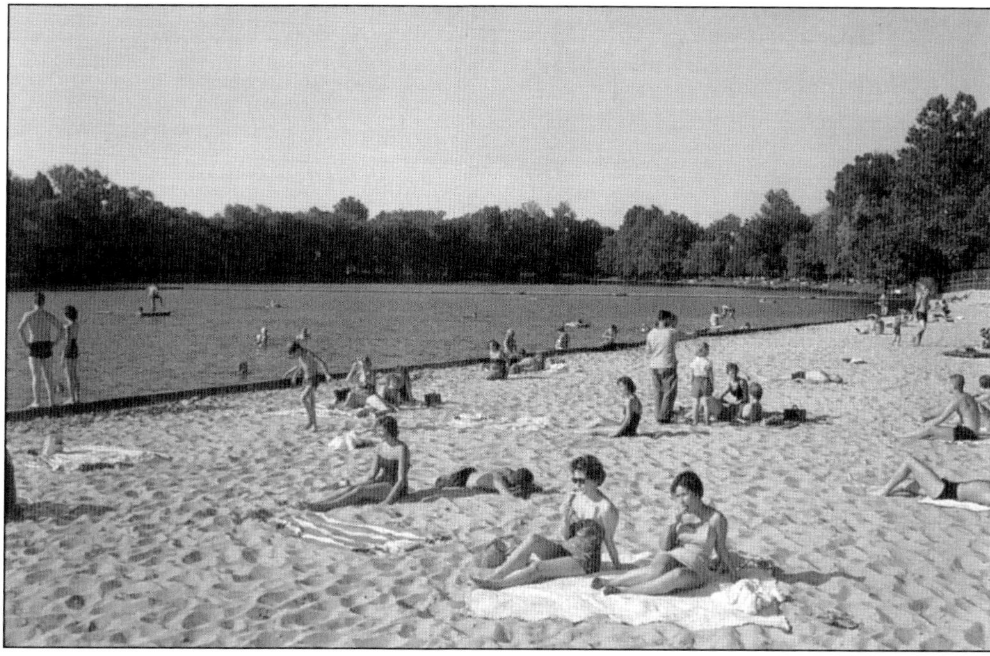

Sand for the beach was shipped from Siesta Key Beach, Florida, near Sarasota beginning for the 1951 season. Surplus sand was stored on the opposite side of the railroad tracks in the parking lot and was a favorite spot for many neighborhood cats.

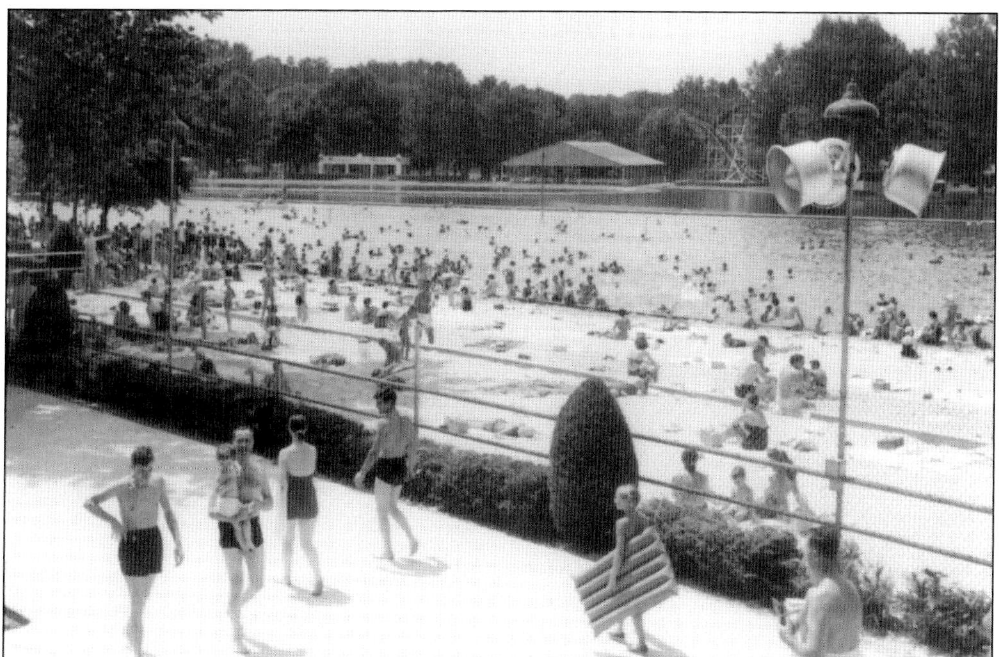

The beach was expanded by 25,000 square feet in 1952 and encompassed nearly four acres. Seen across the lake is the Scenic Ride building (left) and a large picnic shelter that later became the site of the arcade.

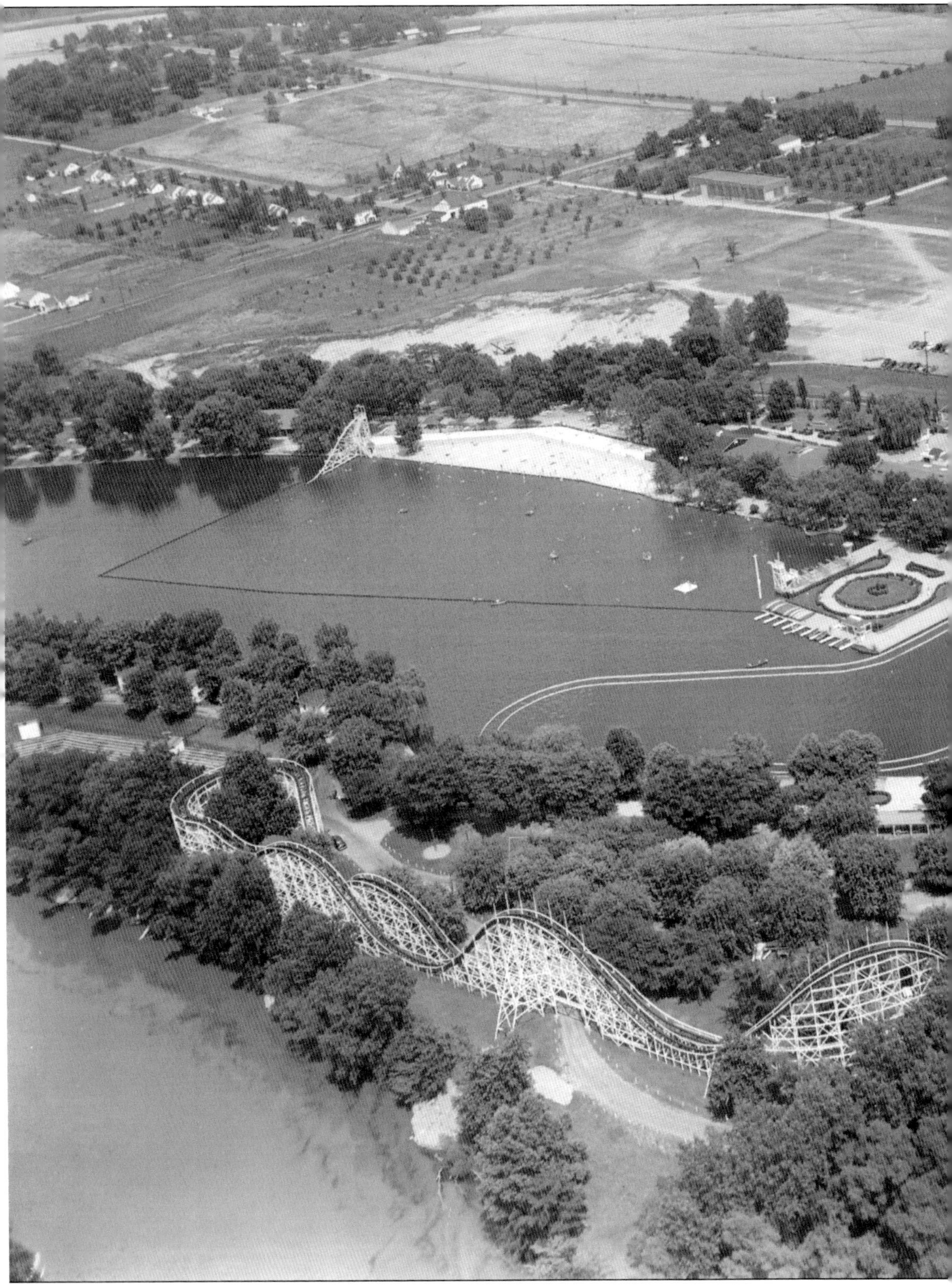

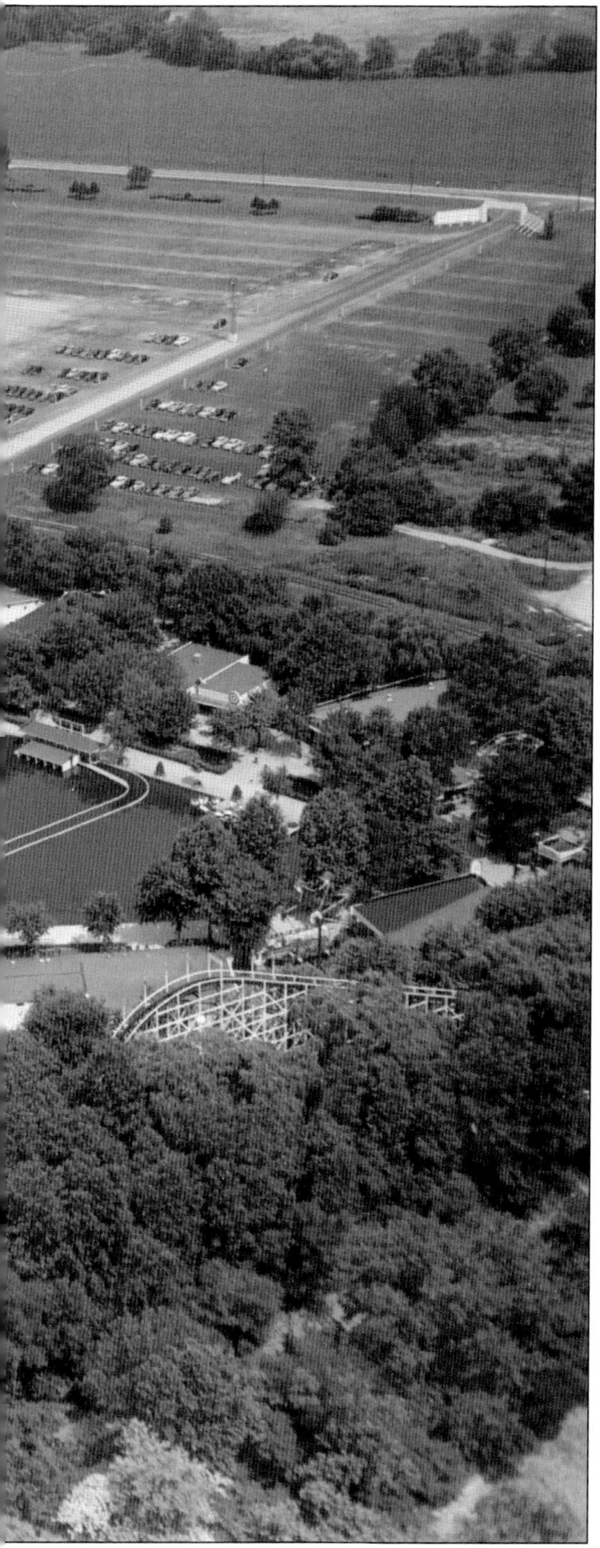

The circular area in the center of this picture was the new promenade area. The pool area was just left of the promenade. The area in the upper left with the tree grove later became Fantasy Farm Amusement Park. The housing development in the far left corner was a subdivision built by Streifthau. The park's ride and attractions line-up in 1951 included the Rock-O-Plane, Fun Parade, arcade, Pretzel, Flying Scooter, Octopus, the Cyclone roller coaster, Dodgem, scooter boats, Ferris wheel, Scenic Ride, carousel, swimming in the temperature-controlled well water lake with a sand beach, toboggans, swings, self-service lunch counters, three large shelter houses, four picnic areas, miniature golf, canoeing, two boats, kiddie playground, kiddie ship, kiddie rocket, miniature train ride, kiddie auto ride, a shooting gallery, and a rifle range. (Photograph by George R. Hoxie; courtesy of the Smith Library of Regional History.)

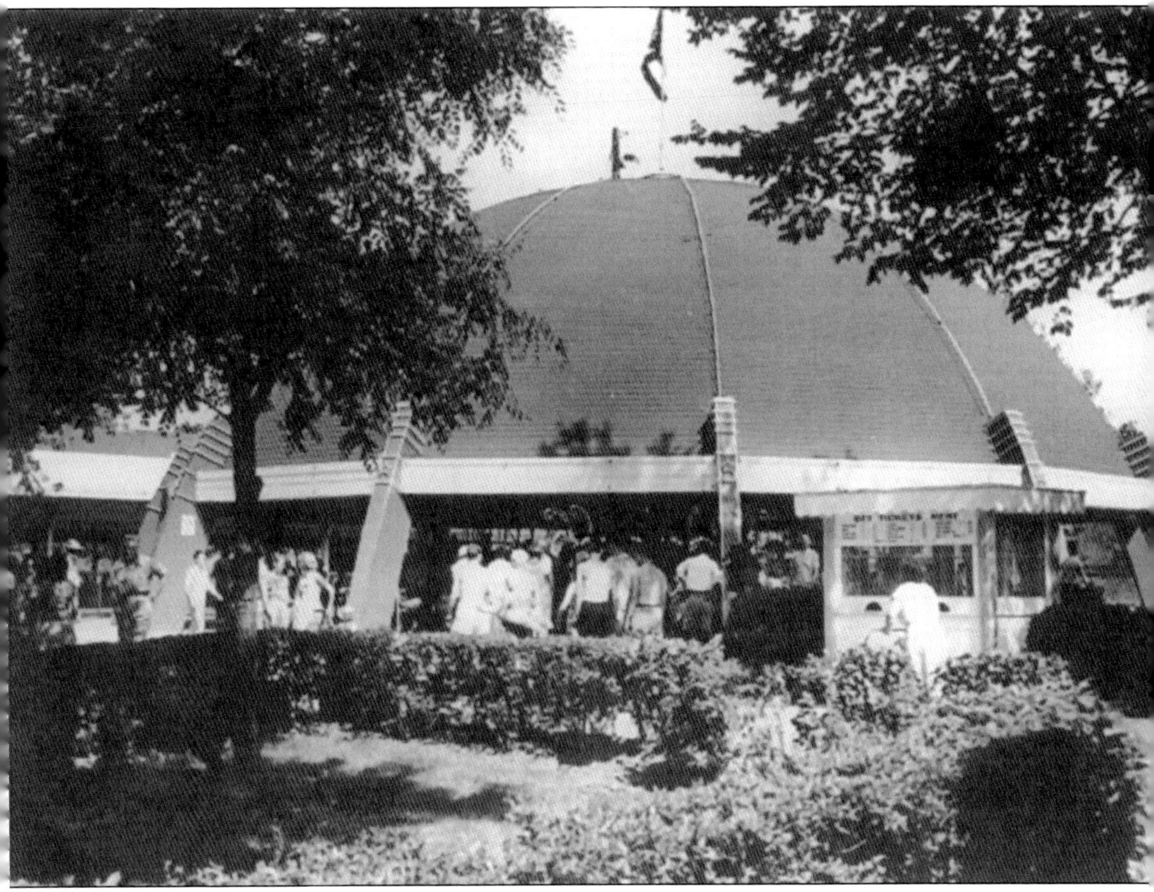

An 80-foot-diameter shell was constructed to shelter the park's historic carousel. The 1924 carousel was one of 87 carousels constructed by the Philadelphia Toboggan Company (PTC). PTC assigned the no. 71 to the structure as an identifier. The three-row carousel consisted of a number of hand-carved horses.

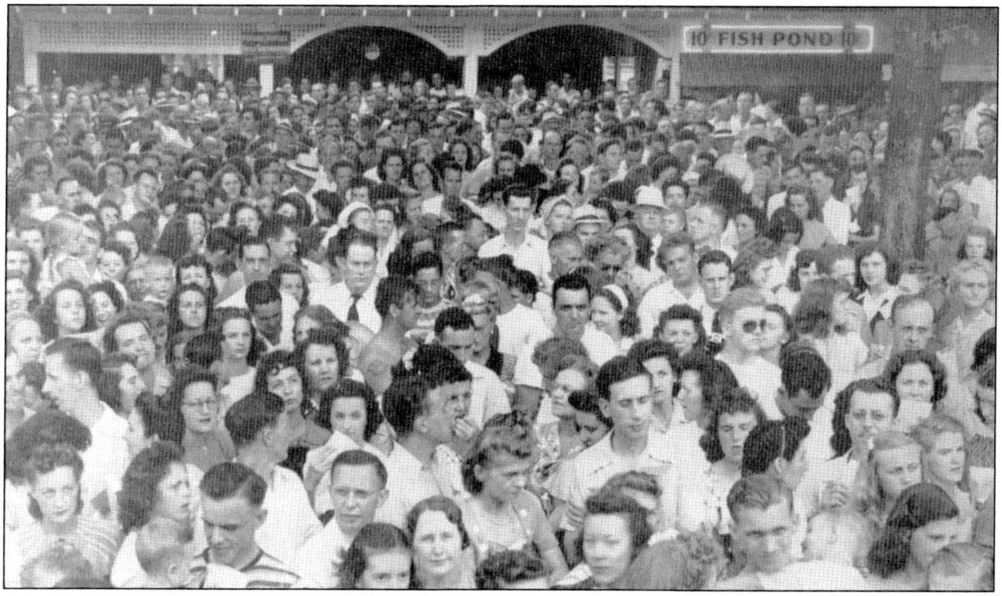

Champion Paper broke the park's one-day admission record, bringing in 32,000 employees and their families at their annual picnic in 1952. (Courtesy of Champion Paper and Fiber Company.)

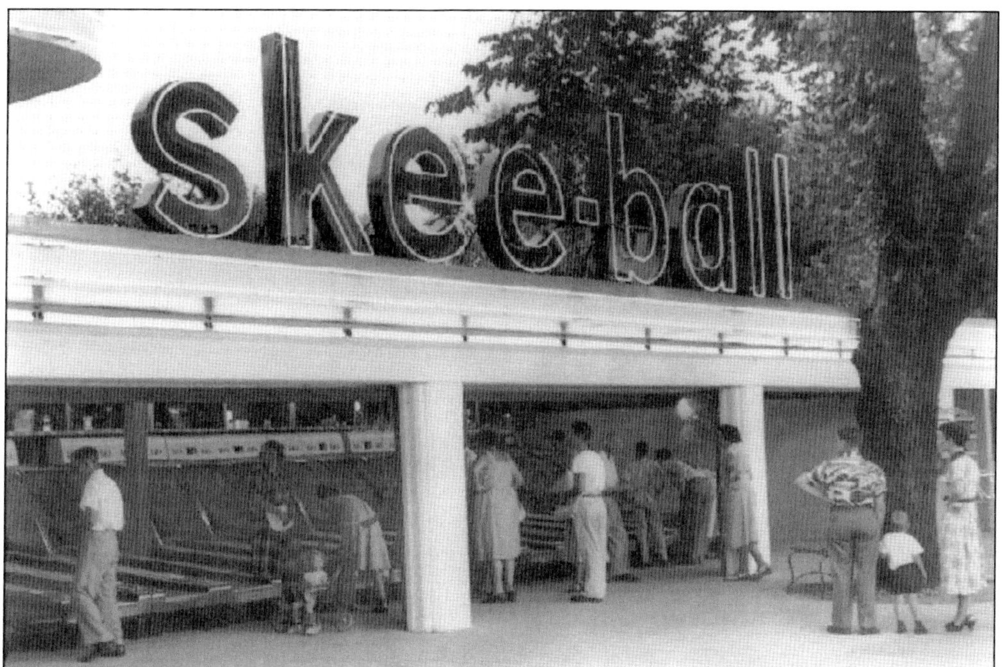

A new Skeeball building was constructed in 1952 at the south end of midway next to the self-service lunch counter. The building would later become the Fascination game building. The park also added a kiddie coaster, a kiddie boat ride, and a House of Mirrors.

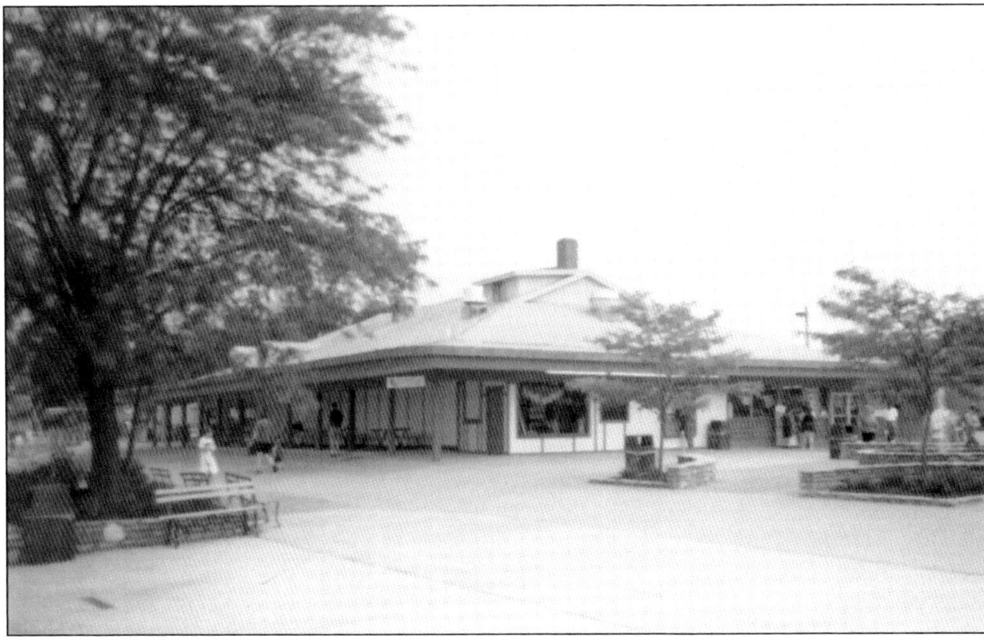

The cafeteria was renovated in 1953 and moved to the side of the building facing the lake. A gift shop opened in the former cafeteria area. When the area was renovated in 2000, the original cherry ceiling molding was uncovered, revealing a style not seen in years.

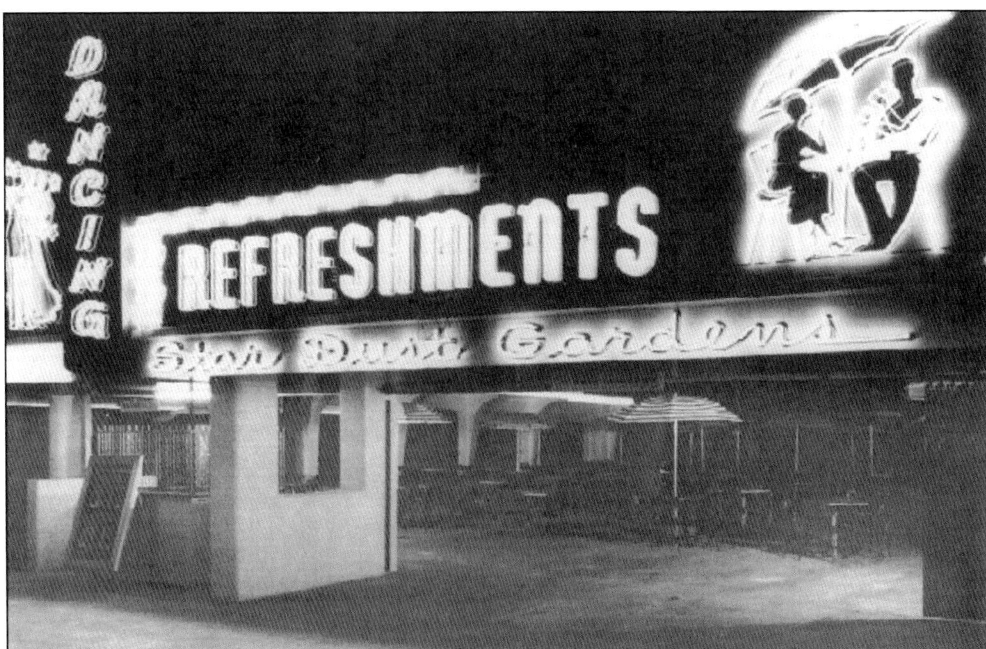

The Stardust Gardens was renovated in 1953 with a new entrance that included a 30-foot-by-15-foot-high neon sign that depicted two dancing figures in motion. The area was painted a blend of pastel blue and rose, and leather booths were added to each side of the dance floor. Five years later, record hops were held on Friday nights replacing the big bands.

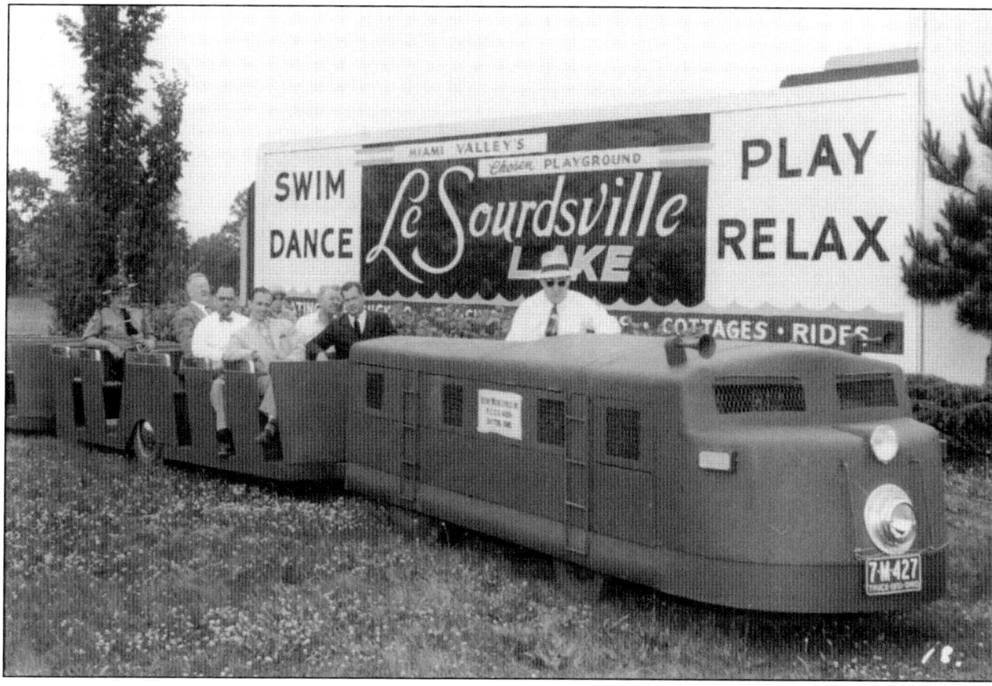

In 1953, the park purchased a National Amusement Device, 32-passenger train called the Century Flyer that was 70 feet long and ran on 1,500 feet of track. It was located just inside the main entrance in Kiddieland and ran through the picnic grounds.

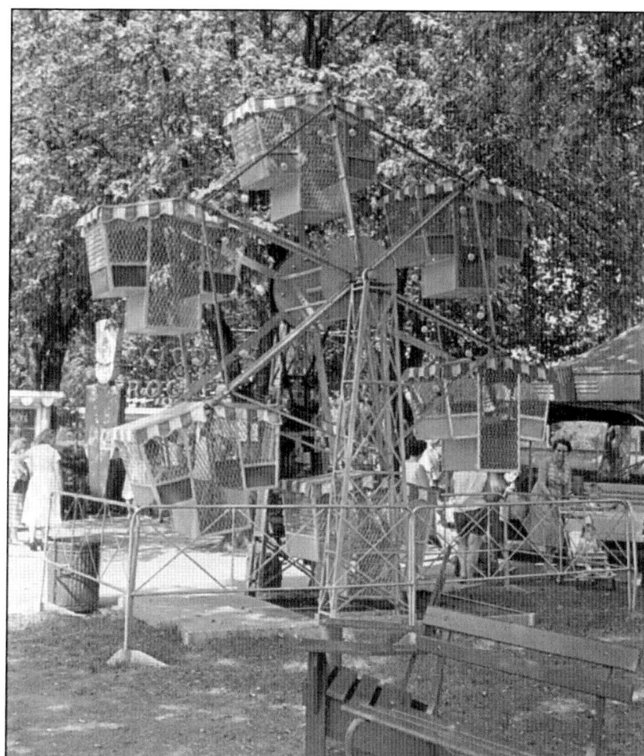

Kiddieland also was the recipient of a Ferris wheel, a Tub-o-Fun ride, and a handcar ride in 1953. The following year, children were treated to a July appearance by Santa Claus. Jolly Saint Nick appeared for three days and gave away actual silver coins. Park lifeguards played elves and sang Christmas carols.

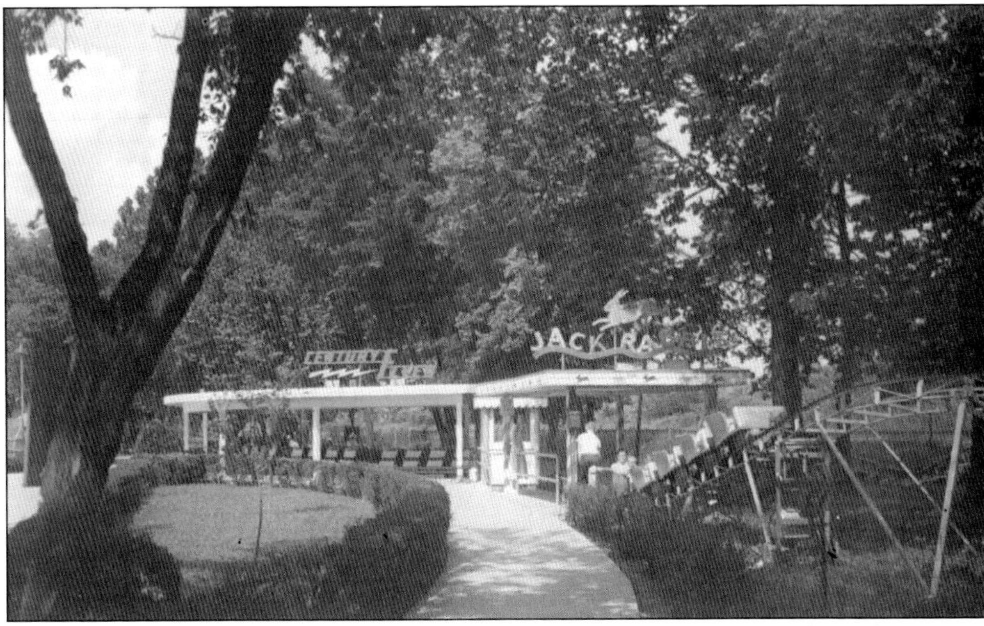

The Jack Rabbit kiddie roller coaster made its debut in Kiddieland in 1955 as the park continued its focus on making the park more family friendly. The coaster was the first steel coaster installed at the park. The ride, which lasted 50 seconds, was replaced by a similar roller coaster in 1968.

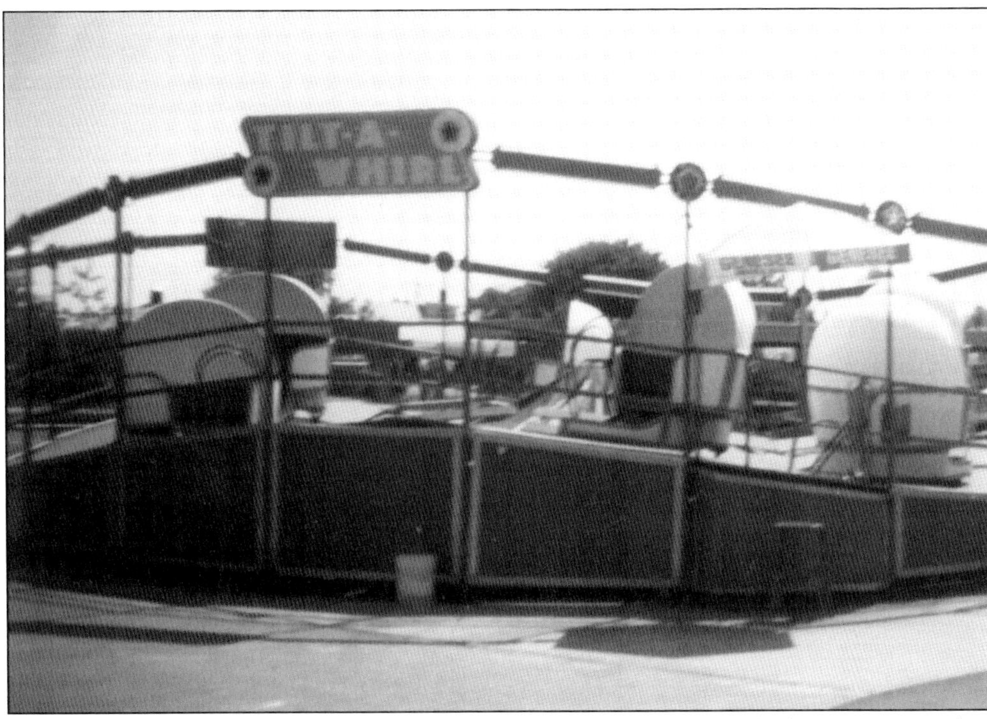

The south end of the midway was extended to make way for the Tilt-a-Whirl in 1956. According the park officials, attendance was estimated at just under a million people annually, and that number stayed fairly consistent through the 1950s.

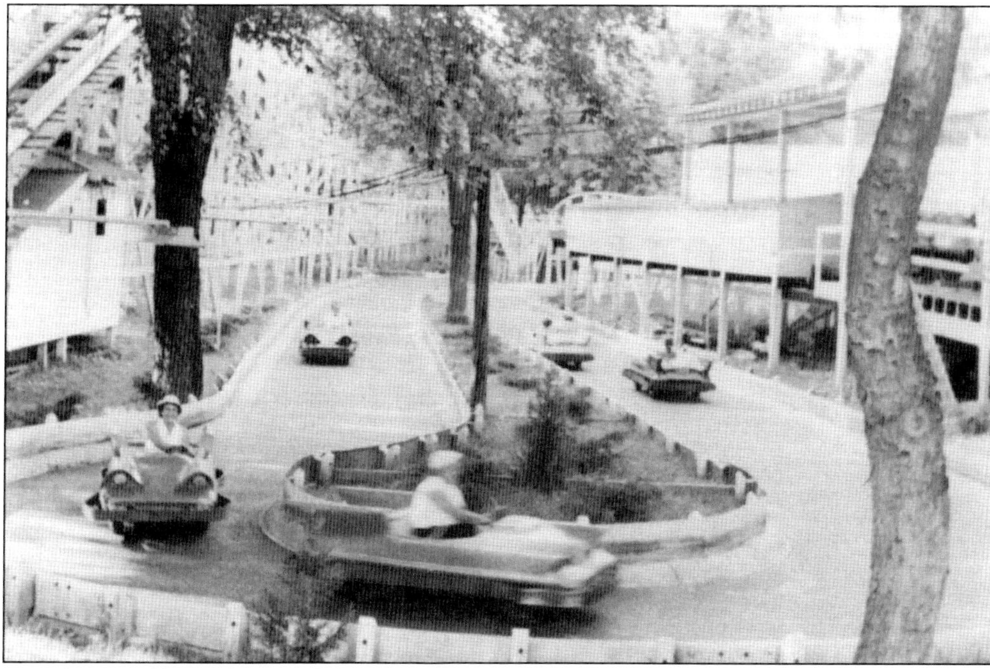

In 1956, Streifthau, along with his son Lindy and Frank Dodd, developed his own version of a turnpike ride that did not utilize any type of guide or rail system. After he realized that he had to have bumpers added to the cars, Streifthau formed the Streifthau Manufacturing Company. The company built and sold turnpike cruisers to parks across the country, including Cincinnati's Coney Island and Camden Park in Huntington, West Virginia.

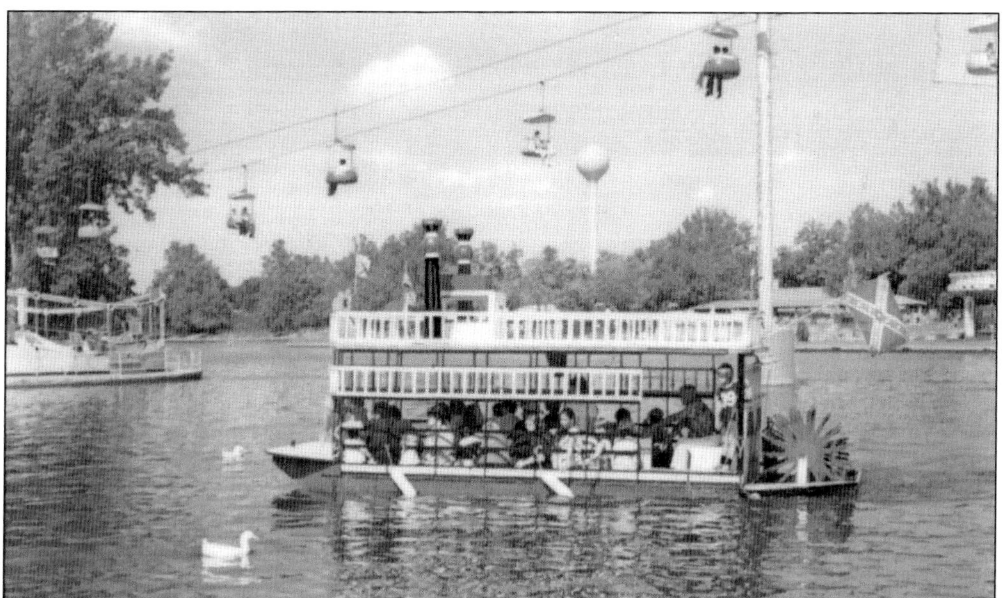

The park added a showboat in 1956 that permitted groups of people to enjoy a peaceful ride across the lake.

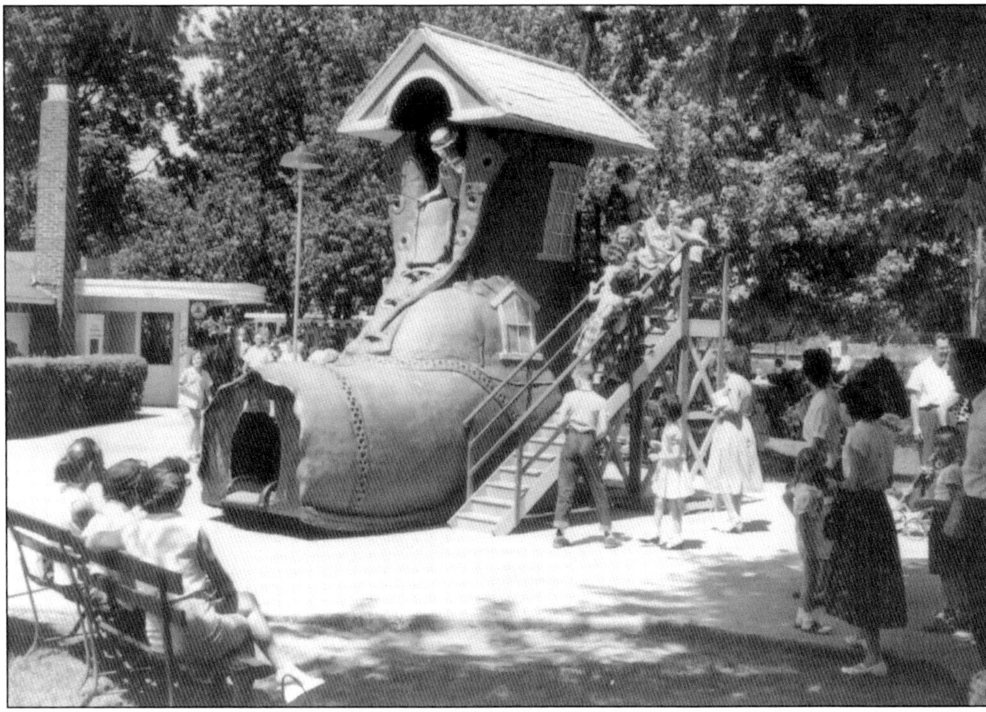

The Old Lady in the Shoe was added to Kiddieland in 1956. It consisted of an 18-and-a-half-foot slide with an animated woman at the top waving a switch as kids slid down.

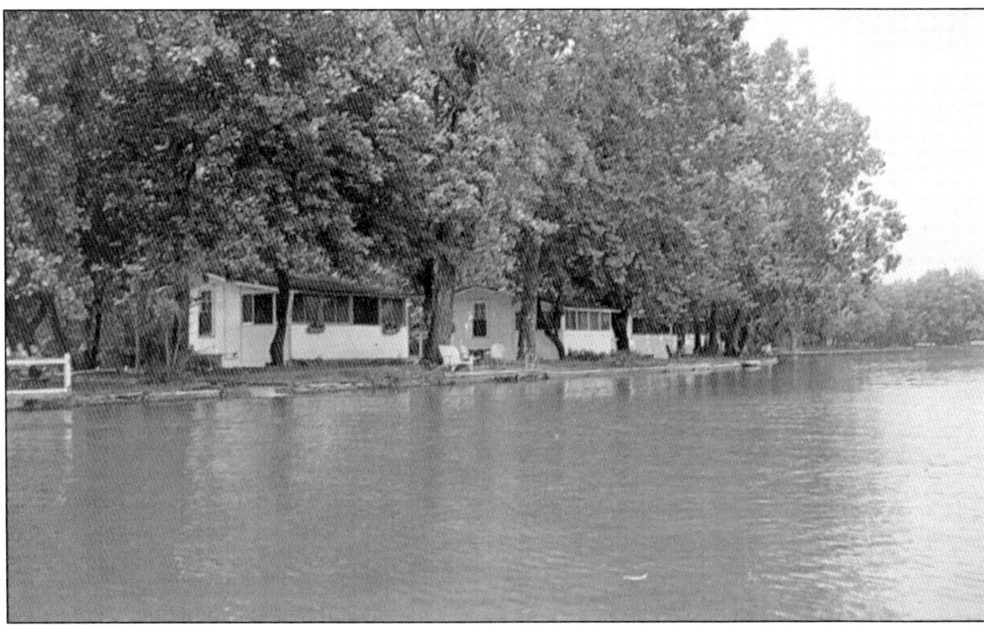

Although the park did not add to their inventory of 33 cabins in years, many of the units were rented on an annual basis, making for a very peaceful setting when the park was not open. In 1956, some of the permanent residents at the lake included Mr. and Mrs. A. R. Green, the William D. Long family, the Packard family, Mr. and Mrs. Walter Delscamp, Mr. and Mrs. Frank Dodd, Mr. and Mrs. John Bitner, Pete Reese, Rolin Johnson, Art Schlagle, and Vance Cummins.

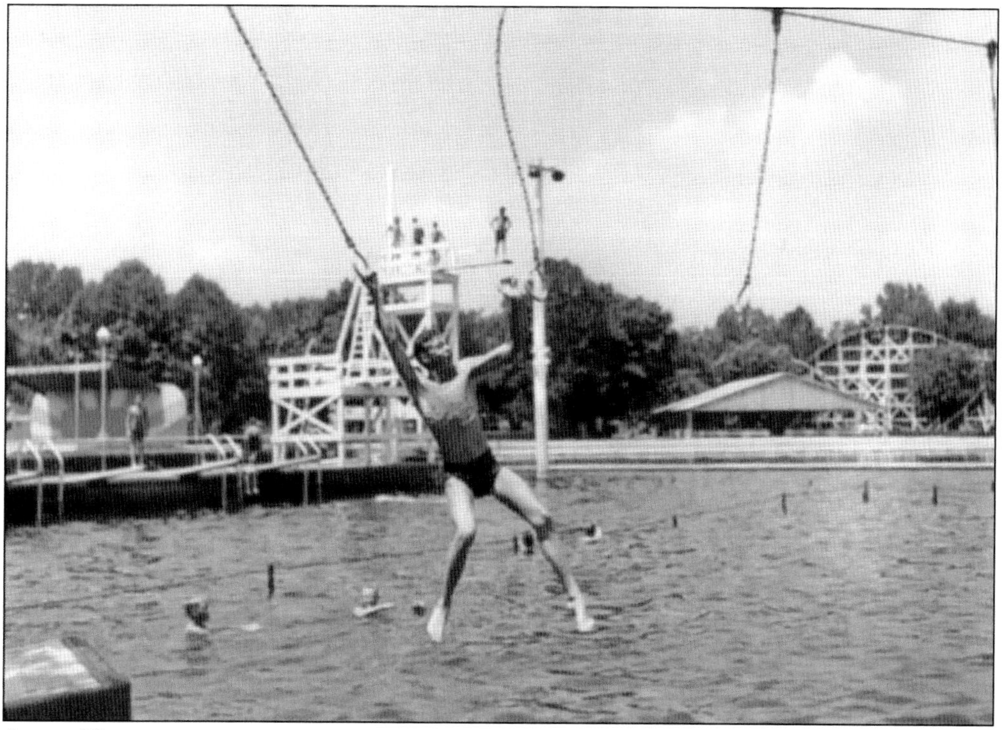

A set of flying rings was added to the beach diving area in 1957. Swimmers would swing from one set of rings to another after jumping from a wood deck.

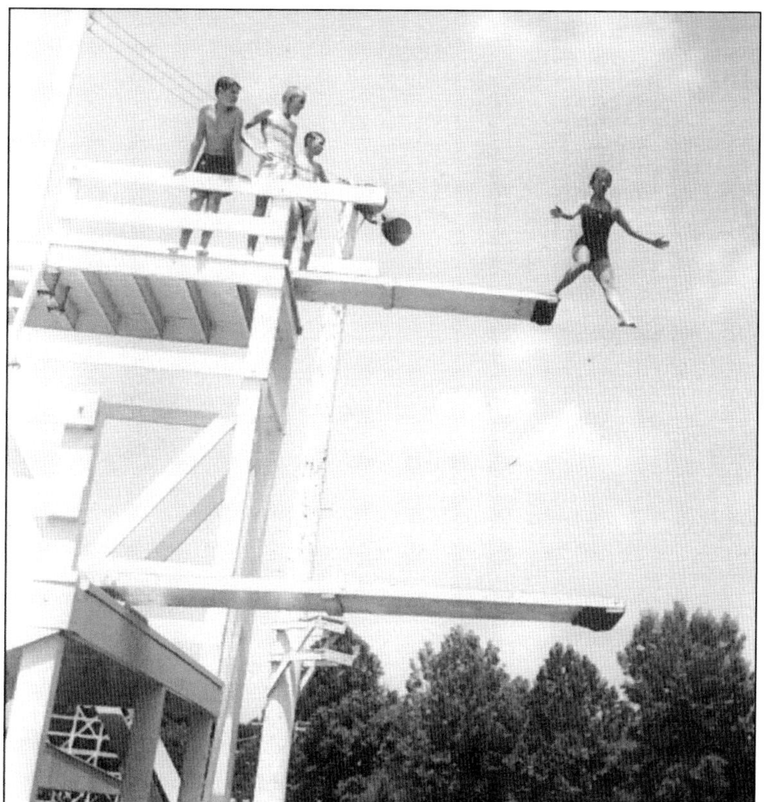

In addition to the flying rings, new diving boards and a cement diving pier was added. Water attractions remained an important aspect of the park's offerings until 1961.

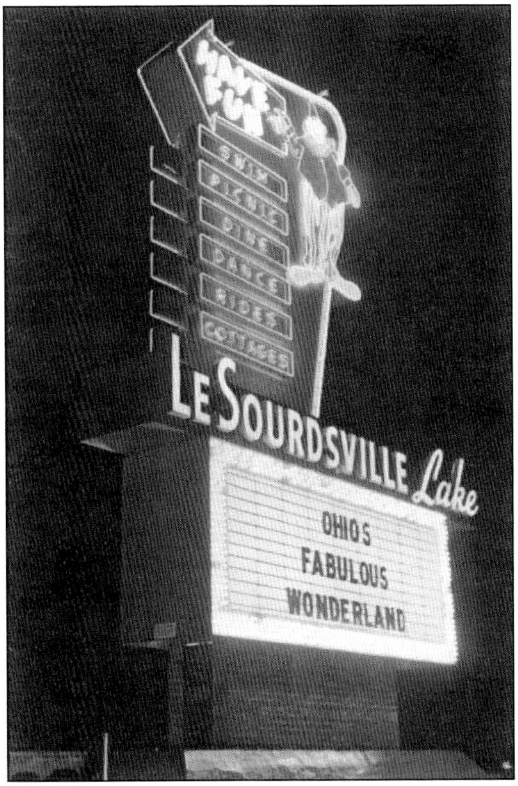

As part of a major expansion and update program, a 45-foot-high neon-lit sign complete with a 15-foot-high animated clown was installed at a cost of $20,000 in 1958 after State Route 4 was expanded to a divided four-lane highway.

The Scrambler was added for the 1959 season. The ride was a staple to the main Midway ride line-up until the late 1980s, when it was moved to the Logger's Run area.

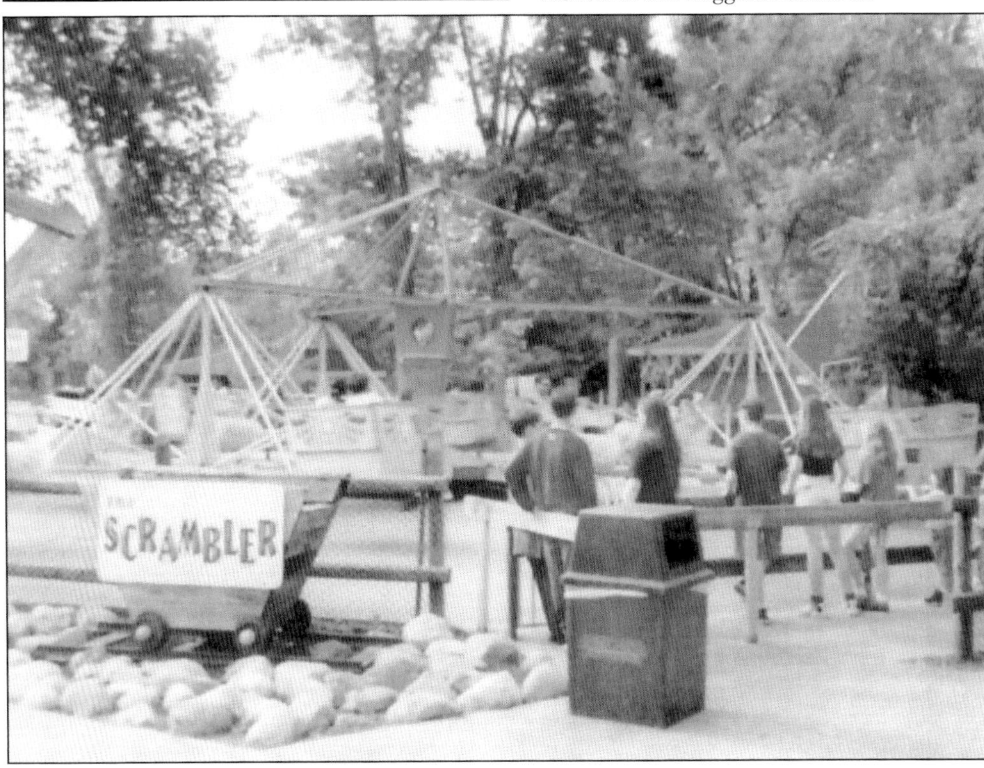

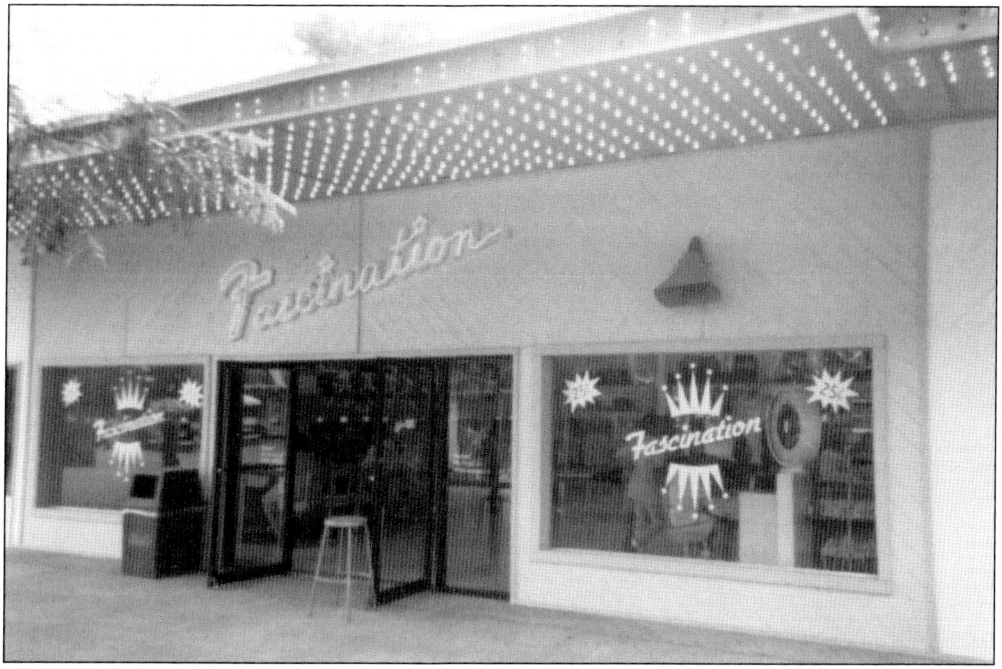

The popular game of Fascination was added to the midway in 1959 and provided an air-conditioned oasis for many players. Potential prizes were displayed on the walls surrounding the 32 game tables.

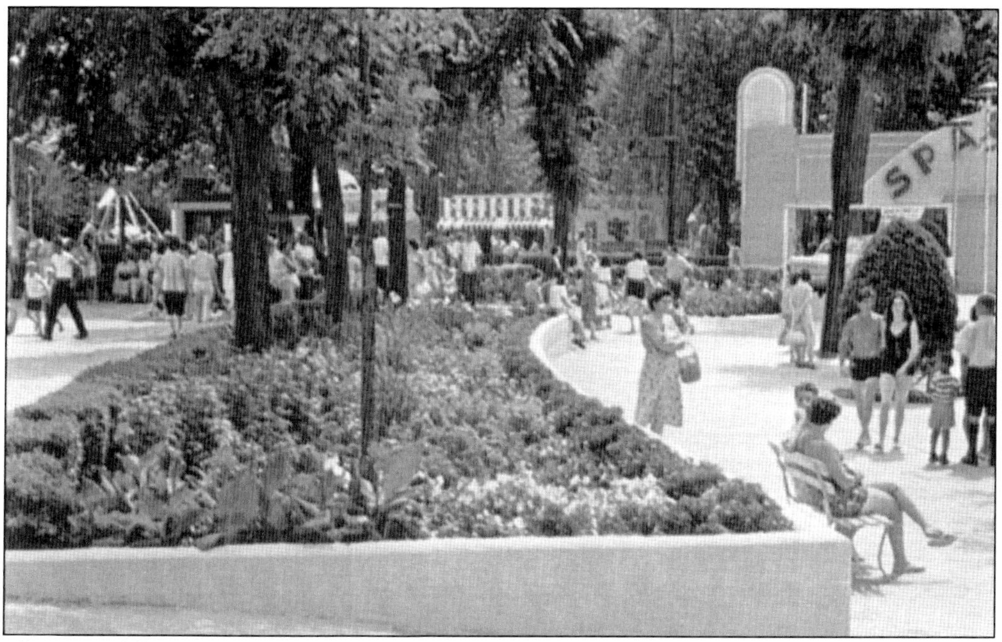

This peaceful scene of the main midway was in stark contrast to what was going on behind the scenes in 1959. Don Dazey had suddenly passed away, and a local bank wanted to recall the loan issued for the expansion. Edgar Streifthau was also dealing with unhappy concessionaires who claimed that not enough people were coming to the park. After much consideration, Streifthau decided to put the park up for sale.

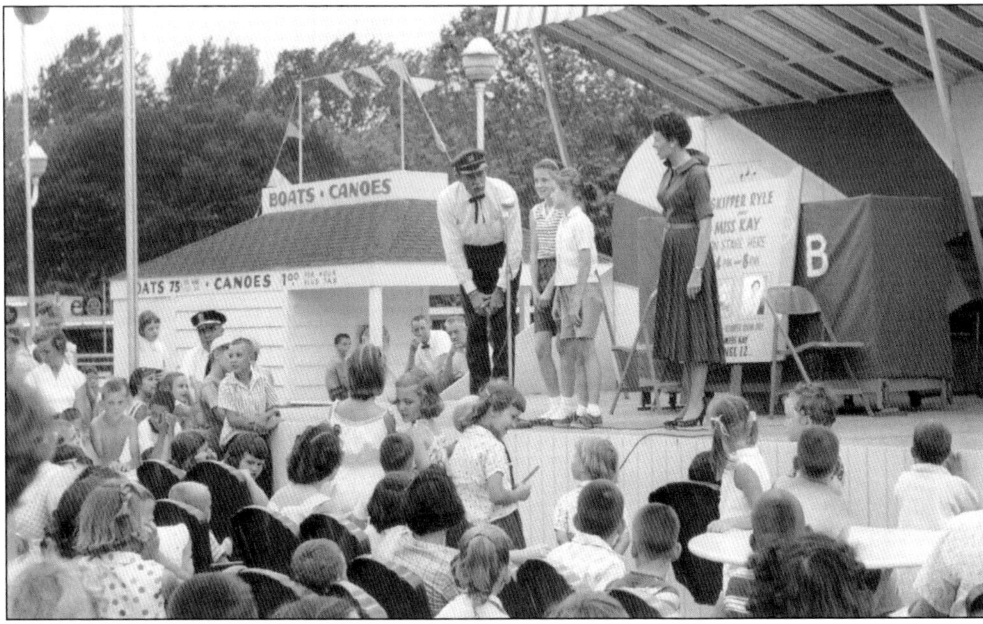

In August 1960, children's television show host Glen "Skipper" Ryle hosted one of his annual shows at the park, sponsored by WKRC-TV and the *Cincinnati Enquirer.* All gate proceeds were donated to charity.

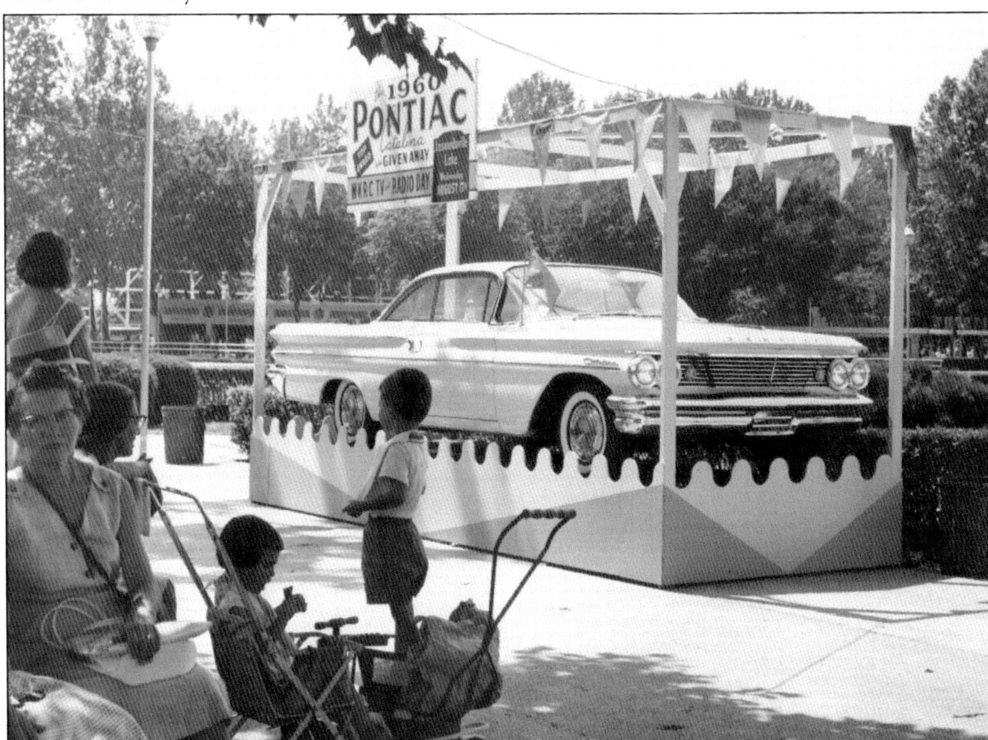

The winner of the WKRC-TV charity raffle received a 1960 Pontiac Catalina that was on display next to the lake during the show.

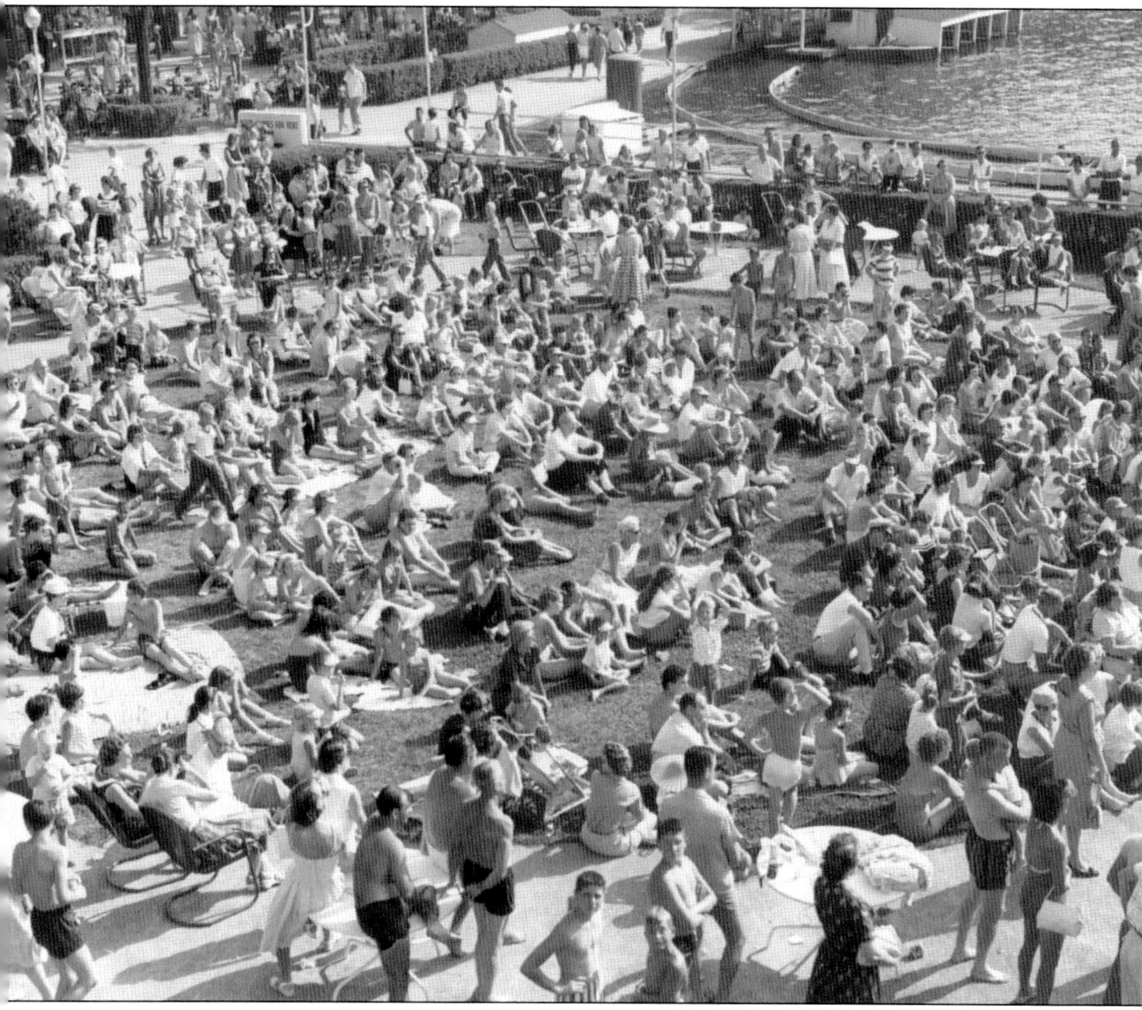

The crowd that came to see Skipper Ryle resulted in standing room only along the promenade and the midway. Local television personalities typically drew very large crowds. Skipper Ryle began his annual shows at the park beginning in 1957. Uncle Al and Captain Wendy from Cincinnati's WCPO-TV began their appearances in 1956. Singers and dancers from WLWT-TV's *Midwestern Hayride* were popular in the 1950s. The most popular local television host was Bob Braun, who cohosted WLWT-TV's the *50-50 Club* with Ruth Lyons and, later, his own show after Lyons retired in 1967. Braun not only sang but hosted a number of events at the park. Singers from the *Bob Braun Show* appeared on the midway stage in the early and mid-1970s. Perhaps the most bizarre television personality to grace the midway was the Cool Ghoul from Cincinnati's WXIX-TV. He was a popular act in the early 1970s at the park and on his late-night television show.

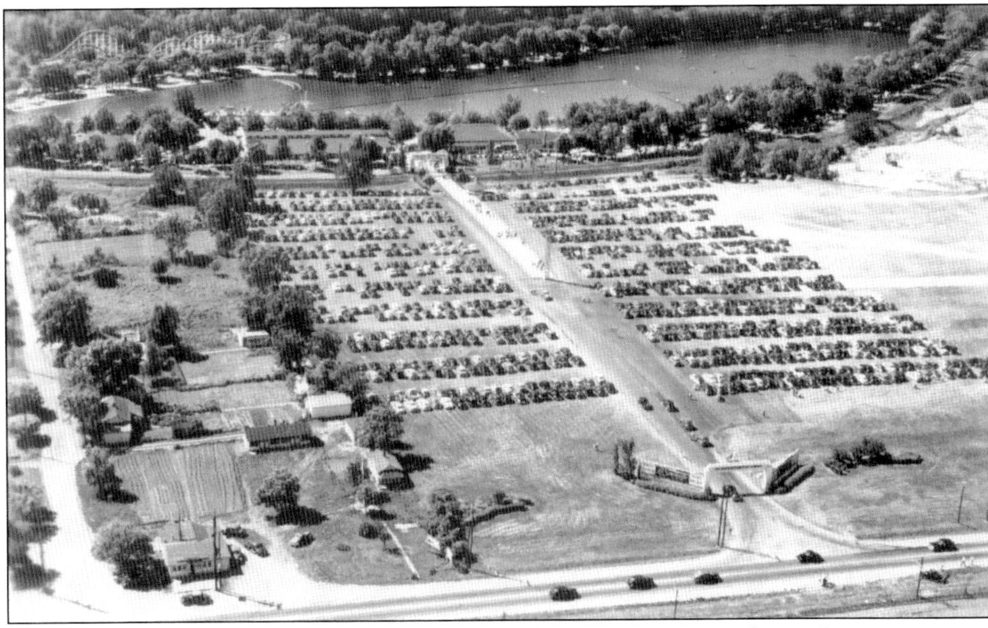

Crowds continued filling the parking lot to enjoy the entertainment, rides, and attractions.

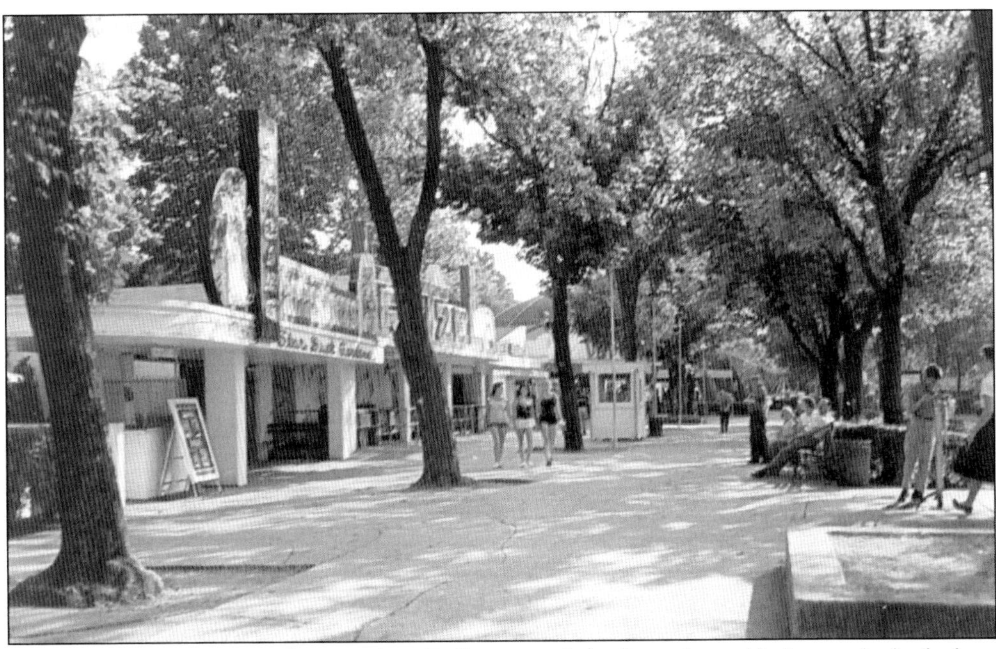

The midway near the Stardust Gardens Ballroom and the Pretzel provided enough shade for a nice, leisurely stroll to the rest of the park. It was small enough that kids could roam freely without parents getting overly concerned. The park was large enough to provide competition to nearby Coney Island. Edgar Streifthau did not want to sell LeSourdsville Lake, but he was under pressure from the bank that issued the improvement loan a couple of years earlier.

Three

The Little Giant Awakens

The 1960s ushered in prosperity for the park. Former Cedar Point concessionaires Howard Berni and Frank Murru purchased the park for $550,000 and took over operations in 1961. In 1964, sales manager George "Bill" Barr replaced Murru and contributed his creative ideas and endless energy. Big bands were replaced by the Byrds, the Beach Boys, Roy Clark, and Ricky Nelson, along with television stars such as Chuck Conners, Dick Clark, Michael Landon, Chuck Morrow, Bob Braun, and others.

By the mid 1970s, LeSourdsville Lake drew 600,000 patrons annually. The opening of Kings Island in nearby Mason in 1972 did not damper the spirits of Berni. In 1975, Barr retired and park veteran Bill Robinson took over managing operations and marketing. Robinson's knack for producing interesting promotions resulted in such events as the "Official" Bicentennial Amusement Park, the Coca-Cola/WSAI Radio Rock, Roll n' Remember concerts, and the Jell-O Jump, where contestants jumped into a barrel of gelatin to find the winning key to a new car.

In 1978, the name of the park changed to Americana Amusement Park after a $3.5 million, three-year renovation.

At the end of 1982, Robinson left the park to open his own marketing firm. He was replaced by Lenny Gottstein. In May 1983, food services director Frank Silvani passed away after a lengthy battle with cancer. In 1987, vice president Guy Sutton left to take a position with an industry consulting firm. Prior to the season opening in 1990, Berni's son Ron accepted a management position at Kentucky Kingdom in Louisville.

In January 1990, a fire destroyed the Stardust Gardens Ballroom that resulted in over a $5 million loss. By May, the area had been redeveloped, but the park experienced claim issues.

Prior to the season opening, the park entered into an agreement with a Mexican college to hire students. The park soon experienced claims of poor living conditions and illegal practices. The local labor unions canceled their outings due to the allegations. Attendance plummeted to just under 200,000, and the insurance company paid $3 million of the claim. In December, the park filed for Chapter 11 bankruptcy.

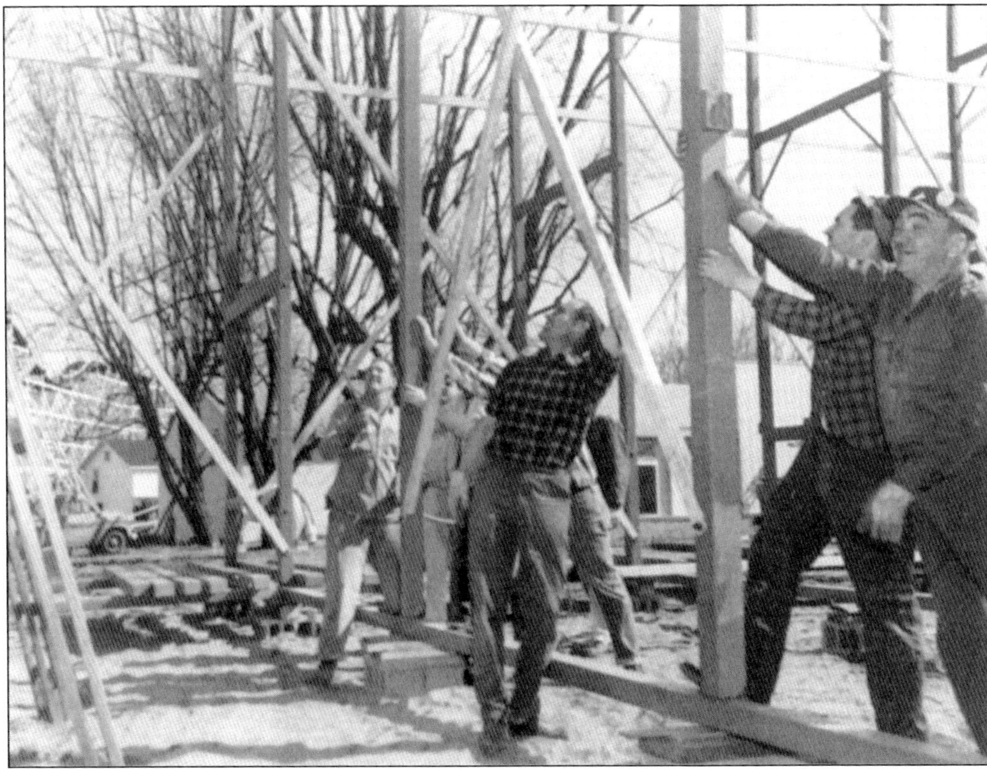

Over $250,000 of improvements were made in 1961, including the addition of an authentic Wild Mouse roller coaster imported from Munich, Germany. The coaster was removed after the 1963 season.

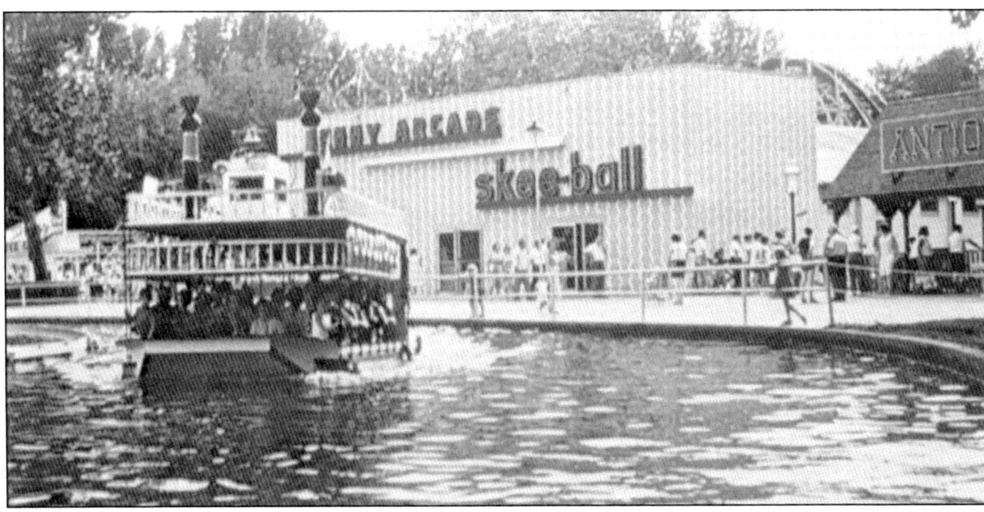

In 1961, a new arcade building complete with terrazzo flooring was built next to the recently renamed Space Rocket roller coaster. In addition, the 18-hole miniature golf course was redesigned and made three times larger than the previous course. New landscaping included a native Hawaiian ornamental garden with a hand-carved tiki and live palm trees. On Mother's Day, the first 2,000 women received a free orchid.

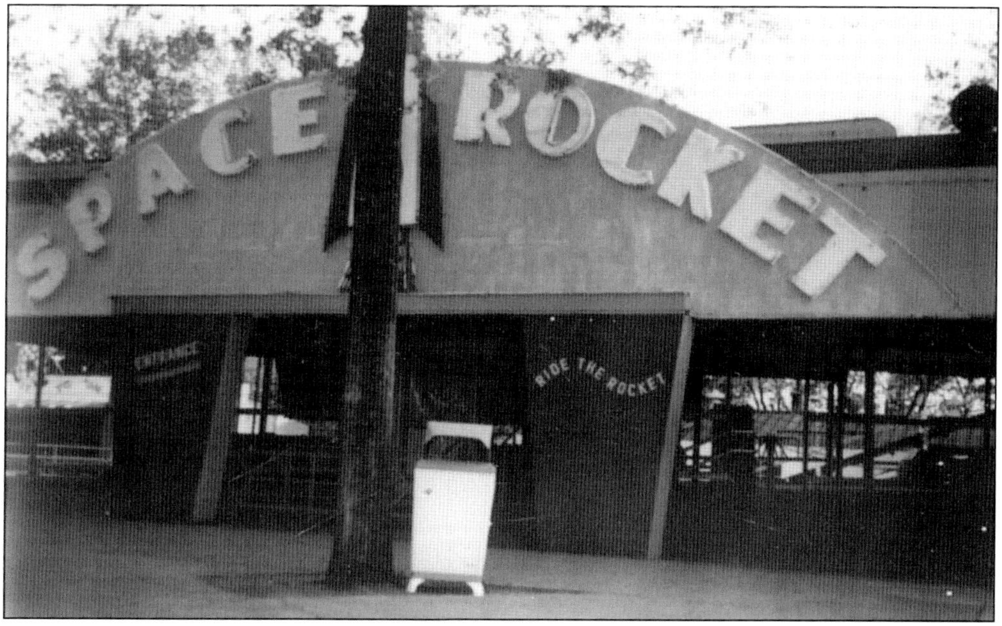

The station for the Cyclone was renovated in 1961, and the coaster was renamed the Space Rocket to coincide with the country's new space program initiative.

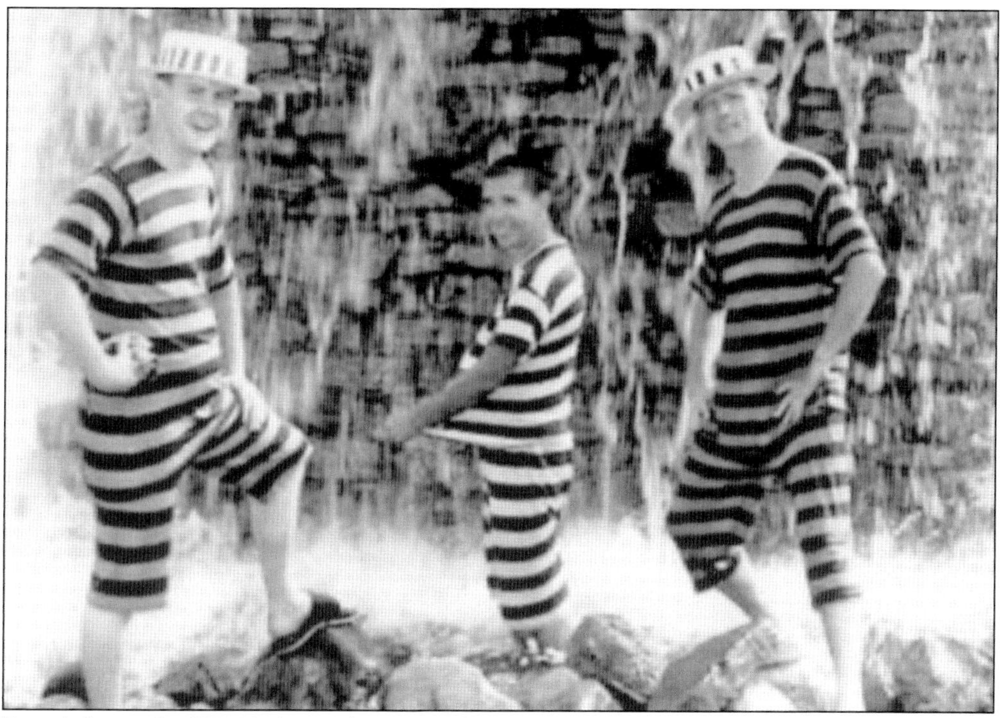

From left to right, WING-AM radio personalities Jim Smith, Rod Williams, and Stan Scott take a swim in the park's stone tower, located in the main gate area, between record hops. WING-AM was part of a Monday and Friday night record hop that was also hosted by personalities from WCPO-AM and WSAI-AM. Big band dancing in Stardust Gardens was still featured on Wednesday and Saturday nights in the early 1960s. (Courtesy of Rod Williams/WING-AM.)

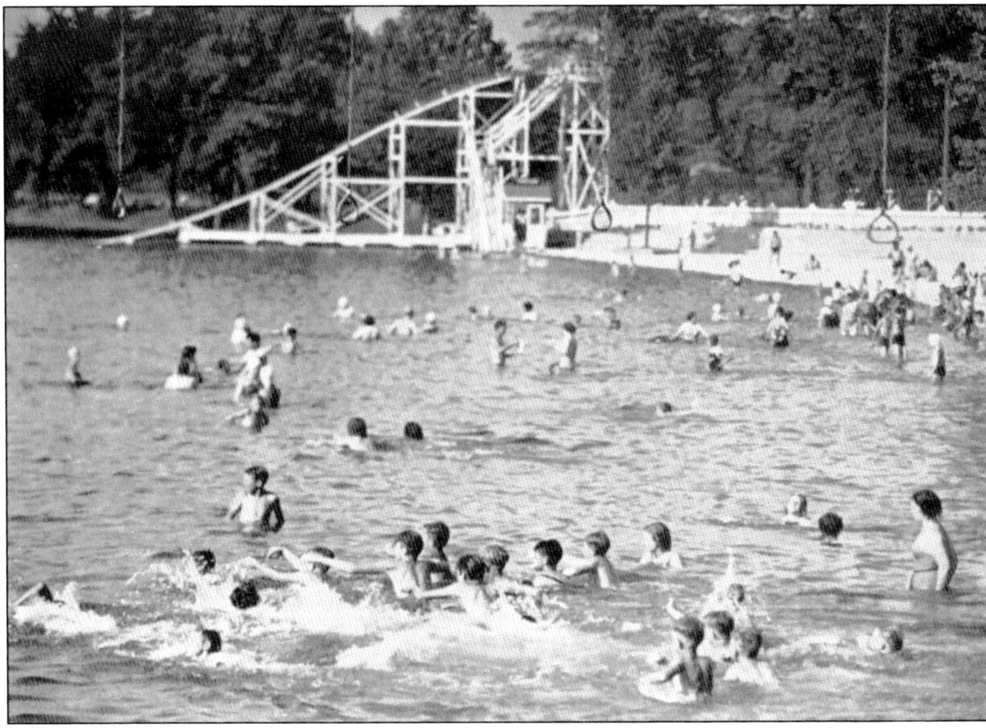

By the early 1960s, emphasis moved to upgrading rides and food services rather than the water attractions; the beach was upgraded once between 1961 and 1975. Ohio governor Michael V. DiSalle visited the park in 1962 and was the first and only governor to visit. New food concessions featured saltwater taffy, caramel corn, spaghetti, and fresh fried perch flown in every Friday from Lake Erie. A new French fry concession was added to the midway.

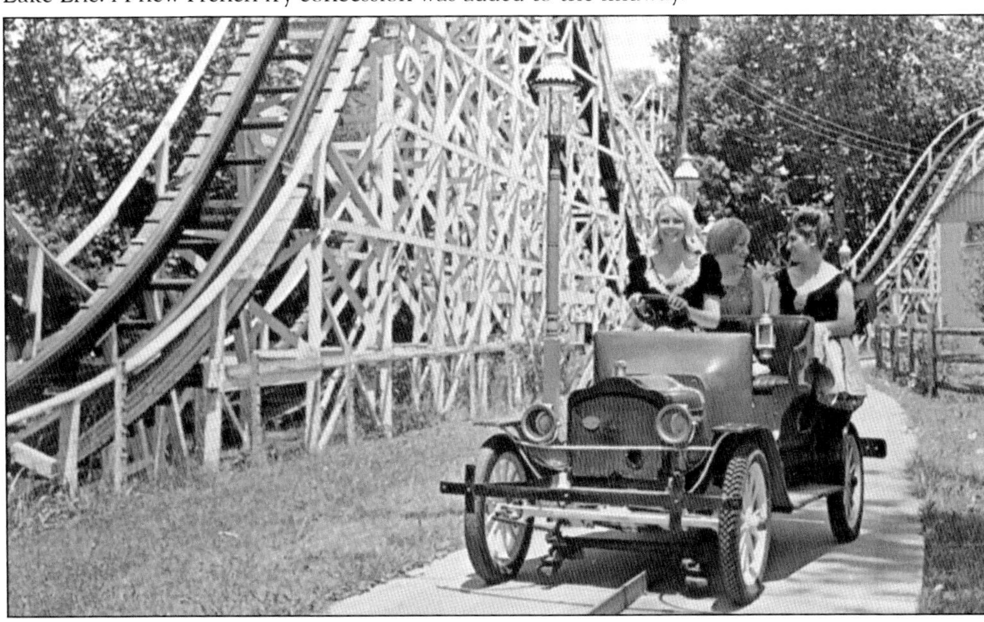

The Antique Autos were installed next to the Turnpike ride in 1962. The ride was designed by park owner Howard Berni.

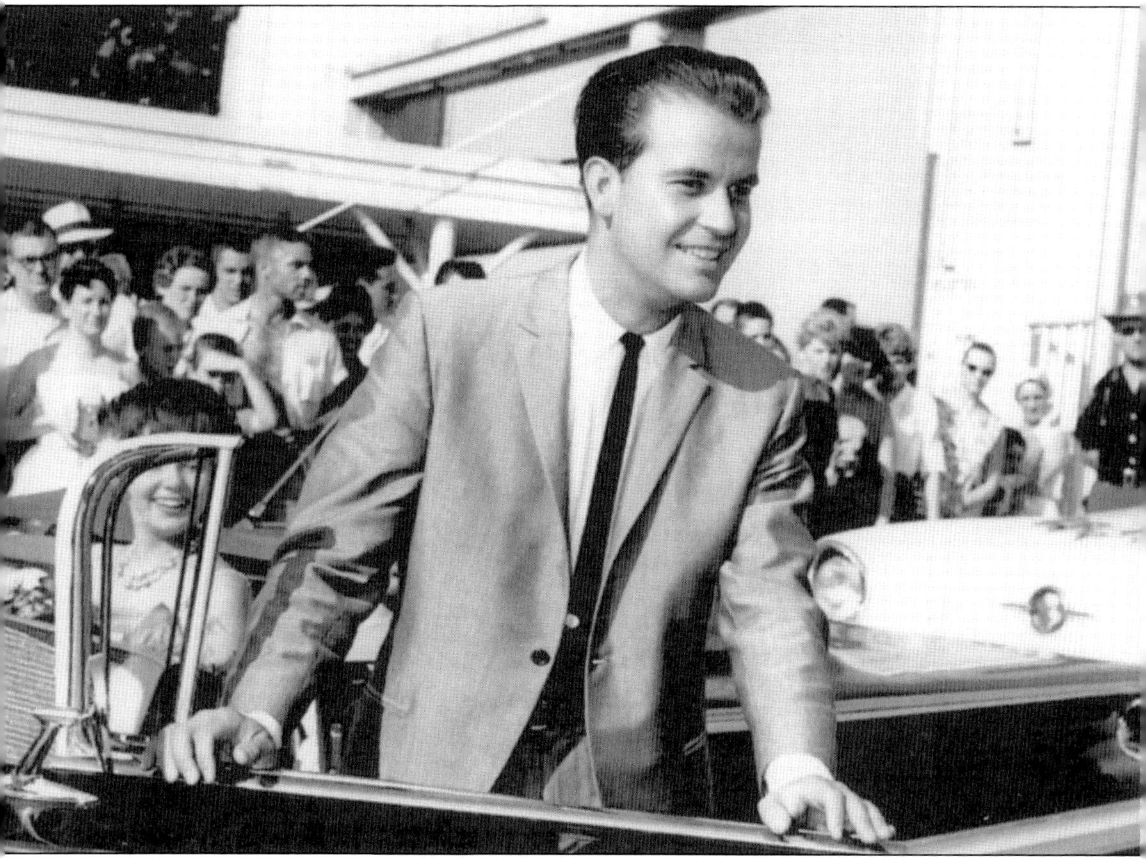

In 1962, American Bandstand host Dick Clark appeared with Bobby Defano and Bob Holliday of WING-AM radio, Dale Wright and the Wright Guys, Teddy and the Roughriders, Carl Dobkins Jr., the Twlighters, and the Casinos. Glenn "Skipper" Ryle of WKRC-TV hosted the event. The appearance of Clark officially welcomed the rock 'n' roll era into LeSourdsville Lake. By 1968, record hops were held in the Stardust Gardens on Saturday nights, hosted by WING-AM and WSAI-AM. One of the more popular local groups in the late 1960s was Teddy and the Rough Riders from Fairborn, Ohio. They enjoyed regional success with such hits as "Tomahawk/Thunderhead" and "Pathfinder." As fickle as the public was with music tastes, record hops were changed to teen dances in 1970 and held on Monday nights. Disco dances started in 1977 and lasted only a couple of years.

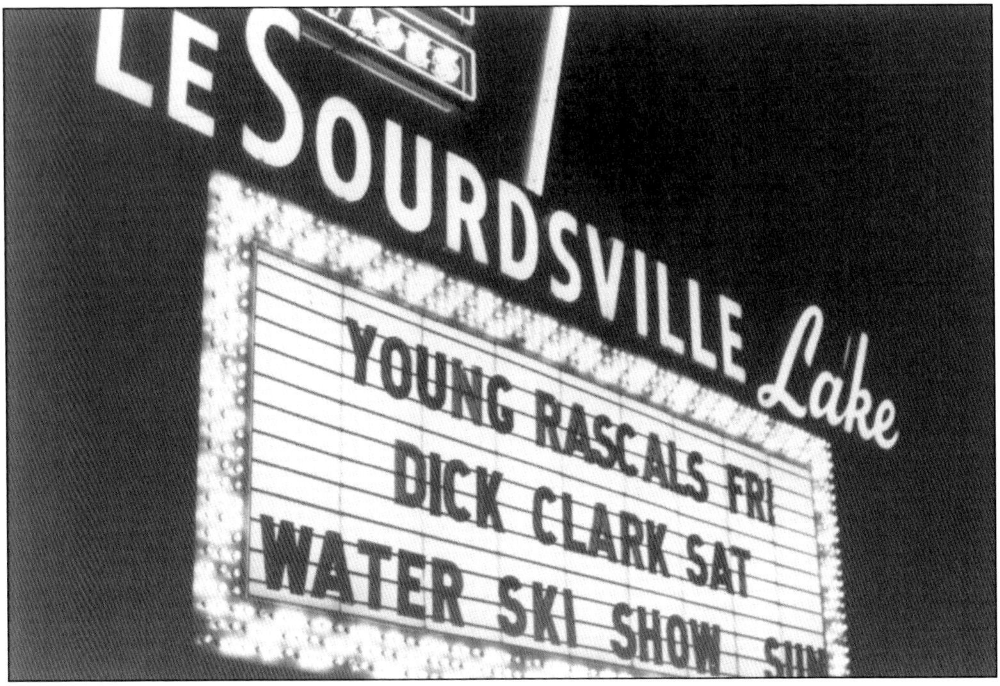

Clark would appear two more times at LeSourdsville Lake, the last being in 1977. Clark was the first major TV personality to appear at the park.

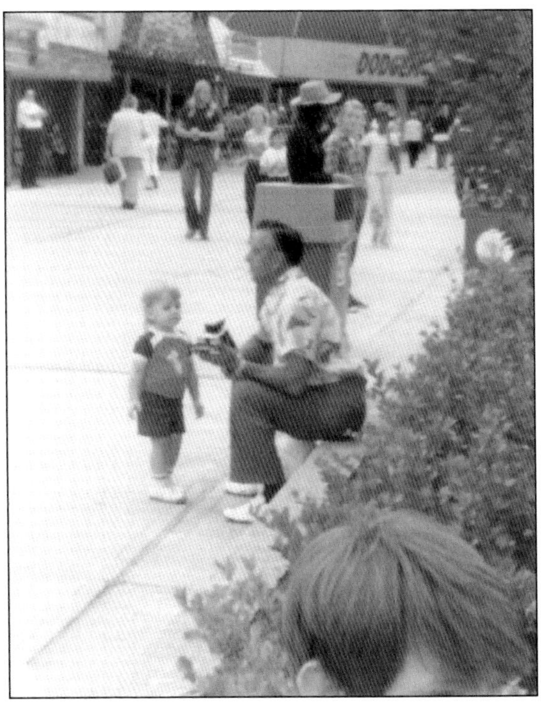
Former Cedar Point concessionaire Lou Faggionato is seen interacting with a small child who is experiencing the midway. Faggionato and his wife, Bea, owned many of the games of chance on the midway from 1962 until the early 1990s. Fagginato's son Joe also managed several games before becoming a part owner in 1991. (Courtesy of Bill Robinson/WHR Inc.)

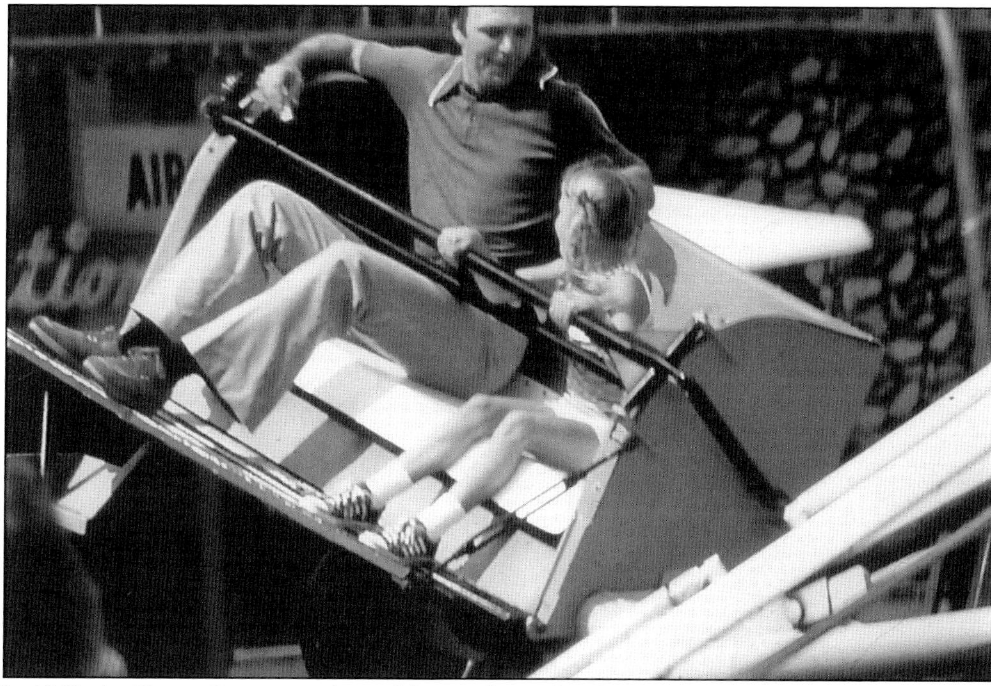

In 1963, the Flying Coaster made its debut at the park. The coaster was on a circular track that launched riders up a 10-foot hill where the car suddenly dropped back down to the track. (Courtesy of Bill Robinson/WHR Inc.)

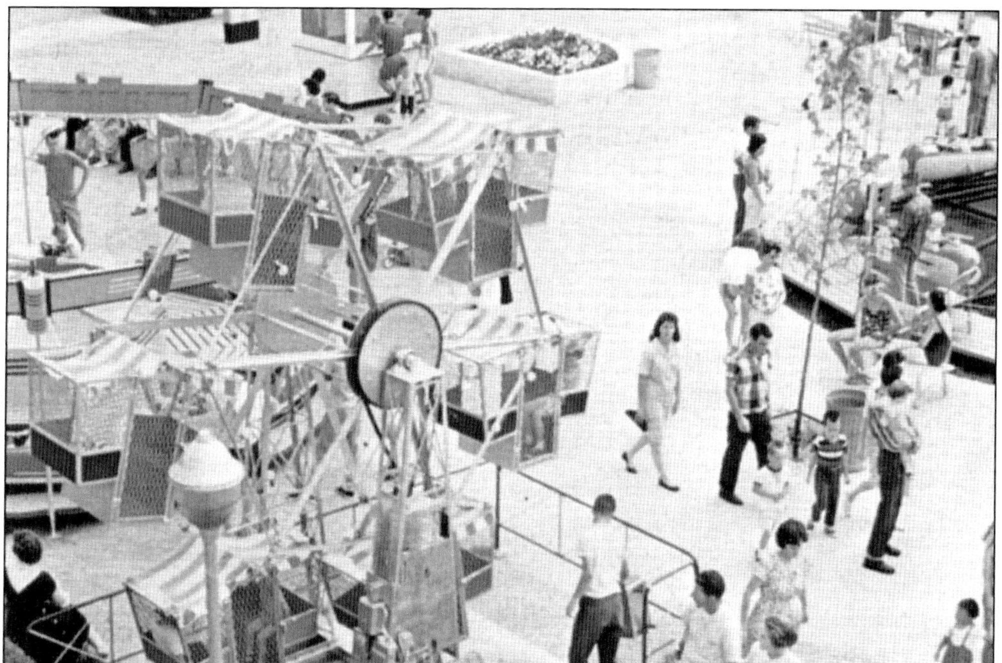

Kiddieland was renamed Pinocchio Land in 1963 and moved from the main gate area to the midway near the promenade area. The Sky Fighters and Hampton Helicopters were added to the rides dedicated to younger children.

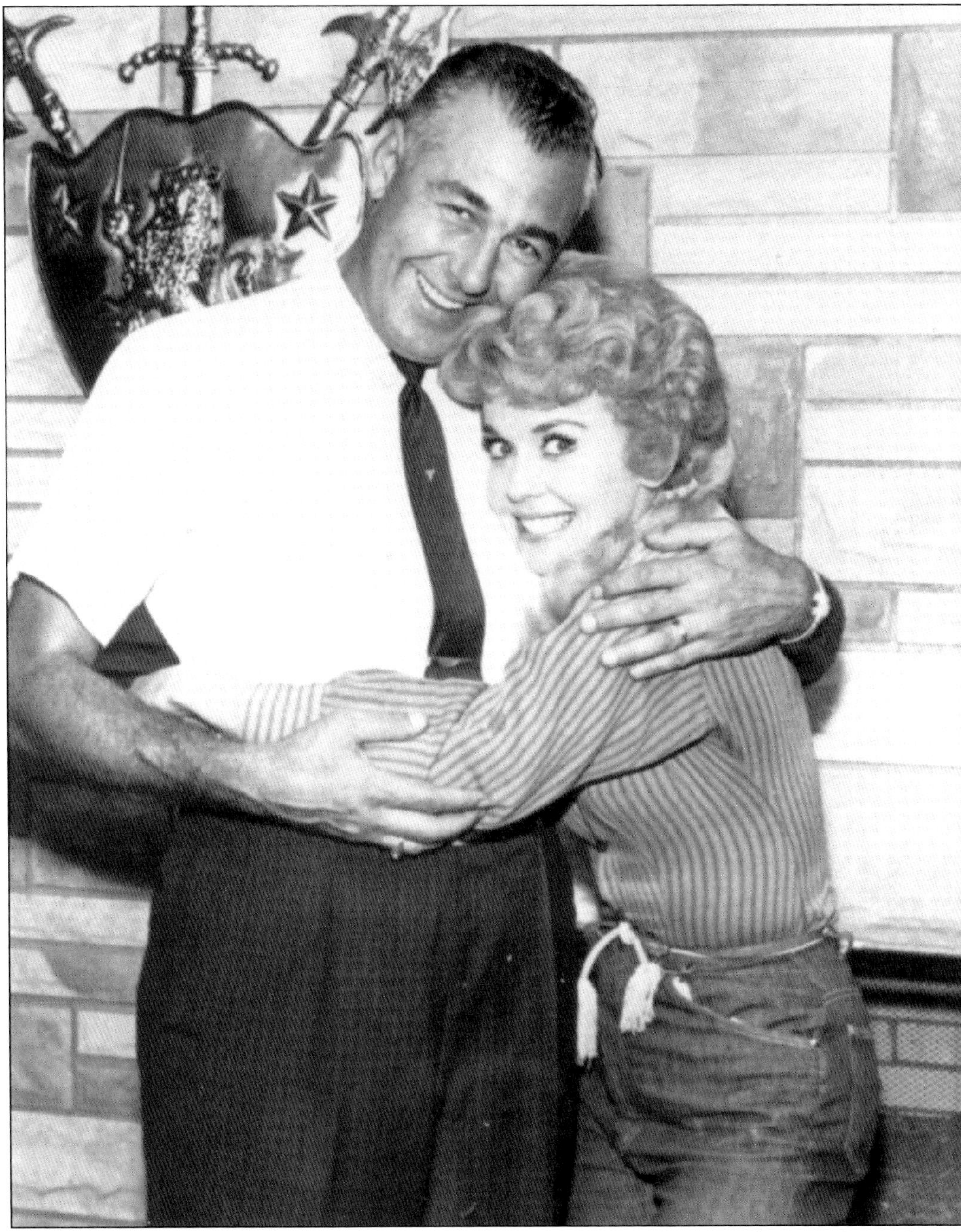

Donna Douglas appeared as her CBS television show character Elly Mae Clampett from *The Beverly Hillbillies* with Howard Berni at his Monroe home in August 1963. During the same month, NBC television star Michael Landon of *Bonanza* visited the park. Musical guests included Johnny Tillotson, Ivan and the Sabres, and the Beach Boys, just prior to their *Surfer Girl* album. The dining room adjacent to the cafeteria was renamed the Celebrity Room, and pictures of all of the stars that have visited the park were placed in frames.

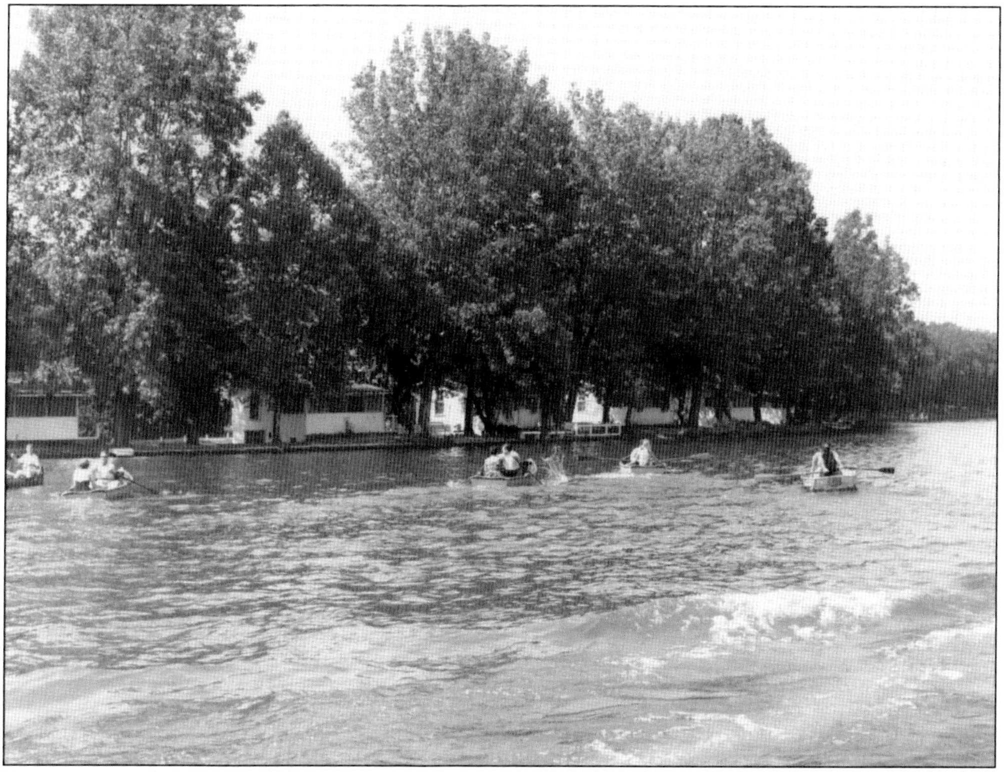

For years, residents were able to rent small cottages surrounding the lake for the summer or the entire year. The upkeep was expensive on the cottages, since they were over 40 years old and constructed of wood. Portions of the lake were filled, and a few of the cottages were torn down to allow for future expansion. The last cottages were torn down in the mid-1970s.

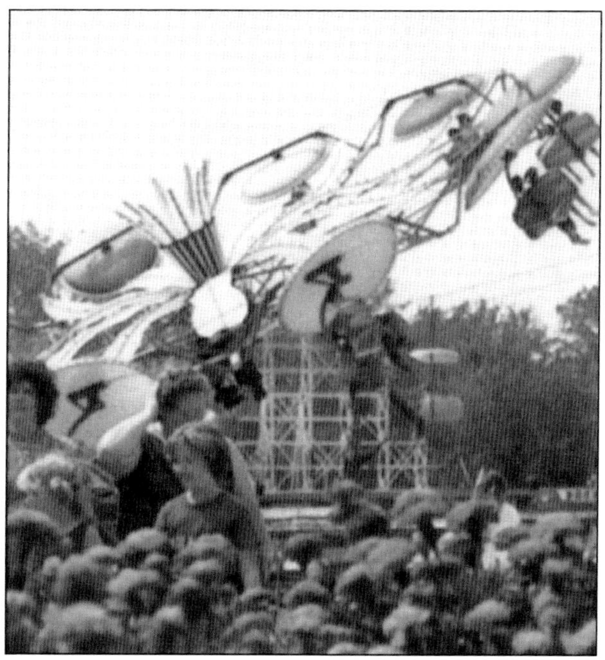

The Paratrooper, a ride that made its debut at the Seattle World's Fair, was added to the LeSourdsville Lake midway in 1964. The ride was retired after the 1987 season. (Courtesy of Bill Robinson/WHR Inc.)

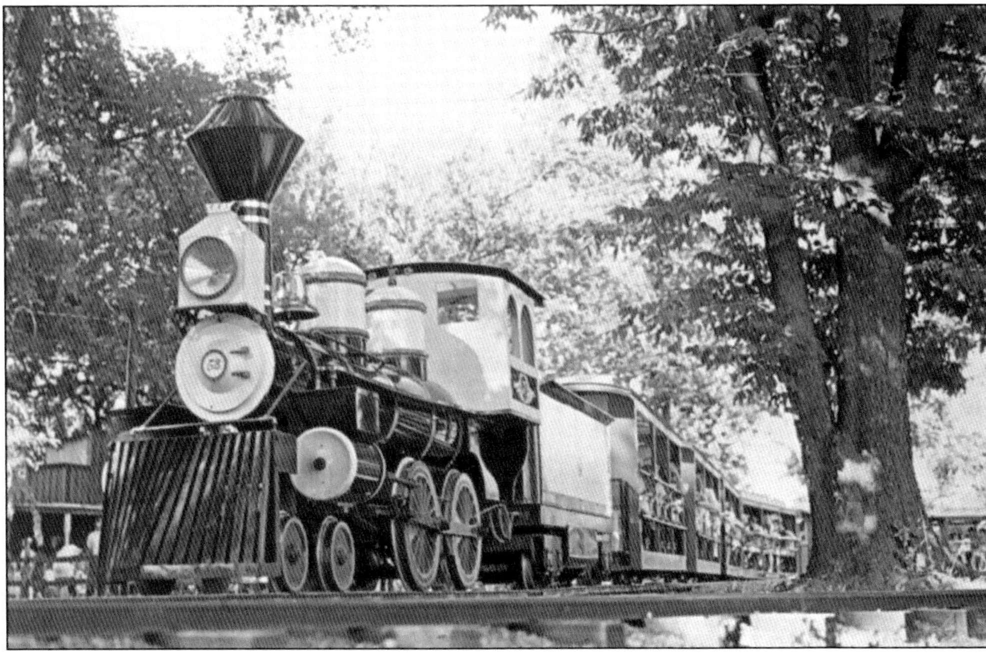

In 1964, the park purchased a National Amusement Device train that became Ohio's largest train ride, operating on 4,000 feet of track. It was named the Iron Horse and was a full-size reproduction of an 1860 Union-Pacific railroad locomotive No. 58, complete with a tender and four cars. Two additional cars were added the following year when a stop was created in Tombstone Territory. The acquisition of the train was part of $250,000 of improvements for the year that also saw the addition of a shooting water game and the expansion of the Turnpike ride from two lanes to four lanes.

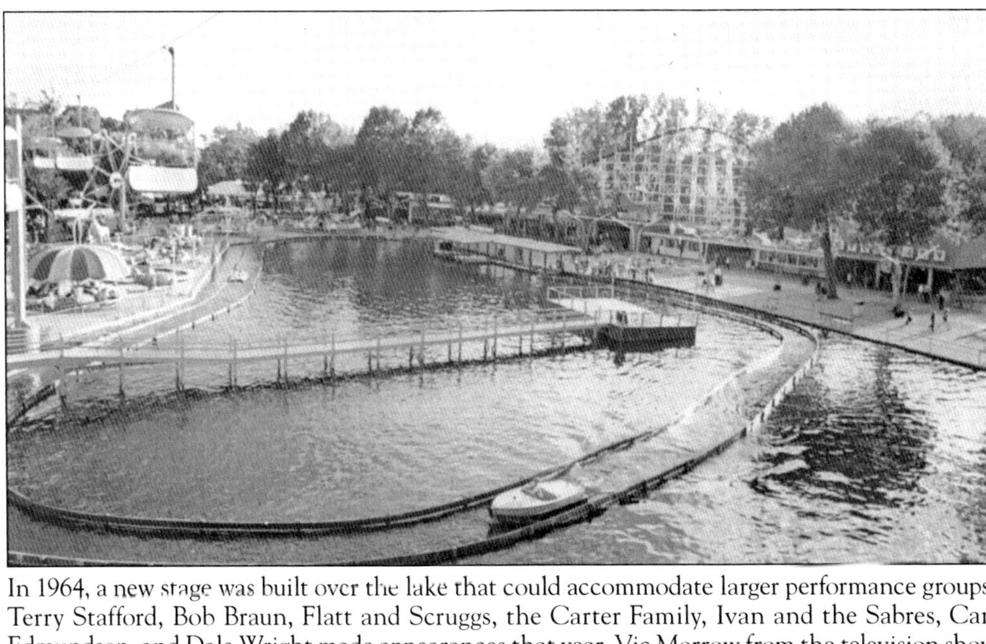

In 1964, a new stage was built over the lake that could accommodate larger performance groups. Terry Stafford, Bob Braun, Flatt and Scruggs, the Carter Family, Ivan and the Sabres, Carl Edmundson, and Dale Wright made appearances that year. Vic Morrow from the television show *Combat* and Tim Considine of *My Three Sons* also made appearances.

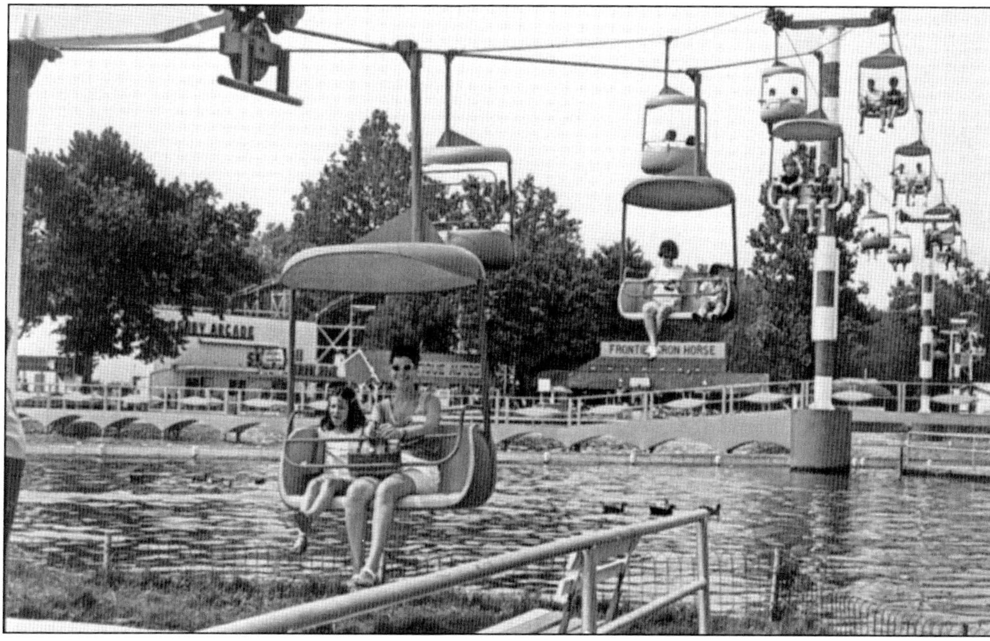

The addition of the Sky Ride was made in 1965. Cars headed across the lake and made a U-turn near the train station and returned back to the midway. The Sky Ride continued operation until the park's last season in 2002.

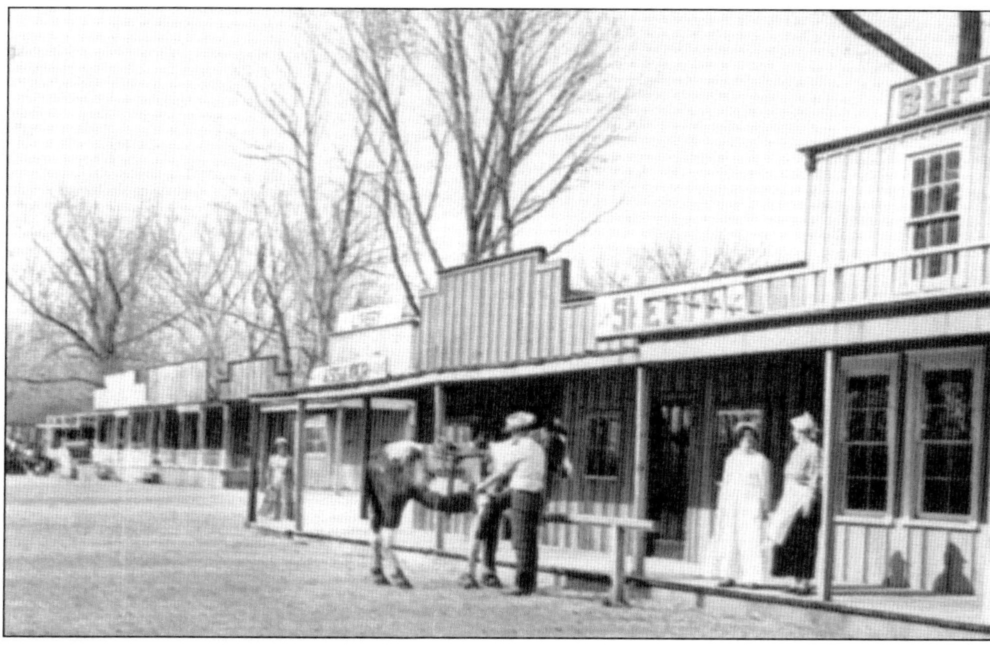

Tombstone Territory was opened in 1965 and became the first and only themed area at LeSourdsville Lake. Originally all of the buildings except for the saloon were fake storefronts. The inspiration for Tombstone came from Knott's Berry Farm in Buena Park, California. Park owner Howard Berni lived in Southern California during the winter months in the late 1950s and early 1960s. One of his visits to Knott's became the vision for the ghost town. (Courtesy of Bill Robinson/WHR Inc.)

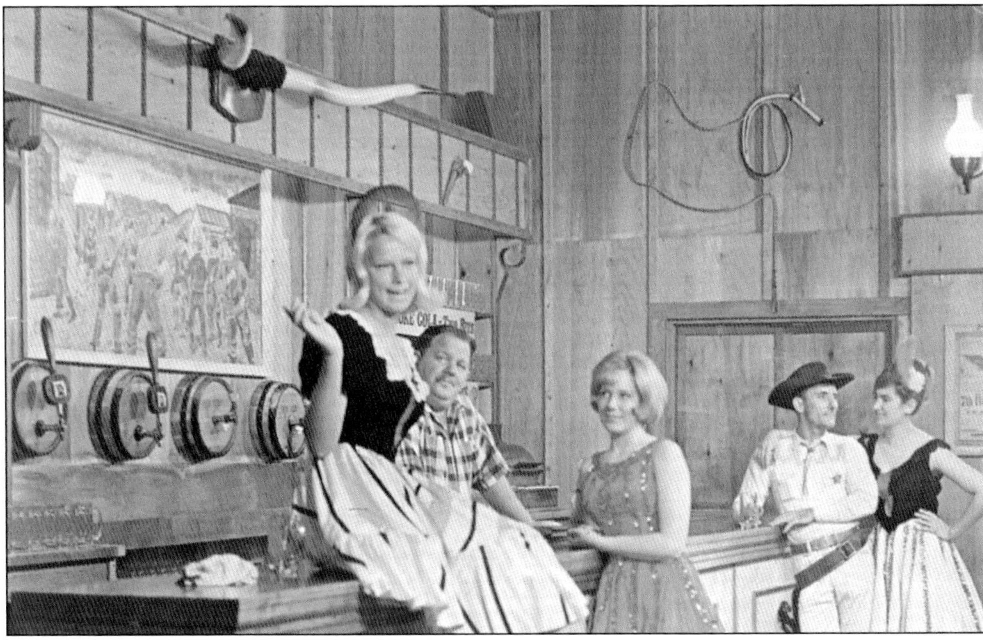

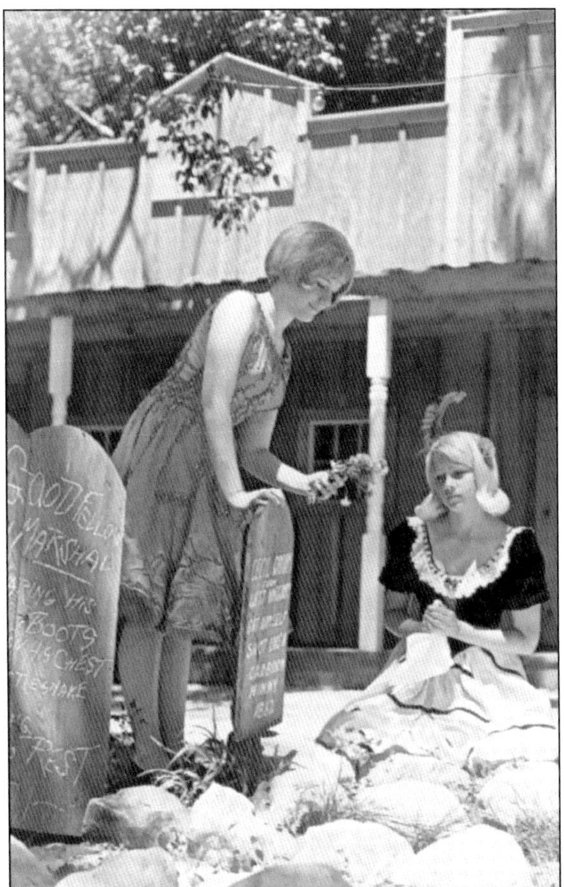

The Dry Gulch Saloon in Tombstone provided a stopping off point for the Iron Horse Train riders. The saloon featured a sarsaparilla drink and beer. Employees dressed in period costumes to add a touch of authenticity.

Boot Hill cemetery was located just outside of the saloon in Tombstone. Humorous epitaphs on each tombstone were featured.

Cowboy and Indian paintings decorated the walls of the Dry Gulch Saloon for years. They were hand-painted by Cincinnati-area artist Bill Rucker.

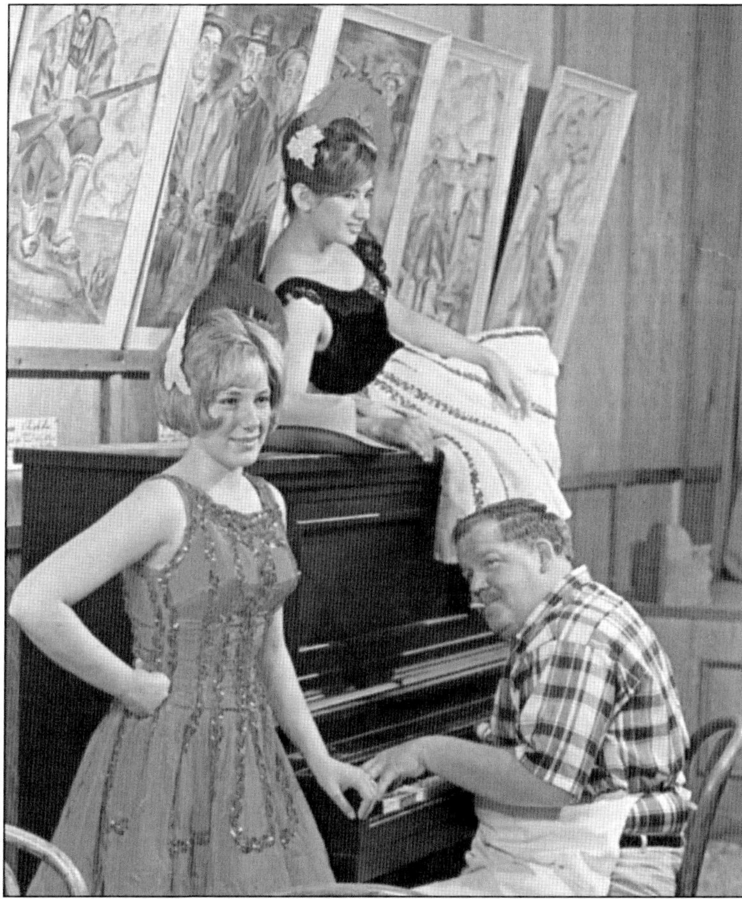

Local residents were recruited to play the cowboy roles. The roles only lasted a couple of seasons because the cowboys were performing too well—when they fell off the buildings, they literally were tearing the structures apart since they were not created for that purpose.

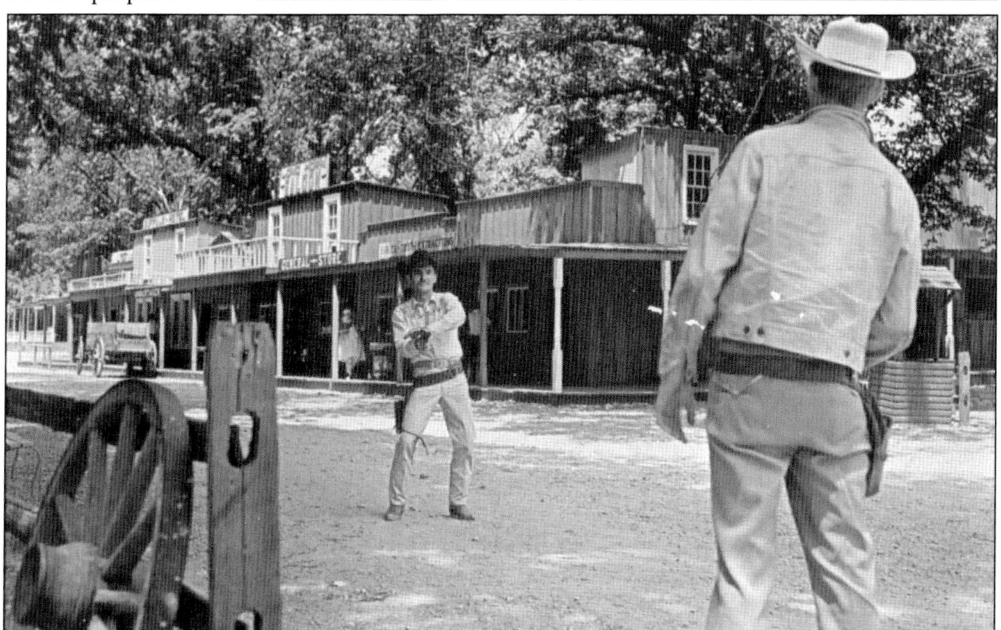

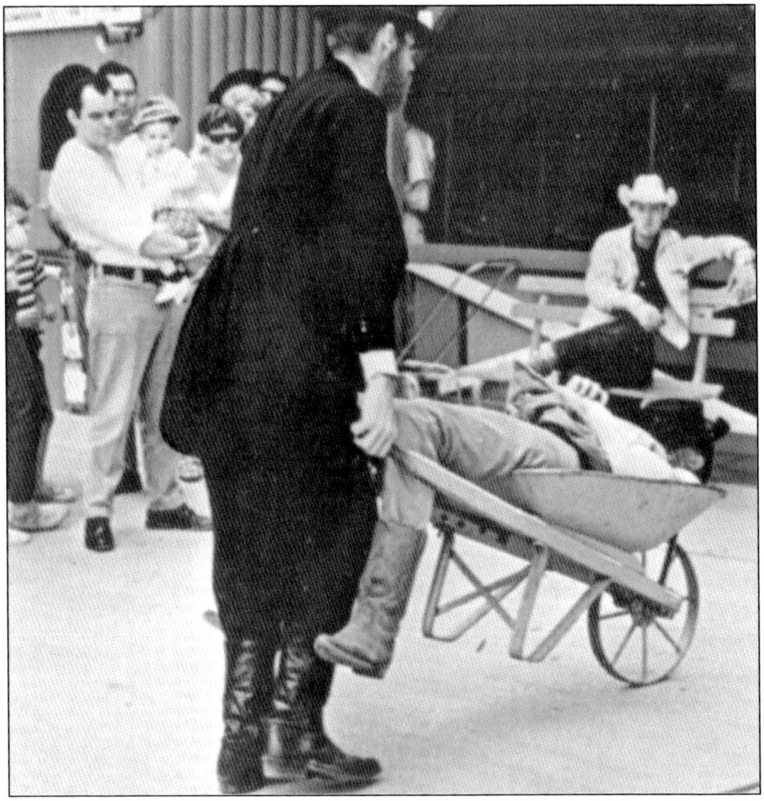

After the shooting and fighting ended, the town preacher would remove the bad guys in a wheelbarrow and dump them near Boot Hill for the final resting. Many of the actors were local police officers.

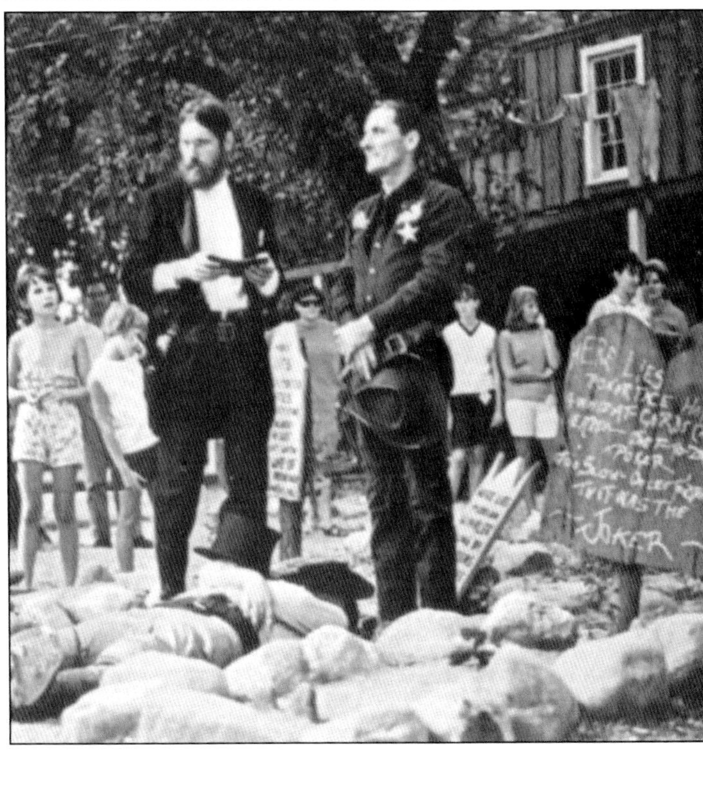

Once in Boot Hill, a few passing words were said by the town preacher. The Wild West Shows were done only on weekends and holidays.

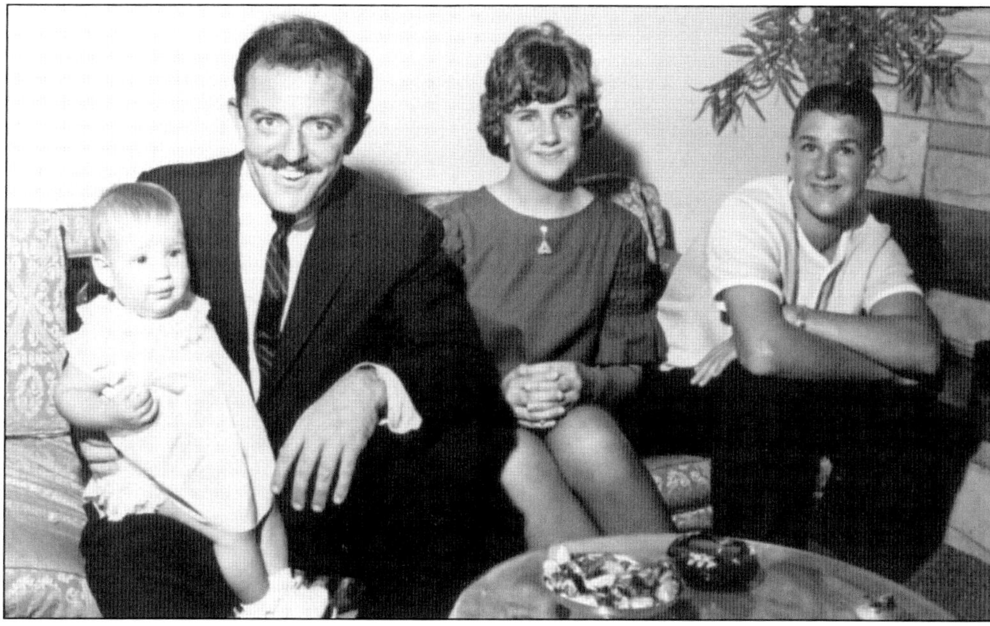

The live performances by some of the country's most popular acts continued in 1965. Actor John Astin from the television show *The Addams Family* is shown holding Howard Berni's youngest daughter, Debbie. Berni's oldest daughter, Diane, and son Ron are seated with Astin. Appearances were also made by Billy Joe Royal, Kitty Wells, Johnny Wright, the Tennessee Mountain Boys, Beau Brummels, Lonnie Mack, and the Sir Douglas Quintette.

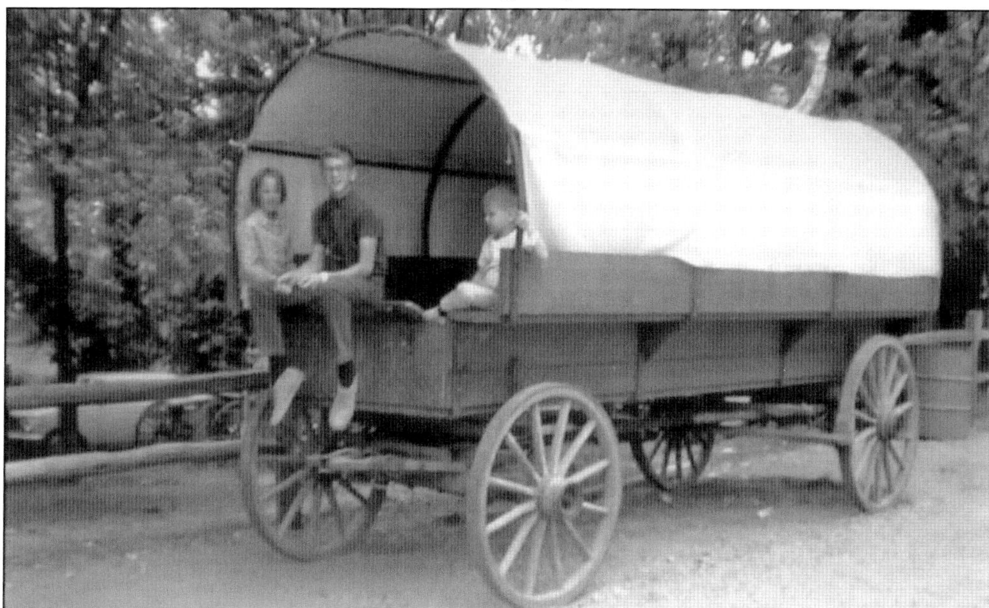

Christa and Todd Shiverdecker are shown with the park's Wagon Train ride that was added to Tombstone Territory in 1966. The park also added some Texas Longhorn steers to the live animal exhibit. A decorative fountain that sprayed water 50 feet in the air was added to the swimming area, and a space ride and motorcycle ride were added to Pinocchio Land. (Photograph by Lewis Shiverdecker; courtesy of Todd Shiverdecker.)

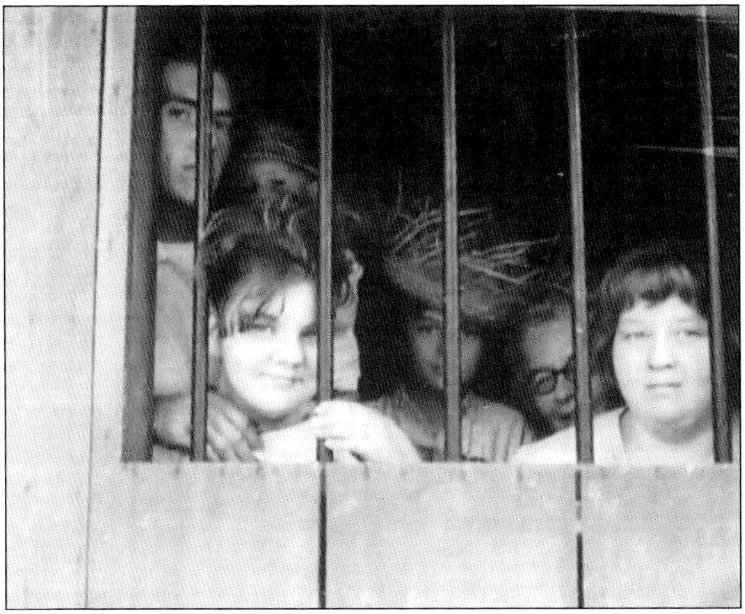

The Robinson family apparently got lost in Tombstone Territory and landed in the jail. Pictured from left to right, Billy Ray Robinson, Jay Robinson, Shirley Robinson, Ray Robinson, unidentified, and Margaret Miser look to be behind bars, but they were released and able to enjoy the show in the Dry Gulch Saloon. (Courtesy of Jay Robinson.)

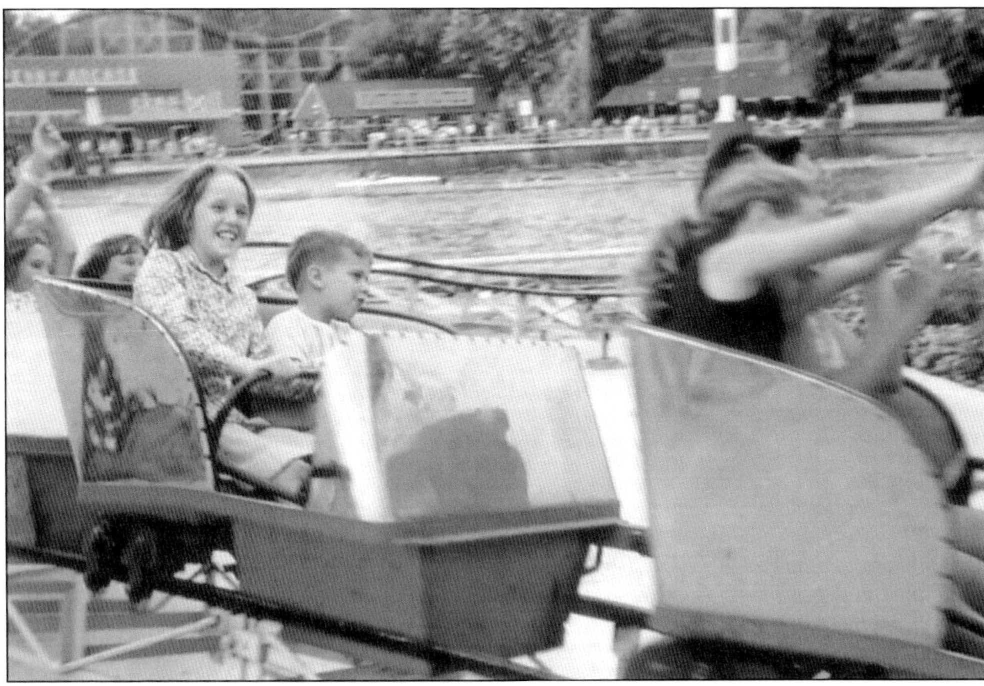

In 1967, the name of Pinocchio Land was changed to Kiddie Kingdom. Christa and Todd Shiverdecker didn't mind as they had a great time on the Jack Rabbit roller coaster. Kiddie Kingdom also added an Old 99 train ride to its lineup. (Photograph by Lewis Shiverdecker; courtesy of Todd Shiverdecker.)

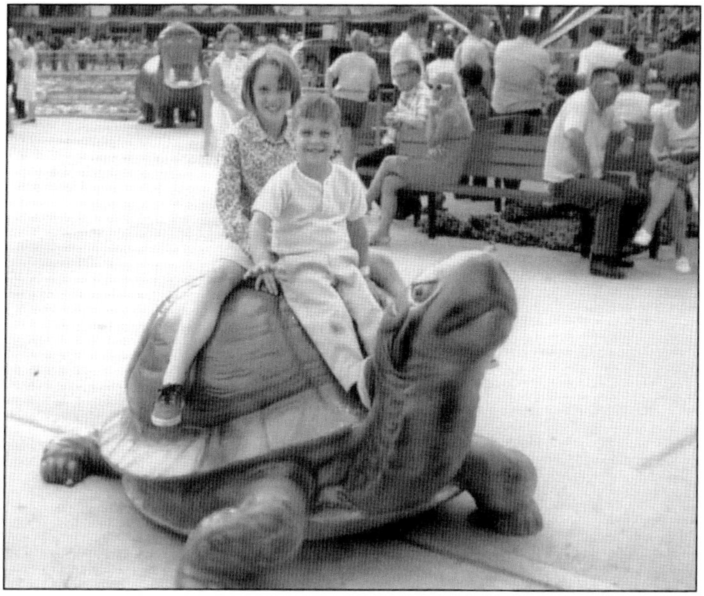

Christa and Todd Shiverdecker of Dayton enjoy their time in Kiddie Kingdom. Plans were in the works in 1967 to move Kiddie Kingdom to a new area and construct a new stage in the area shown here. (Photograph by Lewis Shiverdecker; courtesy of Todd Shiverdecker.)

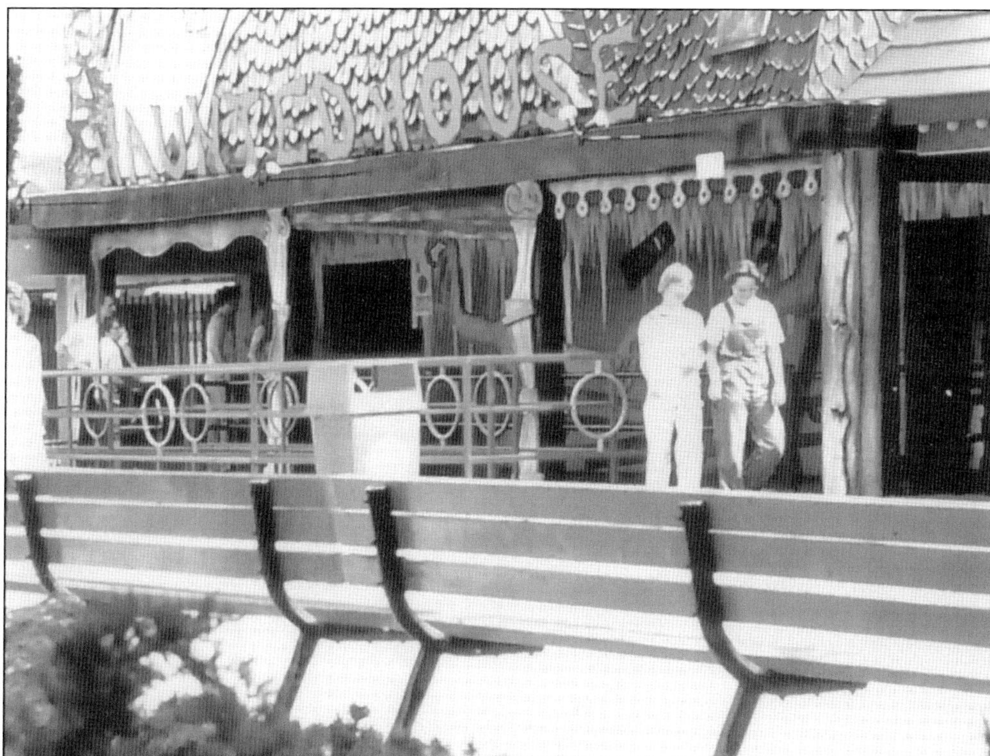

In 1968, the Haunted House was remodeled and touted as a "suspense-filled adventure, as assorted animals and ghosts jump from the darkness to thrill young and old." The attraction was designed by Bill Tracy of Amusement Display in New Jersey. (Courtesy of Bill Robinson/WHR Inc.)

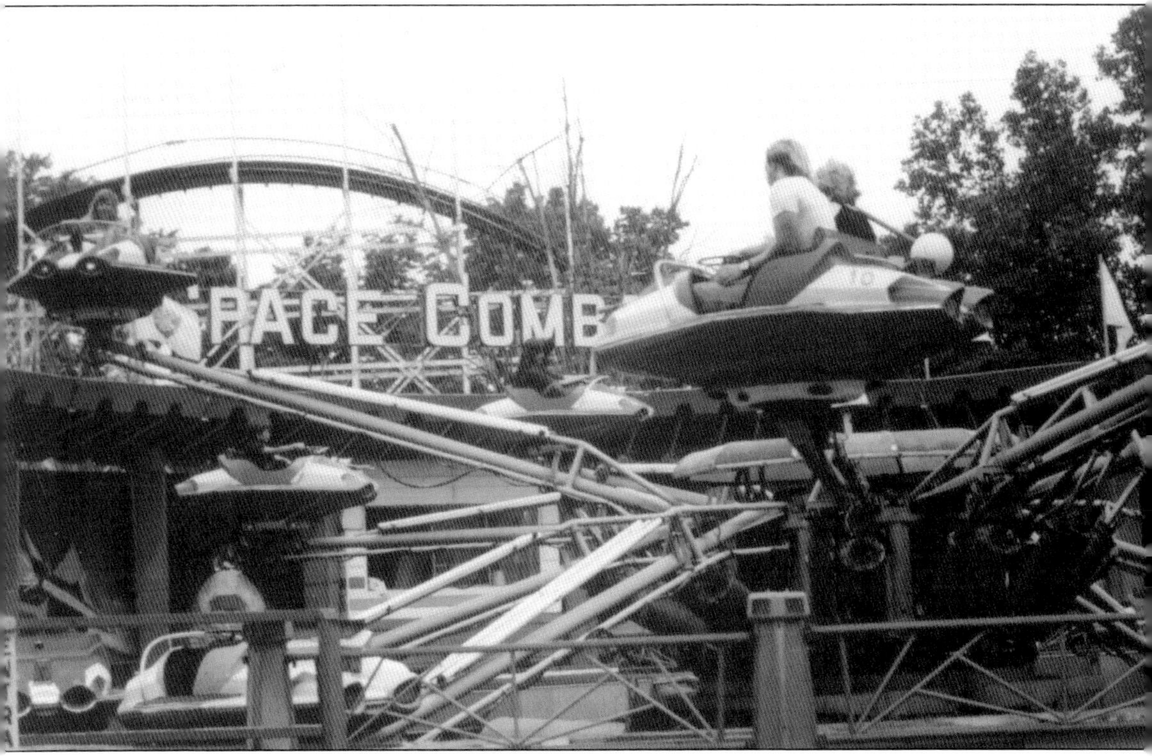

The Space Combat ride was added in 1968. Riders had individual controls that permitted the car to rise and fall on command. There was also a high-pitched horn that riders could use. (Photograph by George Siessel, courtesy of Gale Siessel McCoy.)

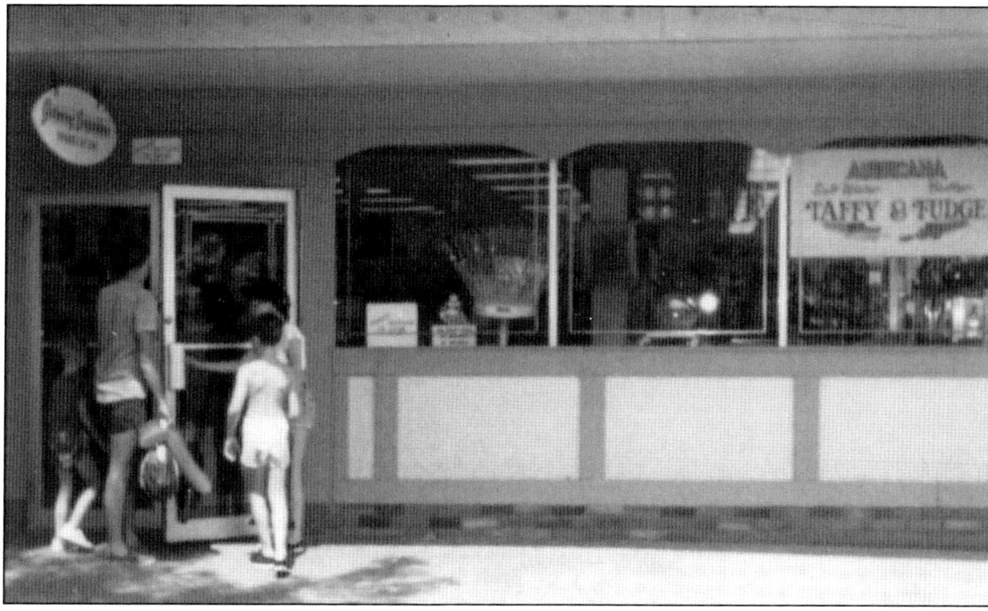

The park gift shop sold a variety of items over the years, ranging from sun wear, handkerchiefs, and plastic toys to hats, shirts, and swimsuits. On the other side of the wall of the gift shop was the kitchen where all of the freshly coated chicken was fried. Cedar Point concessionaire Frank Silvani joined LeSourdsville Lake as director of food services in 1968 and revamped the park's historic restaurant and other food outlets. It was rare not to find Silvani and park owner Howard Berni in the midst of the park's kitchen, surrounded by the scintillating aroma of chicken frying that sometimes would find its way over to the gift shop. (Author's collection.)

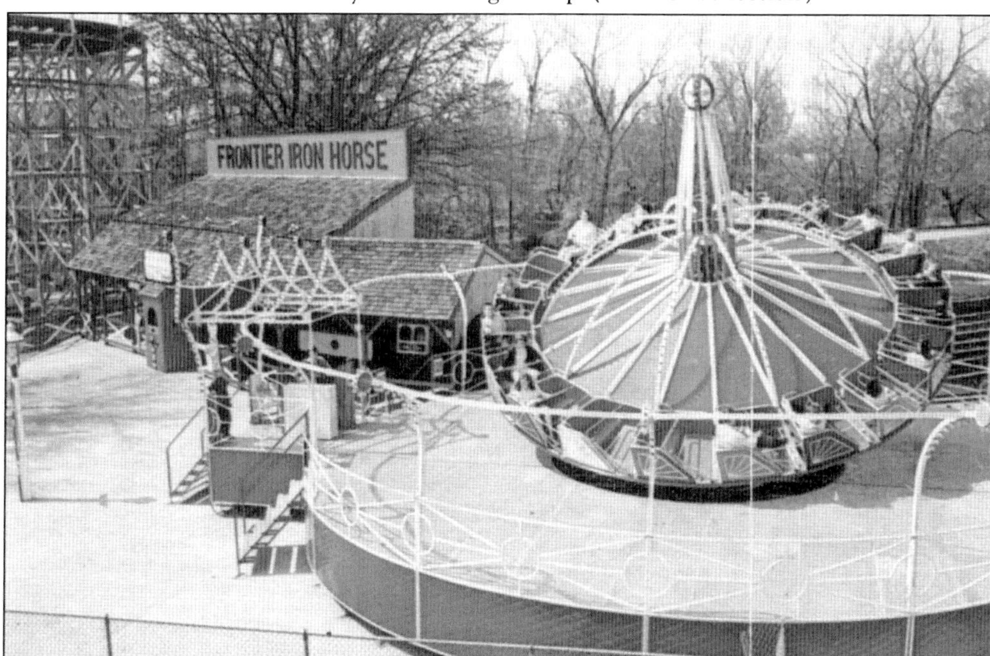

The Trabant was added in 1969 and quickly became a favorite. It was installed between the Iron Horse train ride and the lake and provided guests with something to do while waiting for the train.

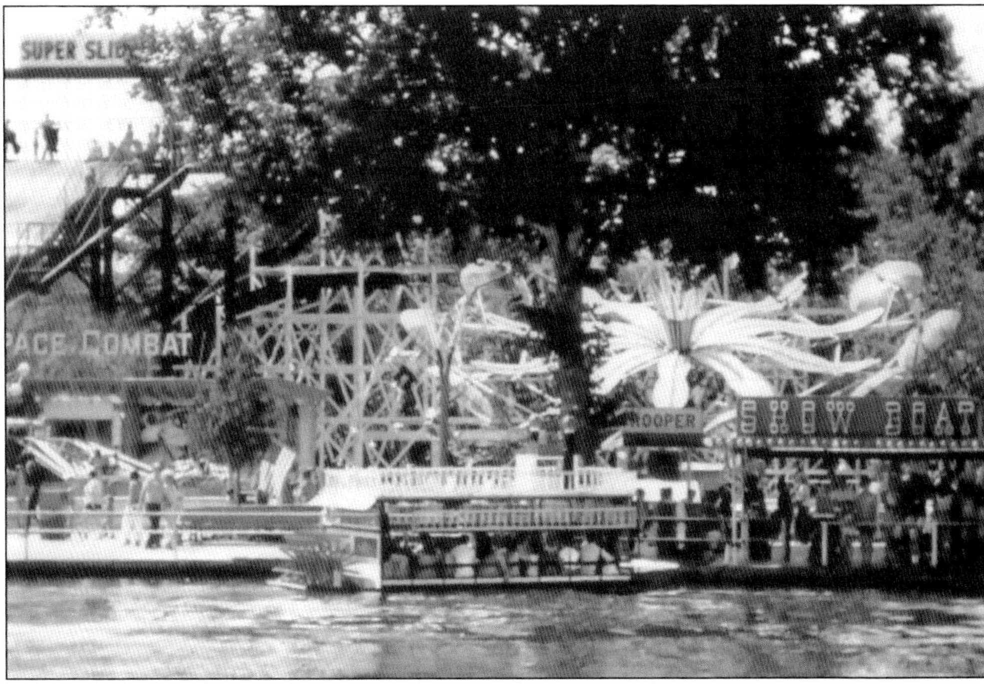

The following year, a 160-foot slide appropriately named the Super Slide (left) was built in place of the miniature golf course. Tombstone Territory added an Indian village, while deer, burros, exotic fowl, and ducks were added to the wildlife exhibits. (Courtesy of Bill Robinson/WHR Inc.)

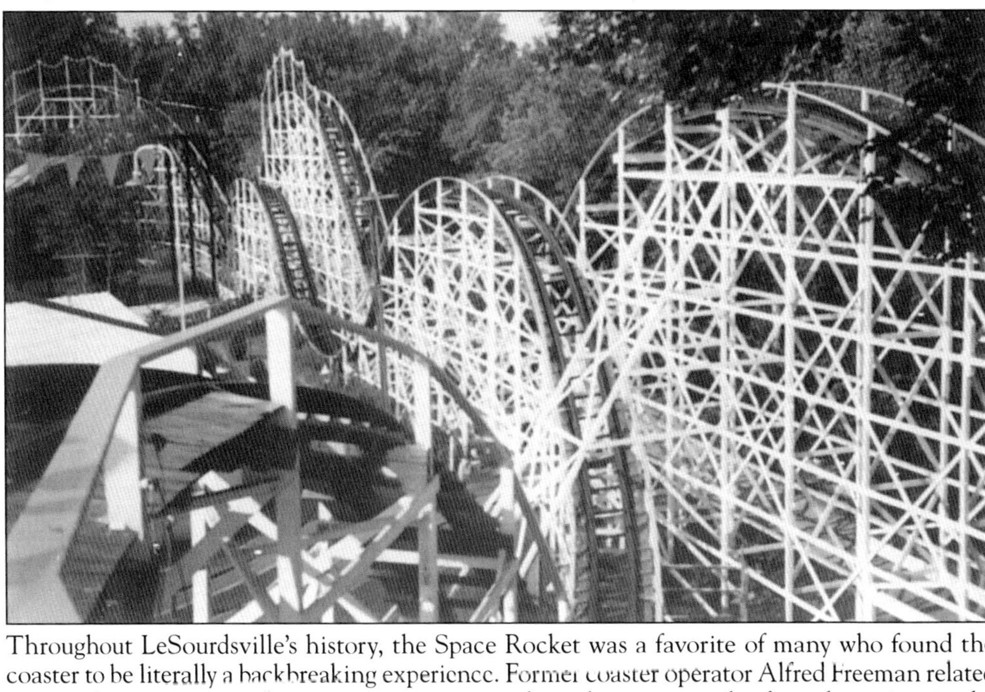

Throughout LeSourdsville's history, the Space Rocket was a favorite of many who found the coaster to be literally a backbreaking experience. Former coaster operator Alfred Freeman related a story about a woman who was wearing a paper dress that was popular for a short time in the late 1960s and early 1970s. By the time she returned to the station, her dress was ripped apart. (Courtesy of Alfred Freeman.)

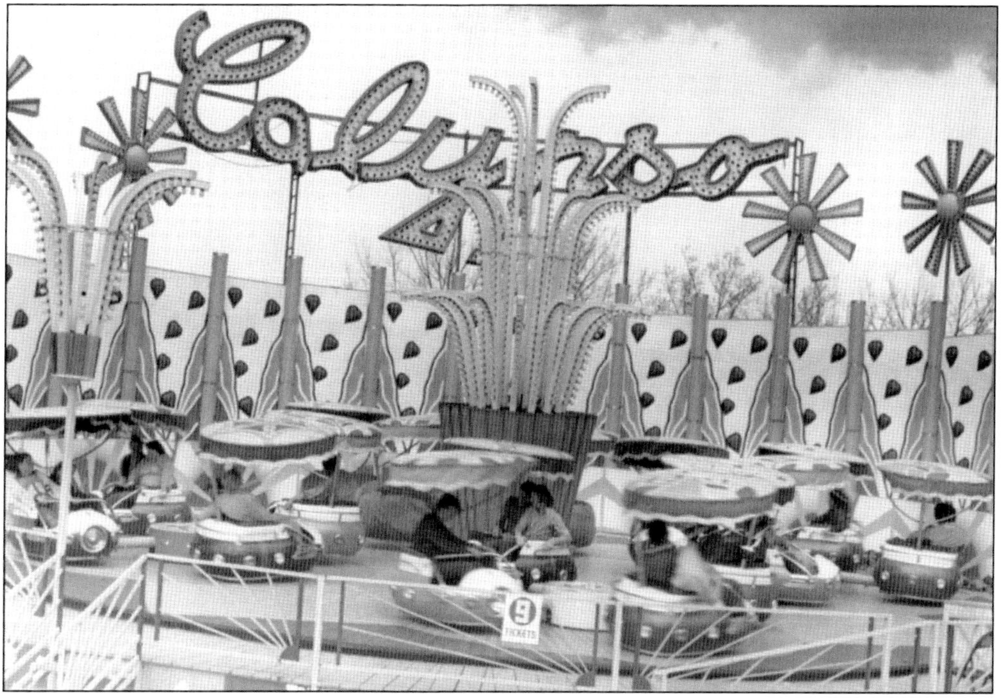

The Calypso was added in 1972 and remained a popular ride until the park closed in 2002. The ride was sold to the Fun Spot amusement park in Indiana in 2006.

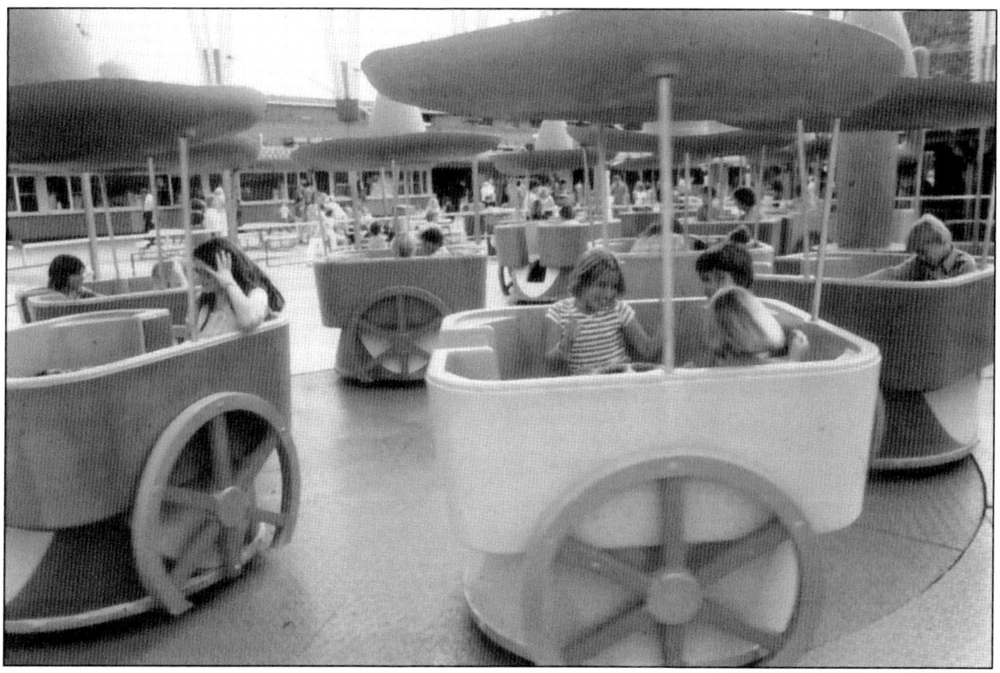

The Sombrero ride was not for the faint of heart. The ride's spinning action created havoc for some parents when their children got sick afterwards. The ride was removed after the 1991 season and dismantled. Some of the ride parts were stored throughout hidden areas of the park. (Courtesy of Bill Robinson/WHR Inc.)

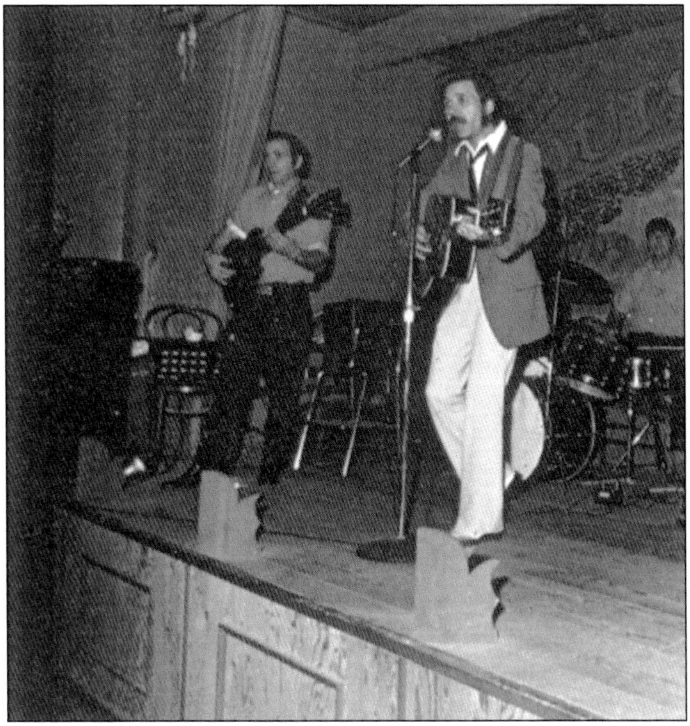

Part of the charm and atmosphere the park was known for was because of Tombstone Territory. The use of live bands on the weekends became a weekend tradition and were broadcasted live on Middletown radio station WPFB-AM. Ken Roberts and the Country Rebels (pictured), featuring teen singer Diane Walker, headlined during the early and mid-1970s. (Courtesy of Bill Robinson/WHR Inc.)

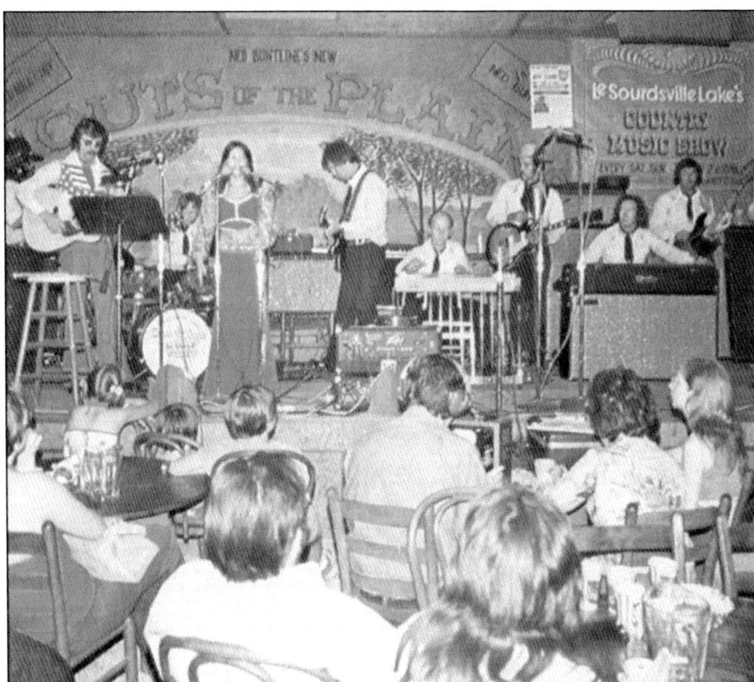

Not only did Ken Roberts and the Country Rebels have a following at LeSourdsville Lake but also throughout the community. Sagebrush with C.D. Craft was another local favorite that often packed Tombstone's saloon with happy patrons. (Courtesy of Bill Robinson/WHR Inc.)

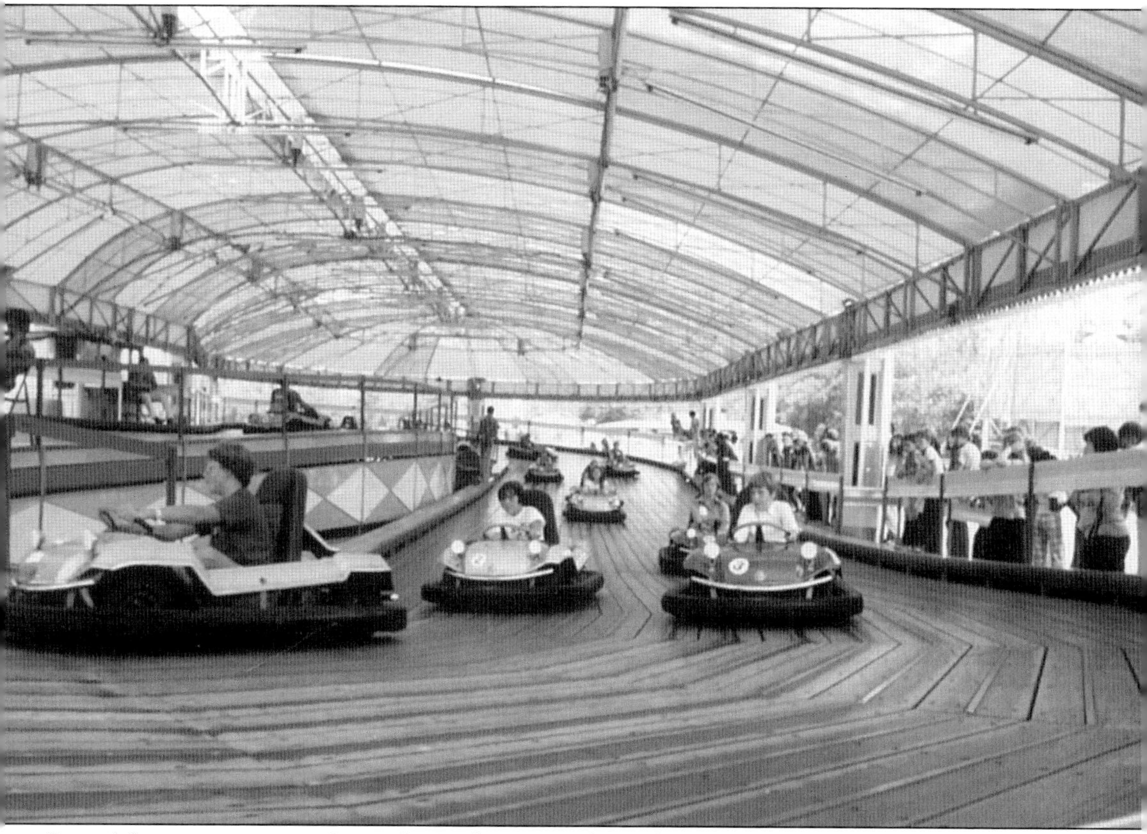

One of the more unique rides in the Midwest was the Indy 500. The ride featured 20 electric cars that were individually controlled similarly to a bumper car and could go up to 35 miles per hour.

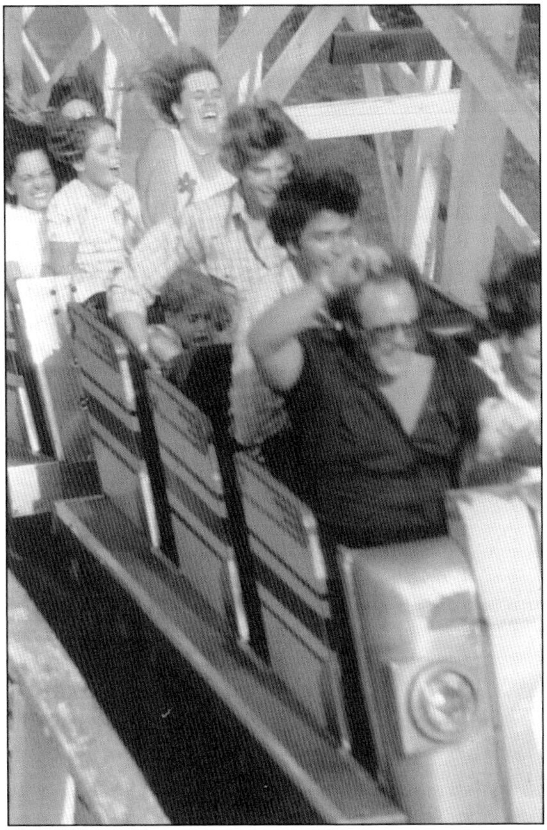

These coaster cars from the early 1970s were very safe despite the fact that a rider would normally lift up out of his or her seat going over some hills. Fortunately, there were very few accidents since the coaster opened in 1940. The last documented death on the coaster occurred in 1973, when a Hamilton man jumped from a car while it was going down one of the hills. (Courtesy of Alfred Freeman.)

New Italian sport cars made their debut on the Turnpike ride in 1973. They replaced the Streifthau cars, which were no longer being manufactured. (Courtesy of Bill Robinson/WHR Inc.)

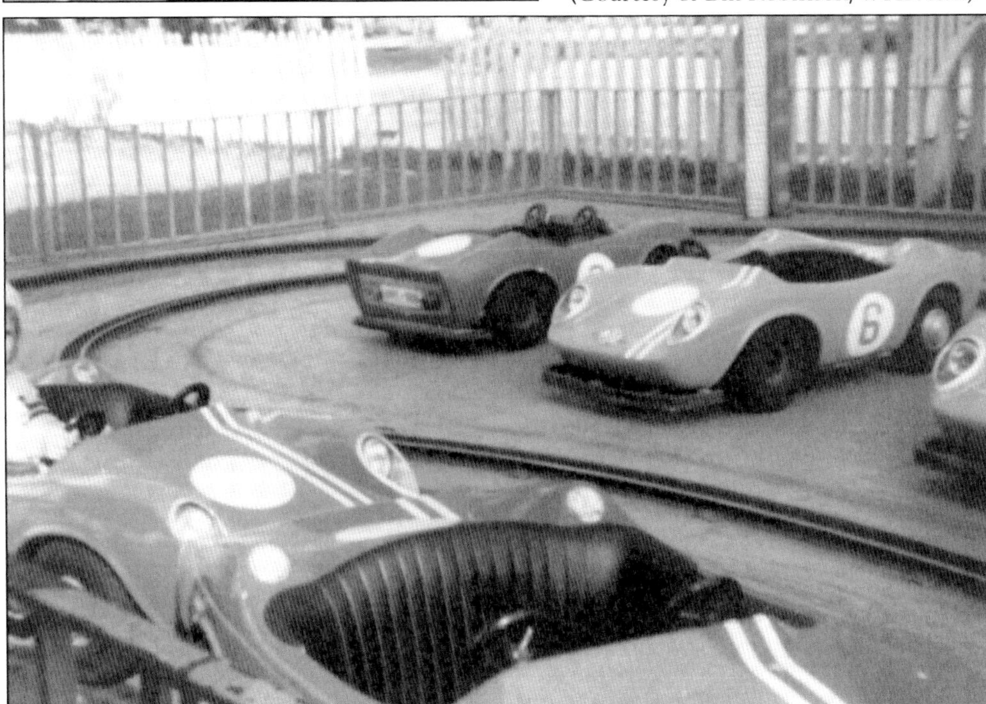

A new high-tech shooting gallery was installed on the midway next to the bumper car building in 1974. The animations were created and installed by Taylor Engineering of Beverly Hills, California. (Courtesy of Bill Robinson/WHR Inc.)

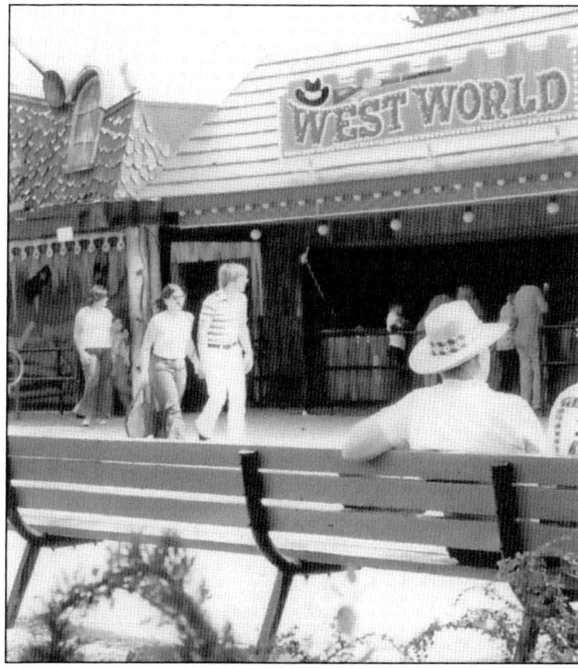

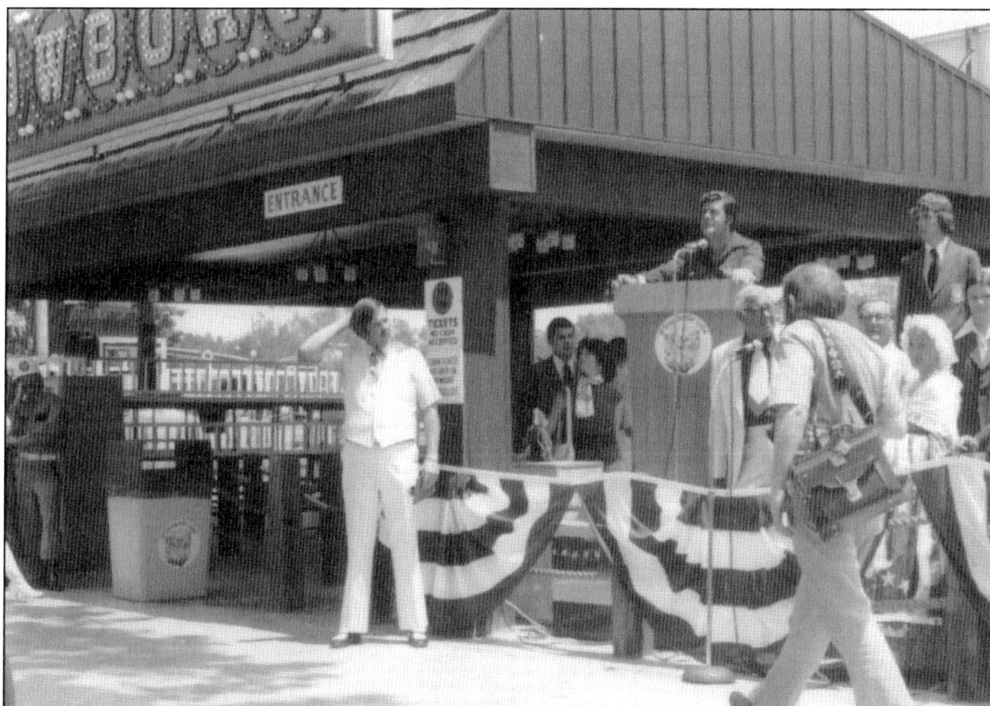

In 1975, television host Bob Braun (at podium) was the master of ceremonies at the dedication of the *Belle of Louisville* passenger boat. The vessel was christened by Sen. Donald Lukens and built by Design Evolution 4 of Lebanon, Ohio. The 50-foot-long boat was designed to carry 65 passengers. The park kept its original boat and both boats would ferry guests to Tombstone Territory and the picnic grove on busy days. (Courtesy of Bill Robinson/WHR Inc.)

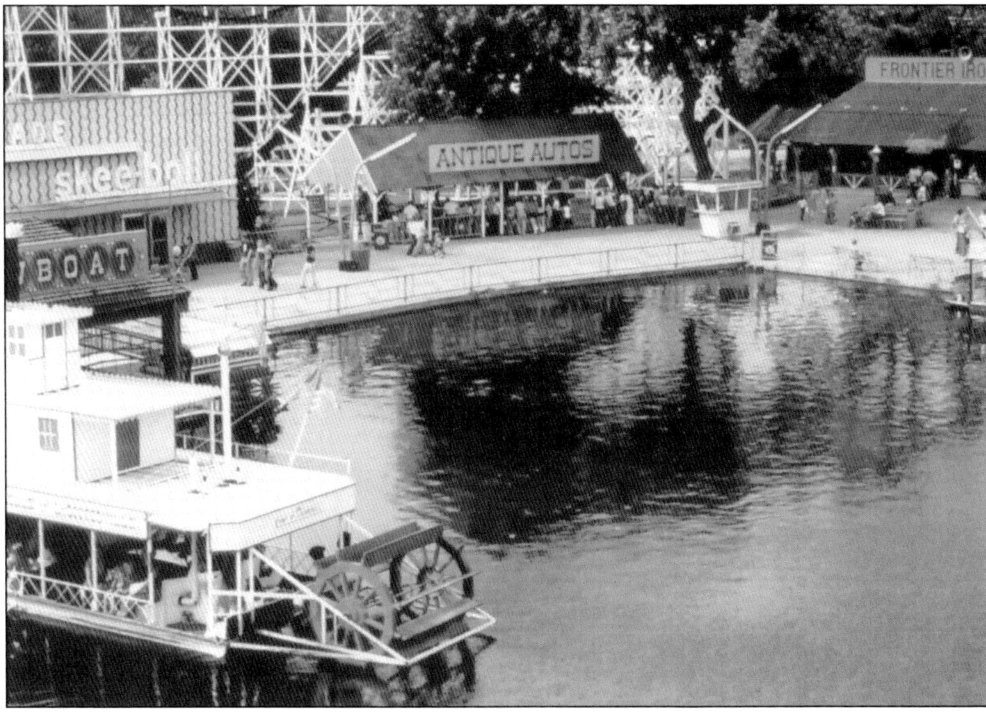

The vessel ran on a six-cylinder Chrysler engine with a 24-inch propeller. The design was patterned after an actual paddle wheeler, the *Chaperon*, built in 1894 in northern Ohio.

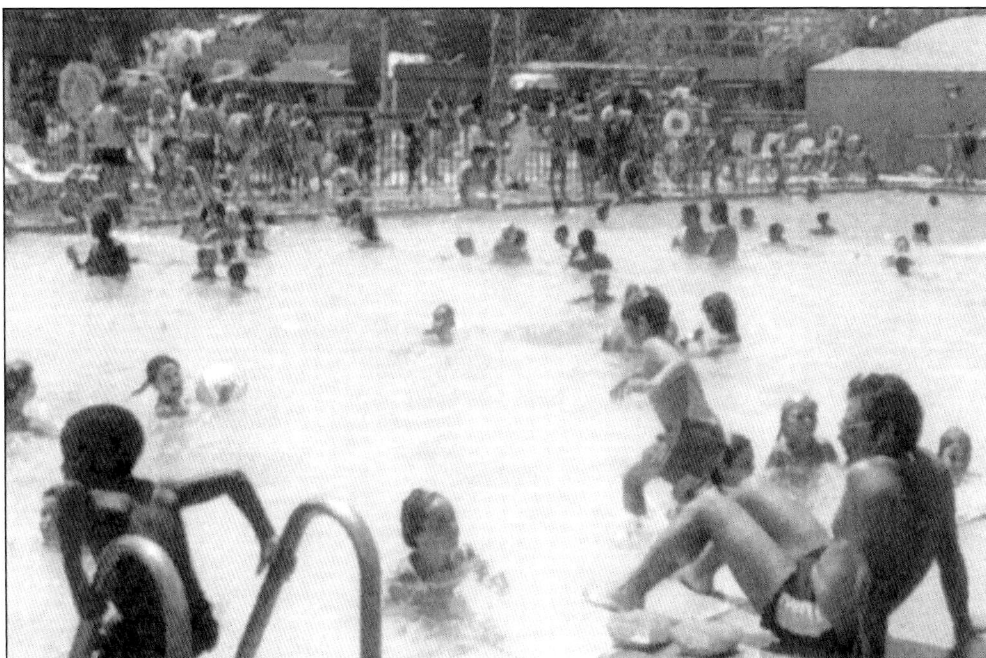

After 54 years of continuous service, the beach and swimming area were removed in 1976 to make room for the Blue Dolphin swimming pool. The Olympic-sized pool was 50 by 100 feet and featured a 30-foot-by-30-foot wading pool for kids. It was built by Dolphin Pools of Columbus, Ohio.

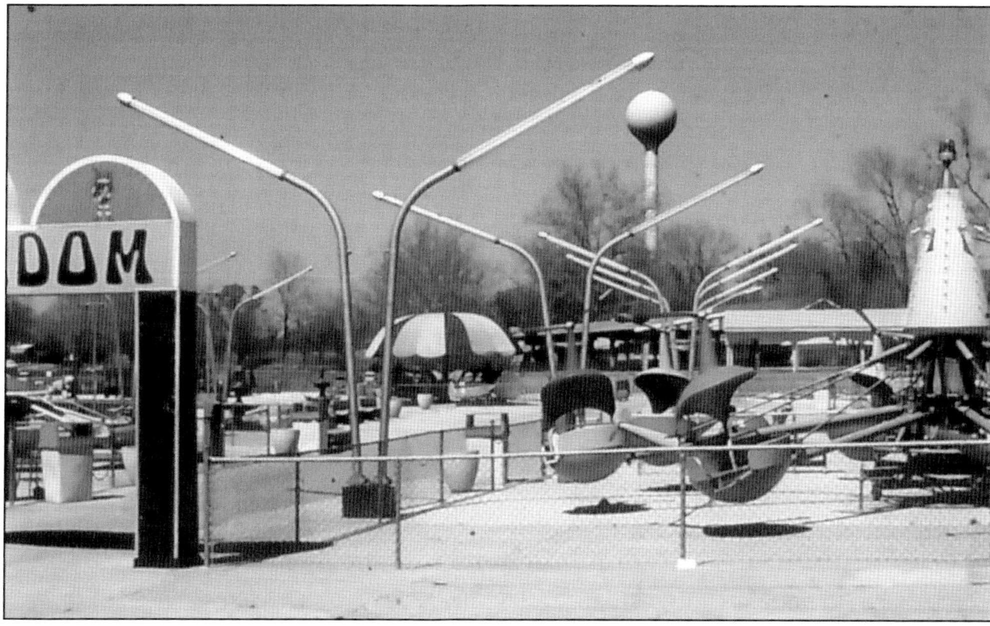

The beach and swimming area were filled in and the Kiddie Kingdom area was moved to the site from the midway. This picture shows the then-new entrance into the area from the midway. (Courtesy of Bill Robinson/WHR Inc.)

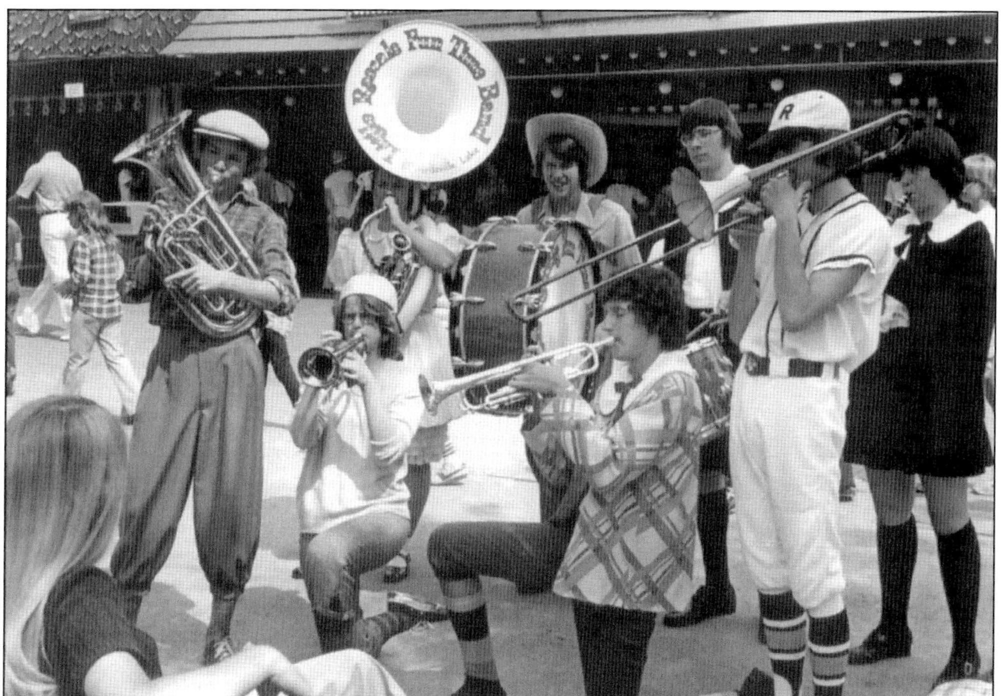

In an effort to provide more variety of live entertainment, the Little Rascals Funtime Band was established, utilizing the talent of local high school students. (Courtesy of Bill Robinson/WHR Inc.)

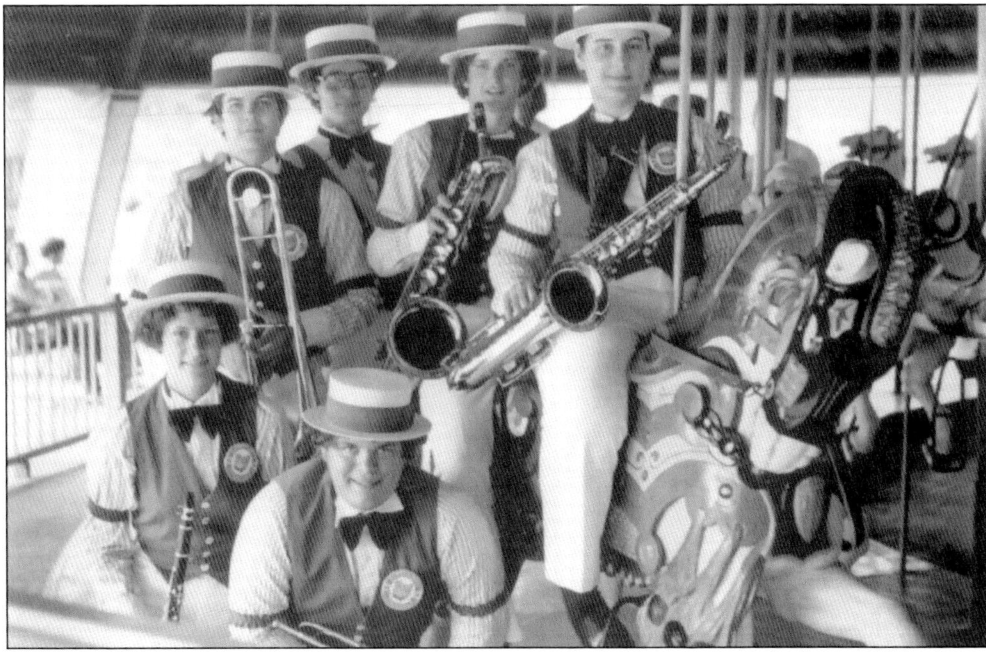

The Funland Dixieland Band also made its debut on the midway. The Entertainers, a group featuring the big band sound, was also established. (Courtesy of Bill Robinson/WHR Inc.)

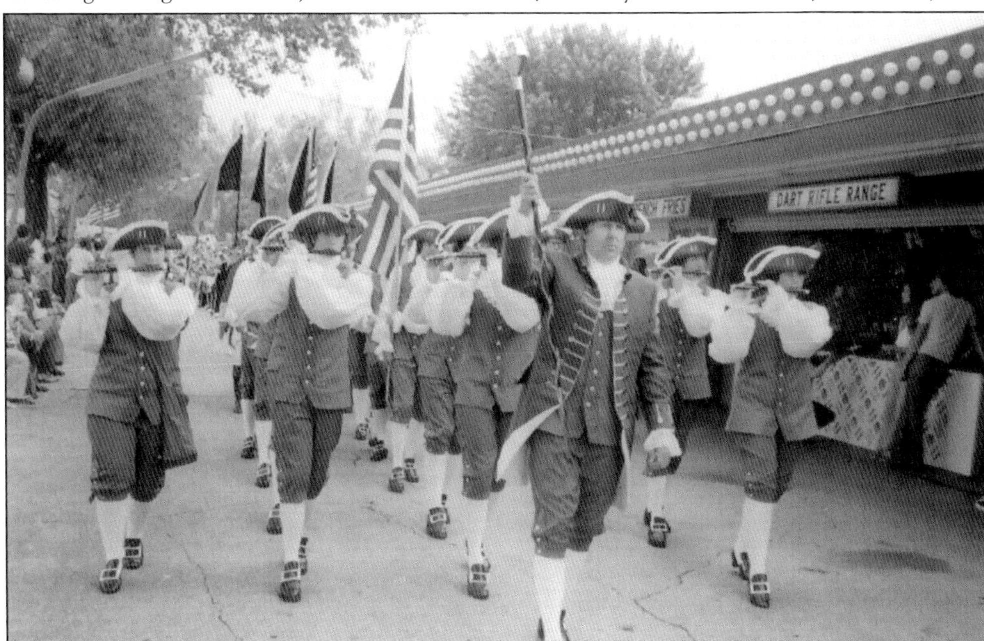

The LeSourdsville Lake Drum and Fife Corps, under the direction of Lemon-Monroe High School Marching Band director Tom Buchanan (in the front), led the parade to celebrate the official Bicentennial Day at the park. A flag-raising ceremony was held at the Liberty Gardens, which featured a replica of the Liberty Bell. Various church choirs performed, as well as dancers from the Lubbers School of Dance in Middletown. The Cliff Lash Orchestra from the *Bob Braun Show* performed in the Stardust Gardens Ballroom. (Courtesy of Bill Robinson/WHR Inc.)

A special bicentennial cake was presented at the ceremony that highlighted events at the only US bicentennial amusement park in the country. The cake was prepared by Herman Albers Bakery on Main Street in Hamilton, Ohio. (Courtesy of Bill Robinson/WHR Inc.)

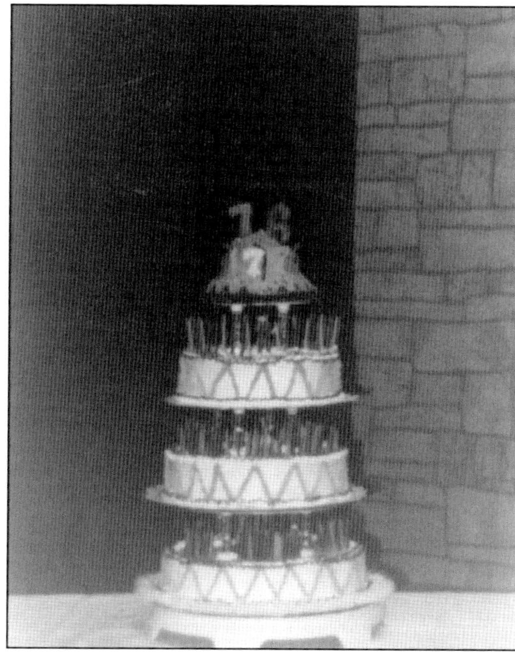

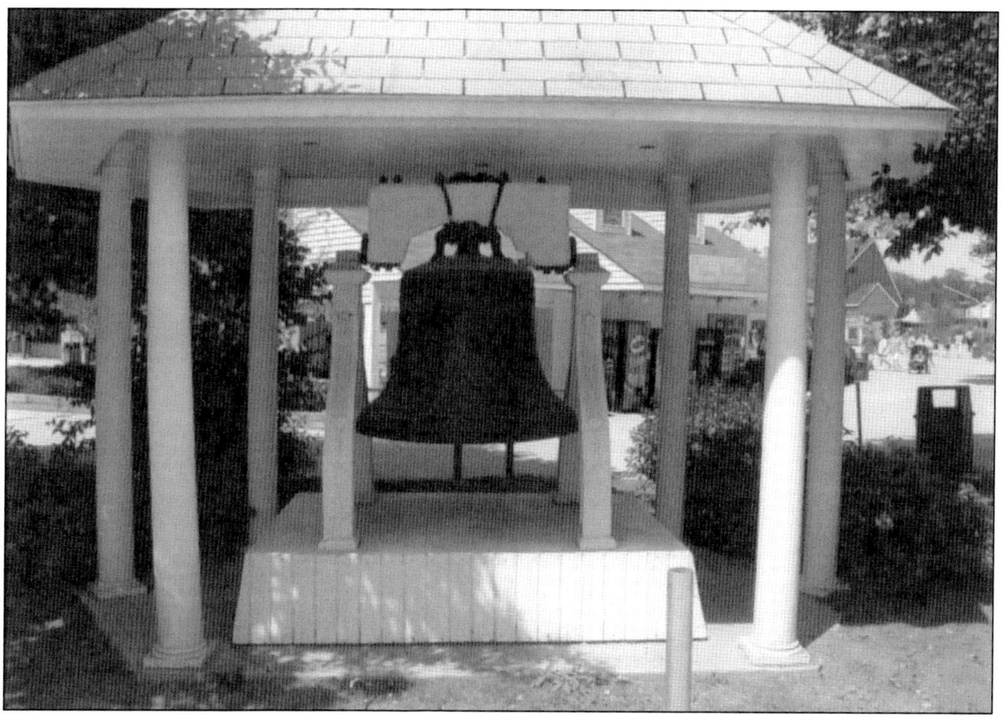

A replica Liberty Bell was dedicated and a specially built shelter was installed. Nancy Kirgan, president of the Butler County Bicentennial Committee, presented Howard Berni with an official bicentennial flag that flew above the bell for the entire season. The Fairfield High School Choraliers sang patriotic songs, and the history of LeSourdsville Lake was read. The Miller Blackhawks Band played the song "When Johnny Comes Marching Home" to culminate the ceremony. (Courtesy of Bill Robinson/WHR Inc.)

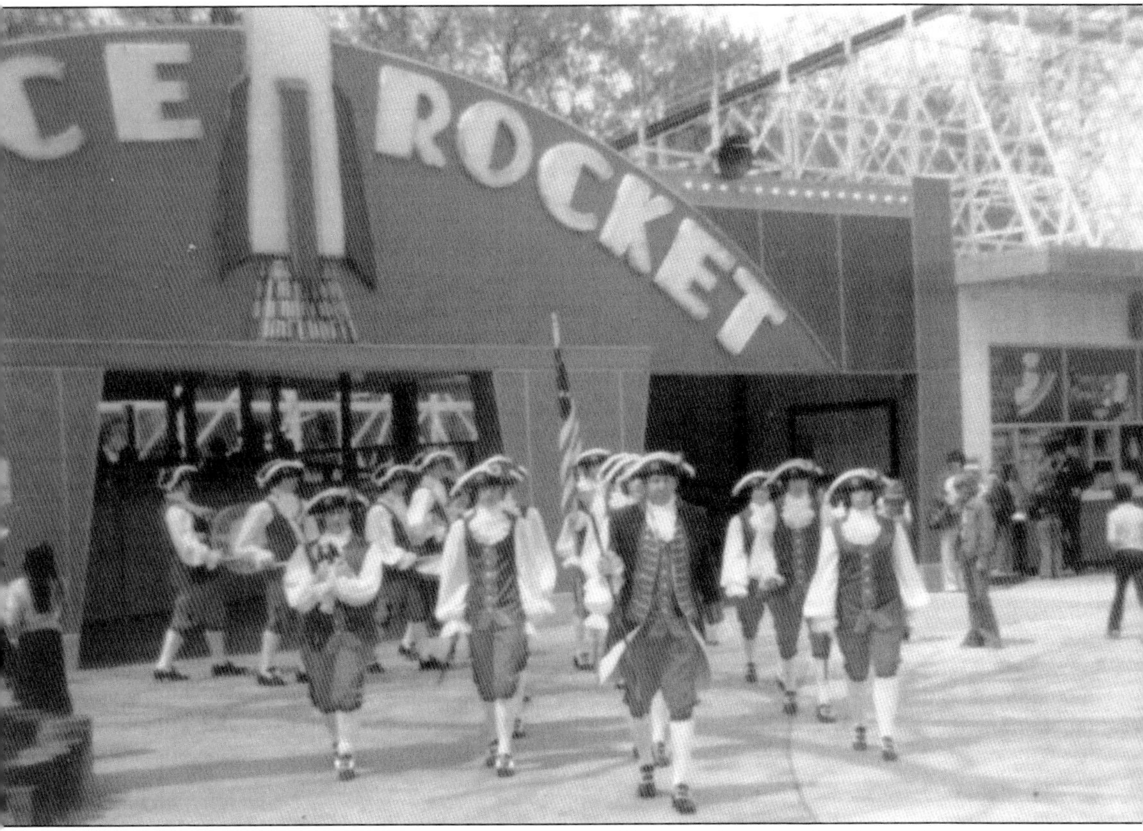

The Drum and Fife Corps performed a version of "Yankee Doodle Dandy" in front of the Space Rocket roller coaster after Sen. Donald Lukens made comments. A Cobra helicopter from the US Army was also on display. (Courtesy of Bill Robinson/WHR Inc.)

Park vice president Bill Robinson created another block of entertainment that included an array of costumed characters led by the park's official mascot, a seven-foot-tall bear called Uncle Freddy, the Fun Bear. Uncle Freddy's original partners included the Crazy Fun Critters, Pierre LeSourd, and Rocky Raccoon. Their appearance complimented the debut of the Rock 'N Remember shows in 1976 sponsored by WSAI-AM. Performers included Ray Peterson, Bobby Lewis, Danny and the Juniors, Jimmy Clayton, Tommy James and the Shondells, and Herman's Hermits. Also appearing that year were Roy Clark, Grandpa Jones, and Bo Donaldson and the Heywoods. (Courtesy of Bill Robinson/WHR Inc.)

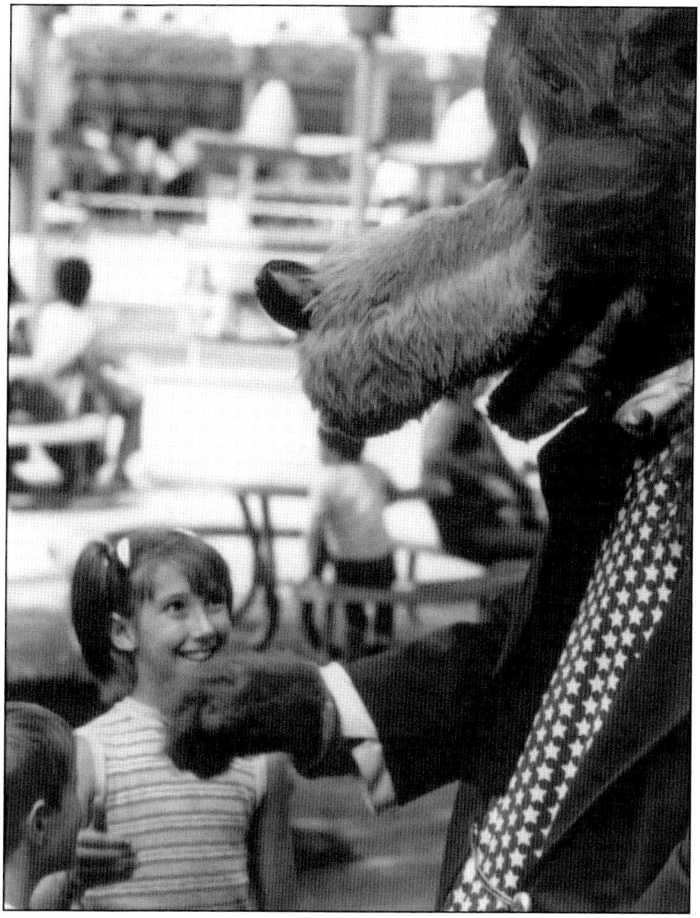

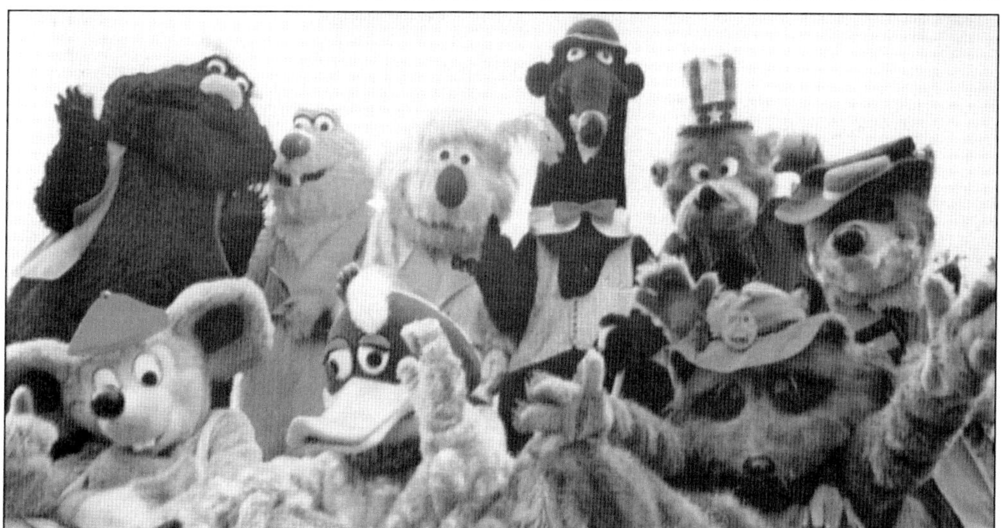

In 1977, the Crazy Fun Critters expanded when Wiley the Weasel, Drake the Duck, and Cheddar the Mouse joined the crew. The Krazy Fun Critter Express Band with Do, Rae, Mi, and Fah made its debut. (Courtesy of Bill Robinson/WHR Inc.)

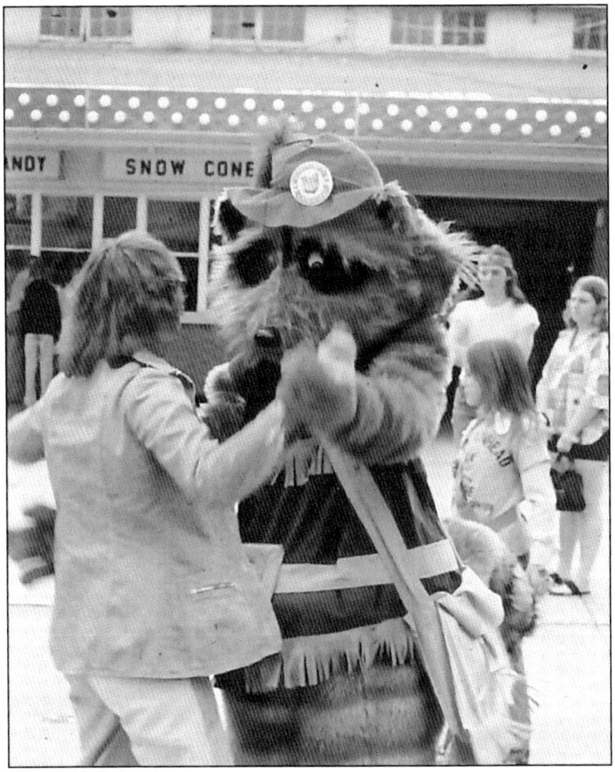

Rocky Raccoon is seen here making new friends on the midway. In the background is a portion of the two-story bathhouse that was destroyed by fire in 1990. (Courtesy of Bill Robinson/WHR Inc.)

The Electric Rainbow was introduced to LeSourdsville guests in 1977. The addition of this ride continued the practice of adding thrill rides to compete with Kings Island. (Courtesy of Bill Robinson/WHR Inc.)

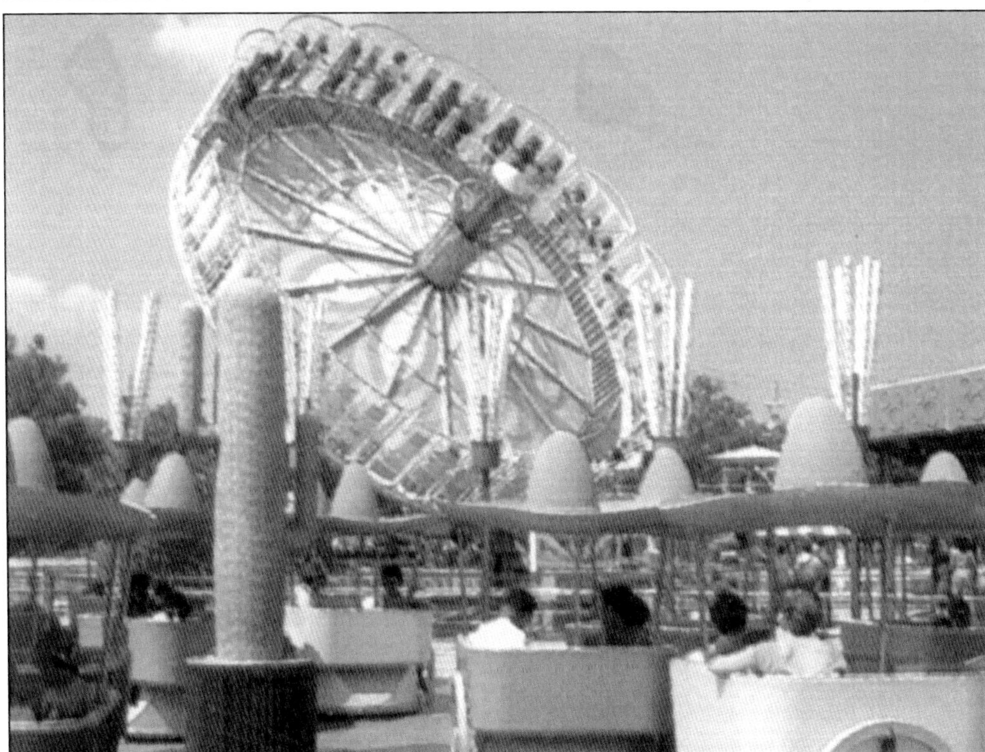

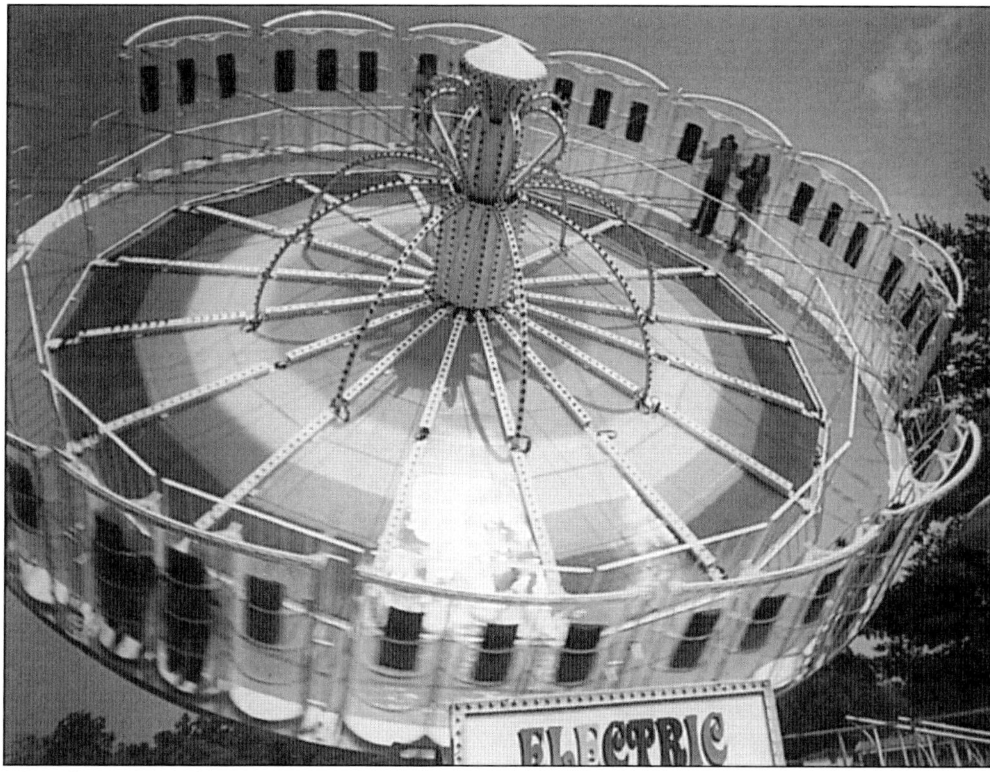

The Electric Rainbow continued operating through the 2002 season. It was sold to Stricker's Grove in 2006, where it continues to operate today.

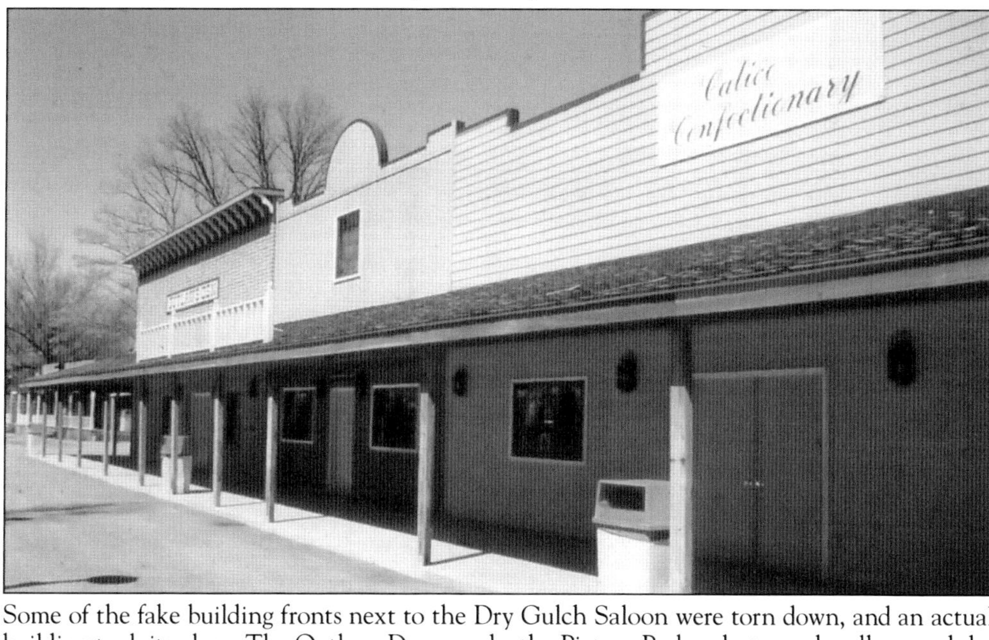

Some of the fake building fronts next to the Dry Gulch Saloon were torn down, and an actual building took its place. The Outlaws Den arcade, the Picture Parlor photograph gallery, and the Calico Confectionary, specializing in homemade fudge and ice cream, opened in 1977. (Courtesy of Bill Robinson/WHR Inc.)

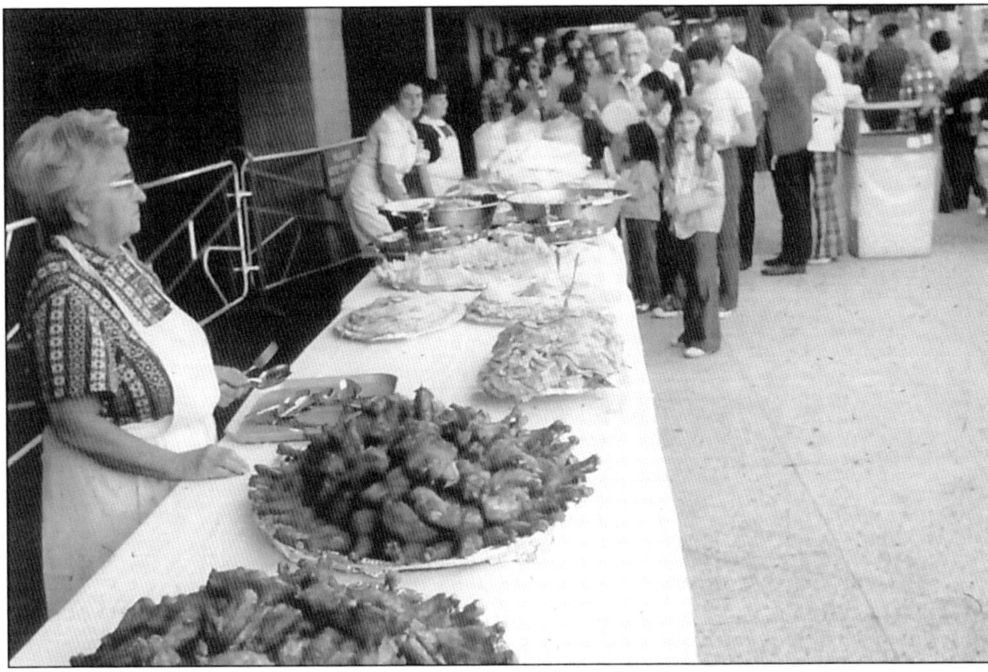

Picnics continued to be popular with companies and churches. The success of these picnics was due to the commitment and dedication that the LeSourdsville management put into serving its delicious menu of fried chicken, mashed potatoes, and biscuits. By 1977, some 200,000 dinners were being served annually. The park was so successful that Kings Island sent people to LeSourdsville to discover the secret to the group's success. (Courtesy of Bill Robinson/WHR Inc.)

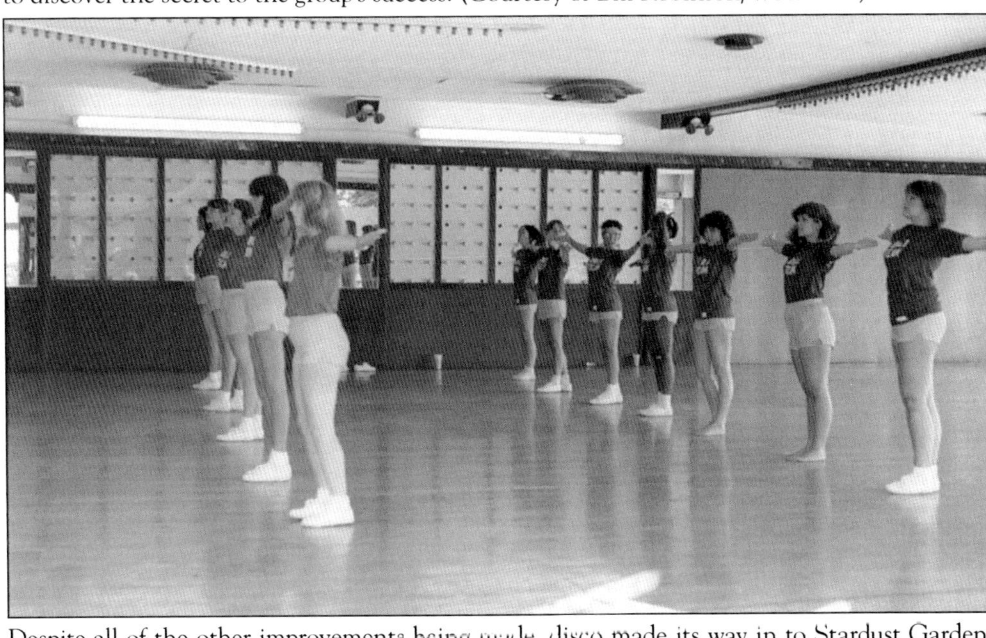

Despite all of the other improvements being made, disco made its way in to Stardust Gardens once a week. During the day, it played host to such events as dance line summer camps, which assisted local high school girls in improving their skills for the upcoming school year. (Courtesy of Bill Robinson/WHR Inc.)

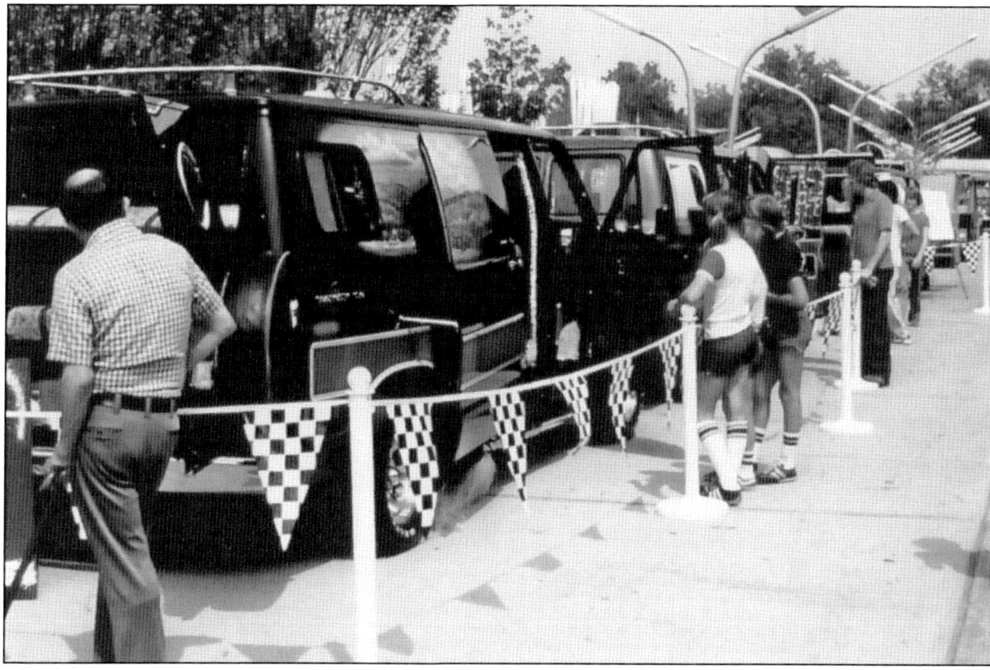

The park was home to a variety of vehicle shows throughout the years, in addition to the annual Miami Valley Boat Show in the early 1970s. In the late 1970s, an annual custom van show was featured. The park's first vehicle show occurred in 1948 and featured Tucker Cars. (Courtesy of Bill Robinson/WHR Inc.)

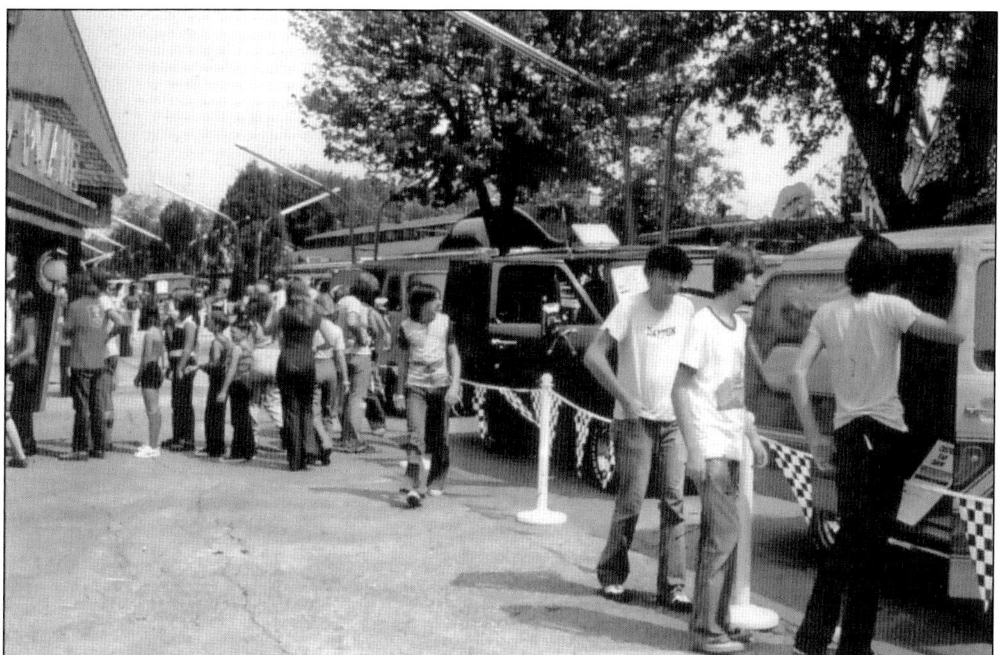

The Tri-State Custom Auto Show, sponsored by the Middletown Pacemakers Club, debuted in 1954 and ran until 1965. In the late 1960s, an antique auto show was held. In the 1970s, a local Corvette club held annual shows on the midway. (Courtesy of Bill Robinson/WHR Inc.)

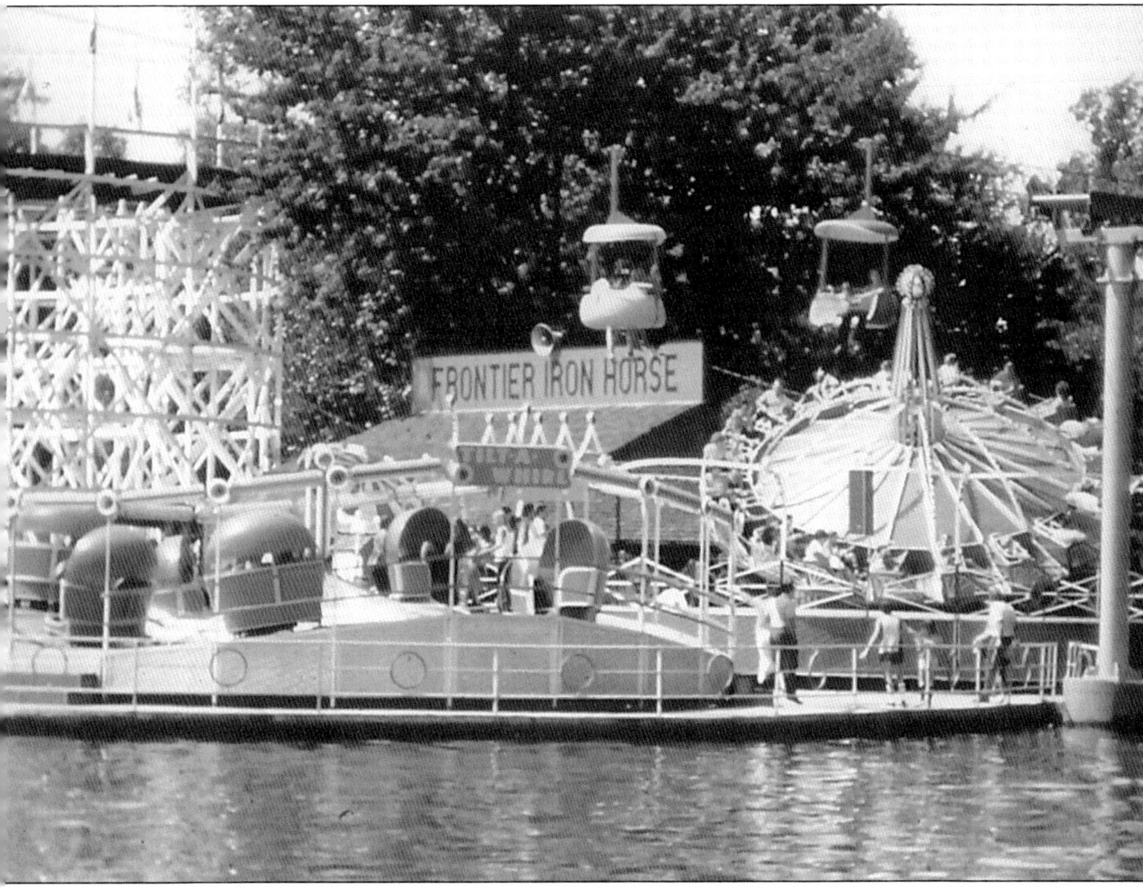

The Tilt-a-Whirl (left), the Iron Horse train station, and the Trabant anchored the end of midway. At the end of the 1977 season, the train station was leveled and the area behind it was filled in to make room for a major expansion. (Courtesy of Bill Robinson/WHR Inc.)

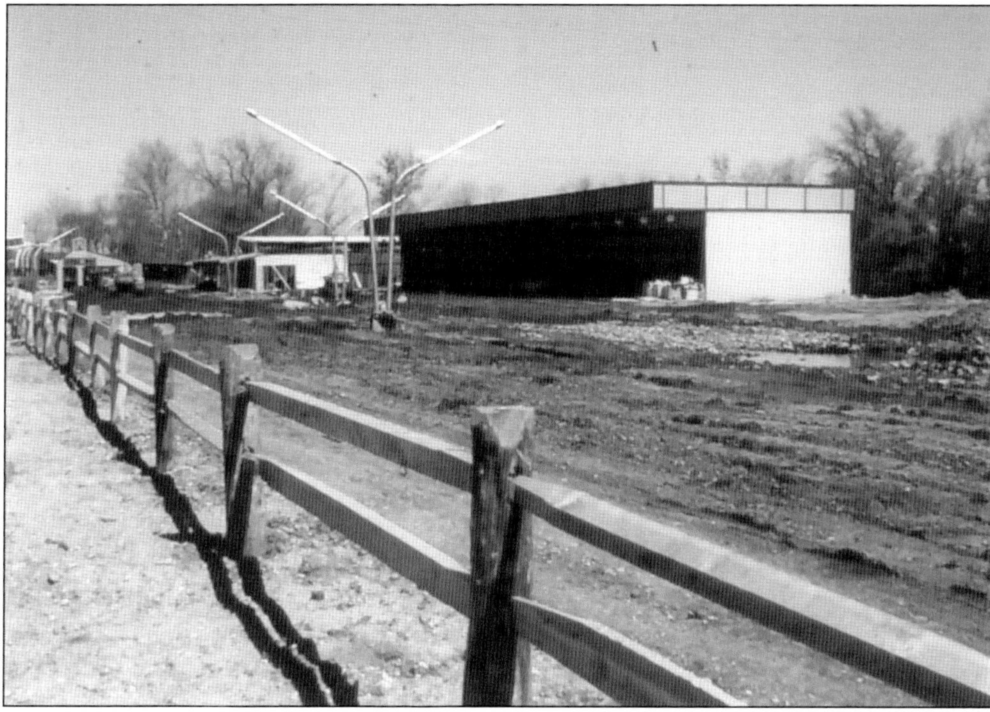

The end of the midway was extended down this fence line to make room for a new games building, an eating facility, an enlarged train station, and a circus tent. (Courtesy of Bill Robinson/WHR Inc.)

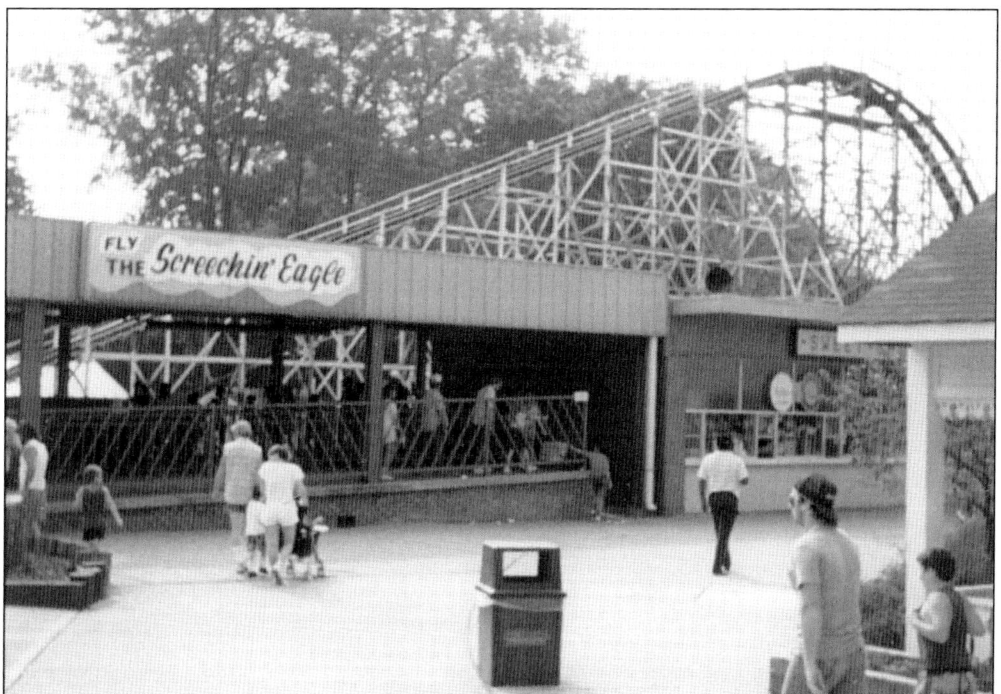

Just after the park closed for the 1977 season, the loading station of the Space Rocket burned down. A new station was built, and the coaster was renamed the Screechin' Eagle. (Author's collection.)

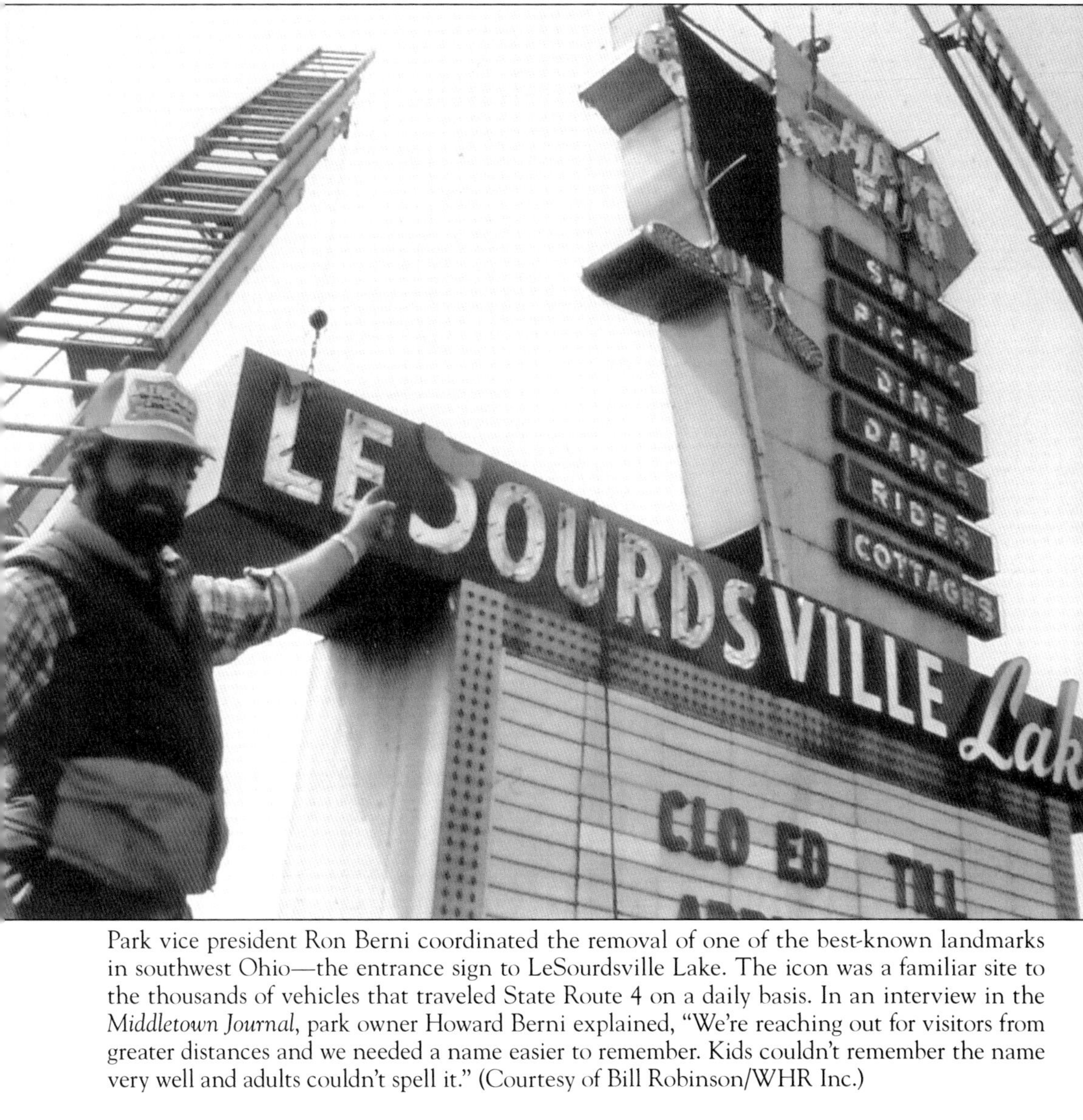

Park vice president Ron Berni coordinated the removal of one of the best-known landmarks in southwest Ohio—the entrance sign to LeSourdsville Lake. The icon was a familiar site to the thousands of vehicles that traveled State Route 4 on a daily basis. In an interview in the *Middletown Journal*, park owner Howard Berni explained, "We're reaching out for visitors from greater distances and we needed a name easier to remember. Kids couldn't remember the name very well and adults couldn't spell it." (Courtesy of Bill Robinson/WHR Inc.)

A new sign reflected the park's name change in 1978 to Americana Amusement Park. The park culminated a three-year, $3.5-million renovation plan to help keep it as a viable alternative to Kings Island. The 800-foot expansion of the midway enabled the park to add a games building, a food complex, an animated bear show, and a structure to house the Hanneford Circus. In addition, Kiddie Kingdom was renamed Kid's World. (Courtesy of Bill Robinson/WHR Inc.)

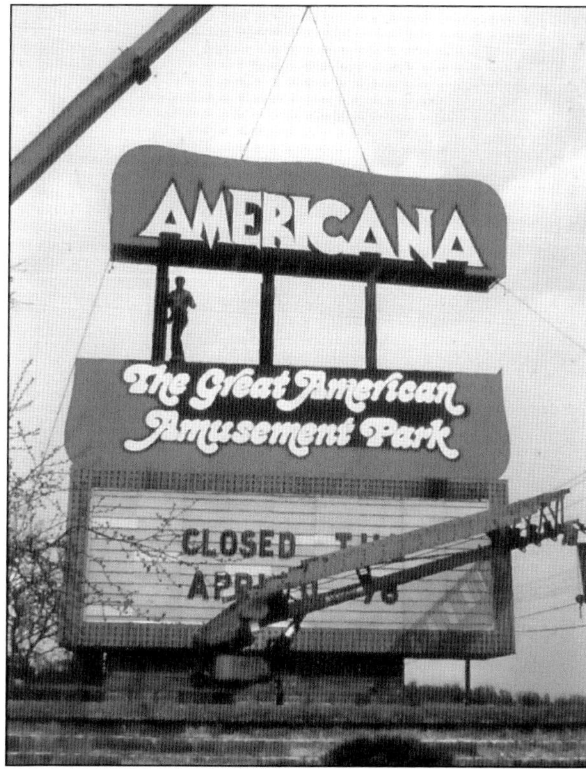

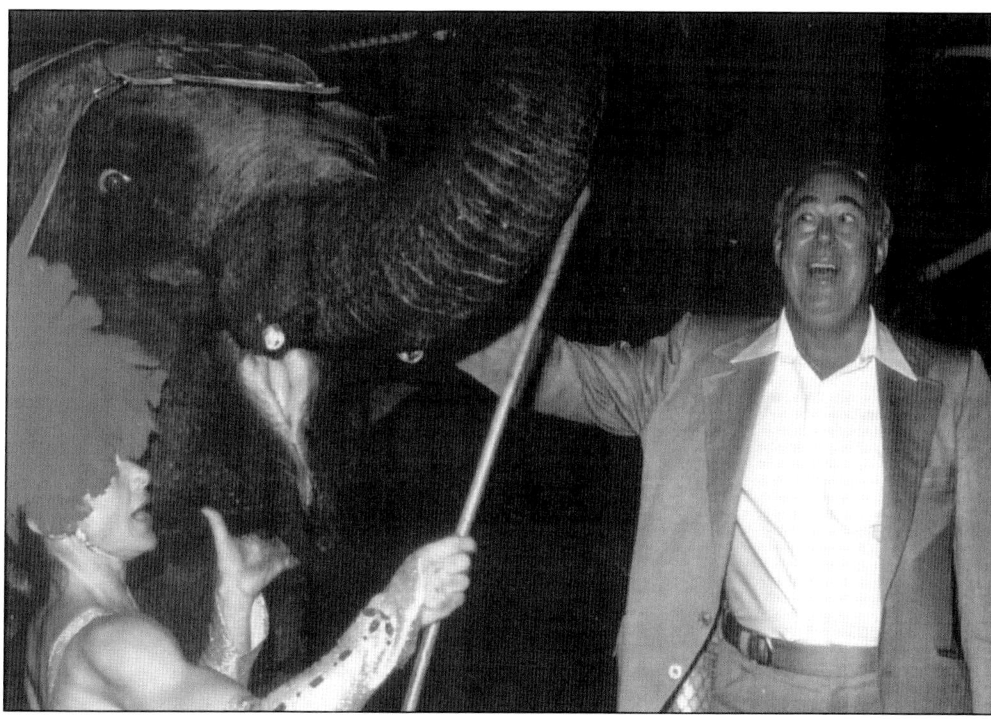

Park owner Howard Berni guided one of the Hanneford Circus elephants to center stage when the circus made its debut in 1978.

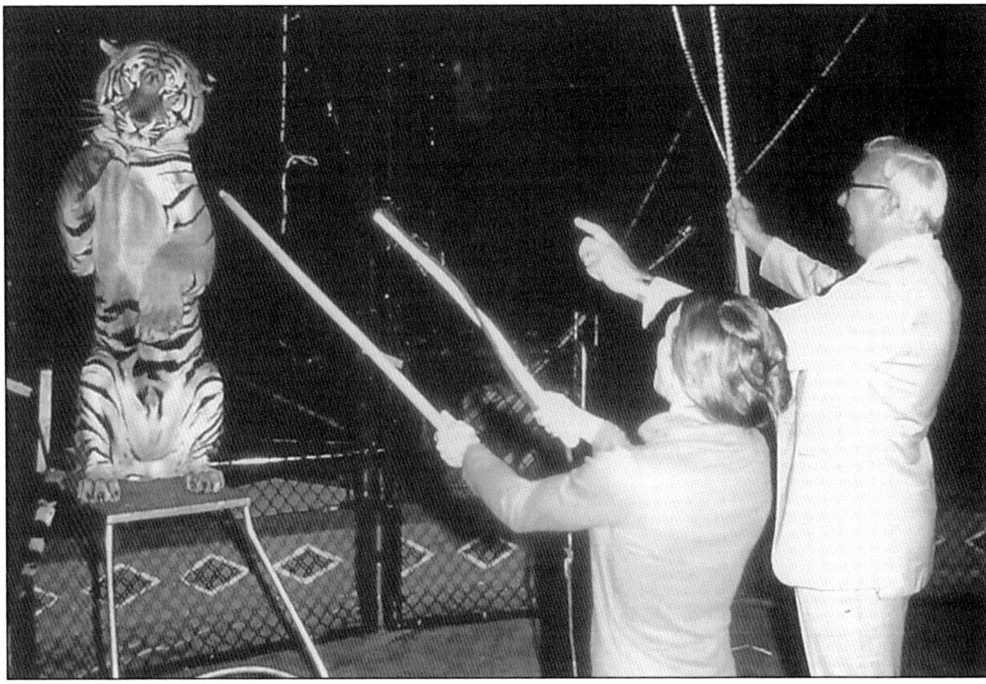

Park owner Howard Berni is being trained to handle one of Hanneford's big cats. The circus performed multiple shows on a daily basis for two years. (Courtesy of Bill Robinson/WHR Inc.)

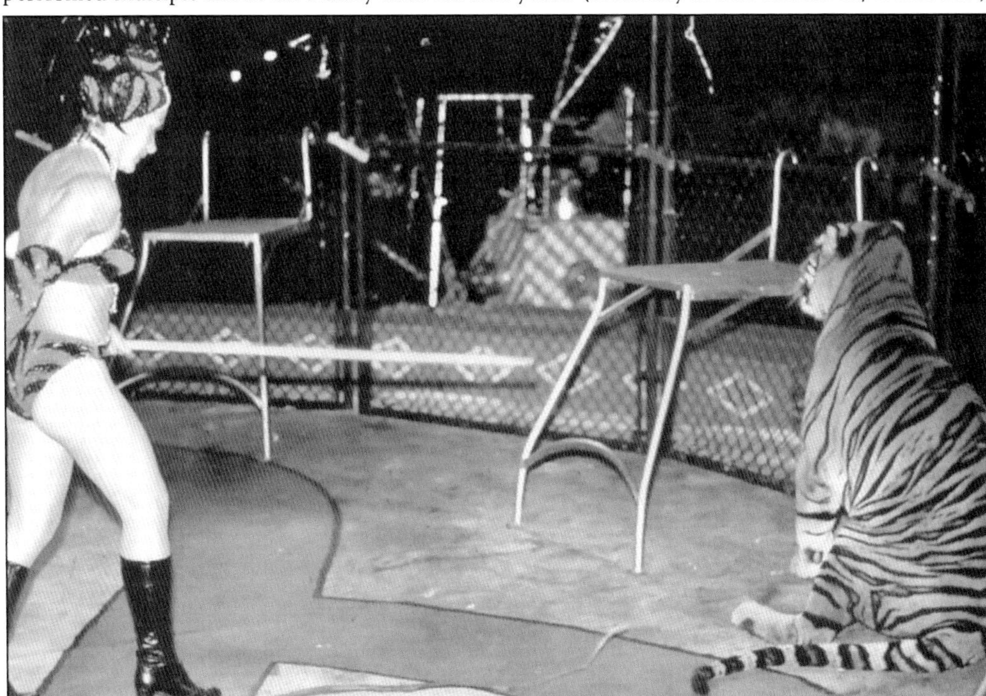

The Hanneford family treated guests to tiger acts, elephant shows, and a high-wire act. The show was replaced in 1980 by Kramer and Company, a nationally known magic show. (Courtesy of Bill Robinson/WHR Inc.)

Guests eagerly participated in one of the new games of chance located next to the Hanneford circus tent. (Courtesy of Bill Robinson/WHR Inc.)

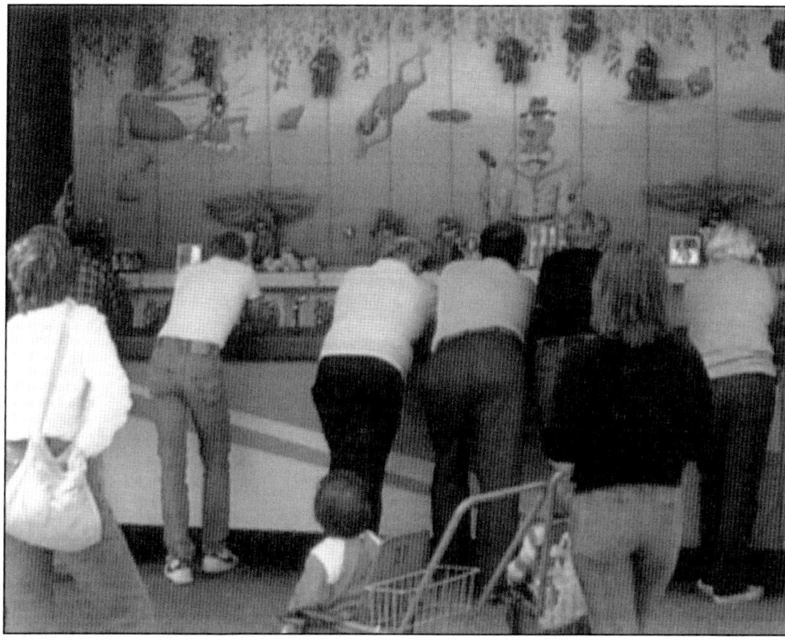

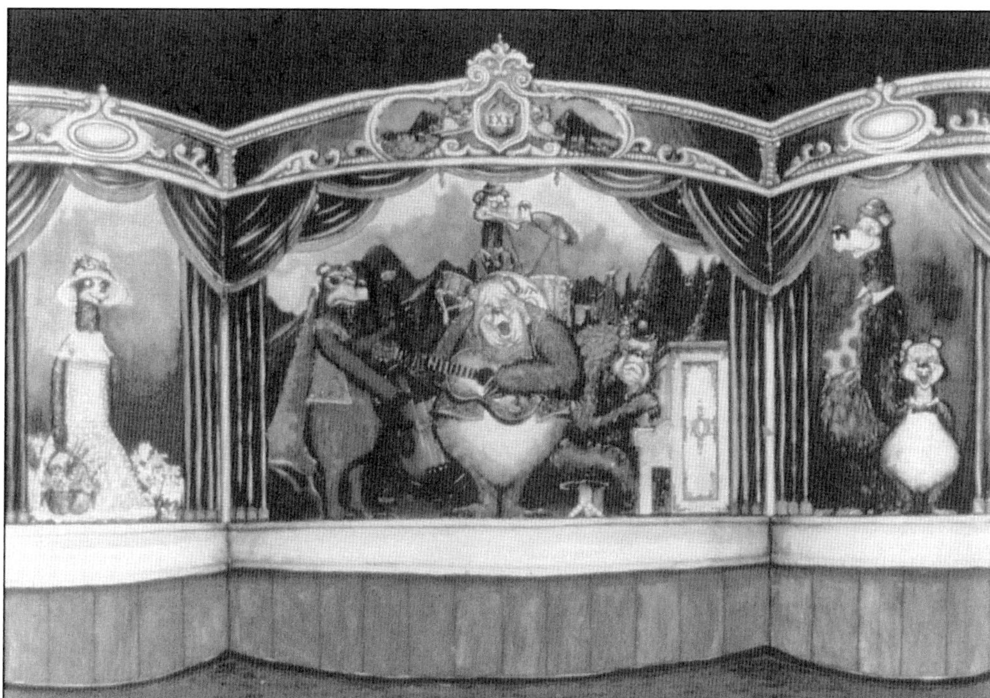

The animated Country Bear Jubilee show debuted in 1978 as part of the expanded midway attractions. The attraction featured animated bears that sang and told stories. The park received a Building Design Award from the American Building Company for creation of the building, which was constructed by Holden Construction in Springboro, Ohio.

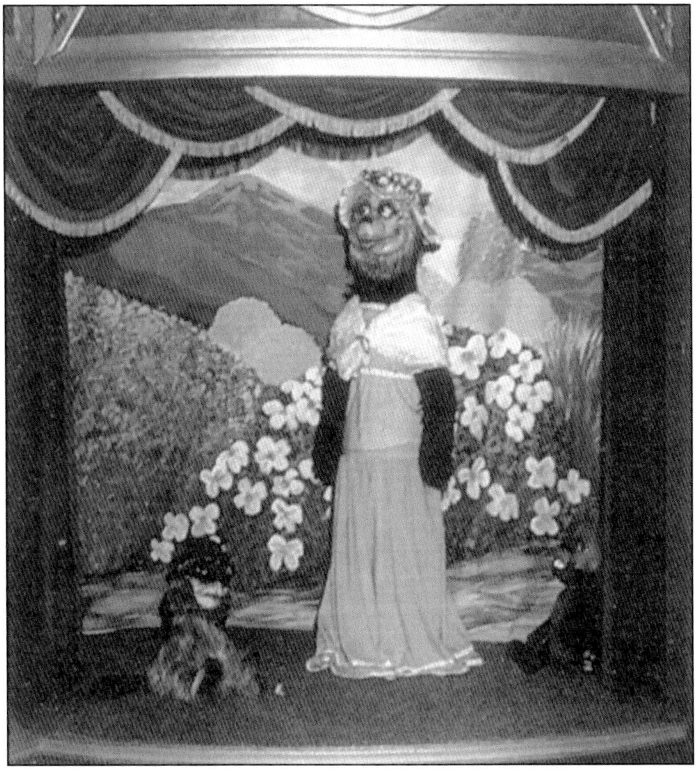

In 1993, the animated Country Bear Jubilee show was sold to the Jungle Jim's Farmer's Market in Fairfield, Ohio. The building housing the bear show remained vacant until 1998 when the LeSourdsville Theatre opened and featured the Heart of Rock and Roll Show.

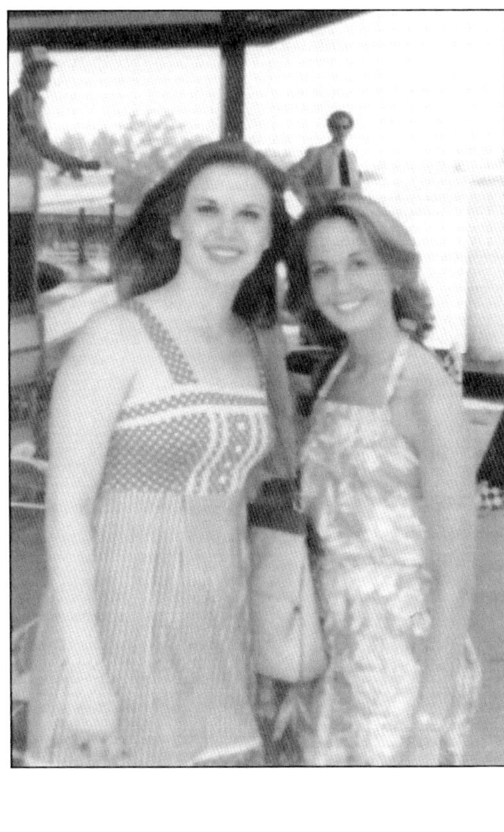

Miss Ohio Susan Perkins (right) and her first runner-up, Joan Gilger, made an appearance at LeSourdsville. Perkins won the title of Miss America in 1978 and was forced to give up her Ohio crown in order to serve as Miss America. Gilger was named Miss Ohio to finish Perkins's term. Perkins is a native of Middletown and was a frequent guest of the park before being crowned Miss Ohio. (Courtesy of Bill Robinson/WHR Inc.)

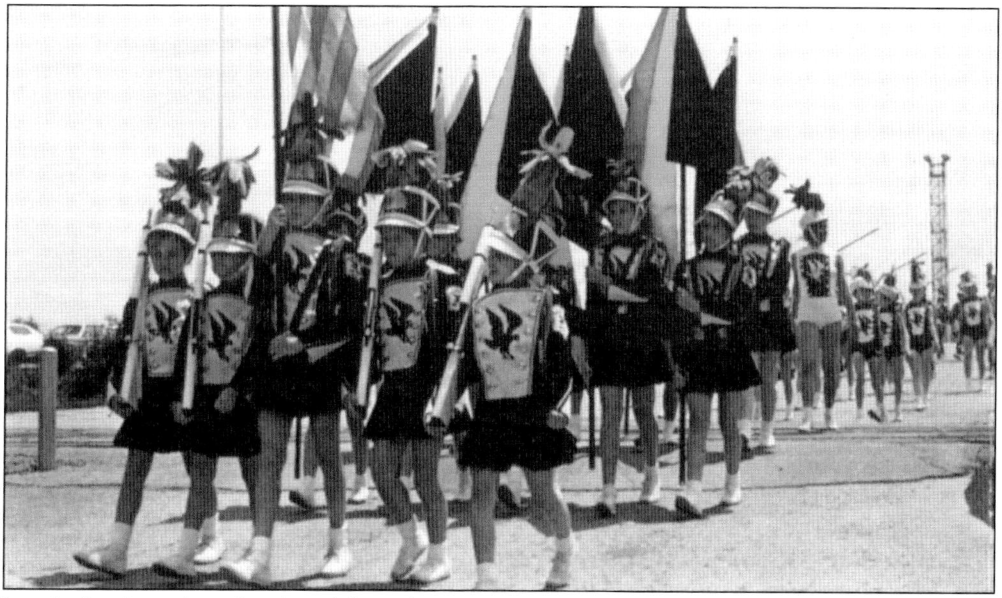

Local school marching bands and dance lines were a common site on the midway. This organization makes its way from the parking area to the main entrance of the park. (Courtesy of Bill Robinson/WHR Inc.)

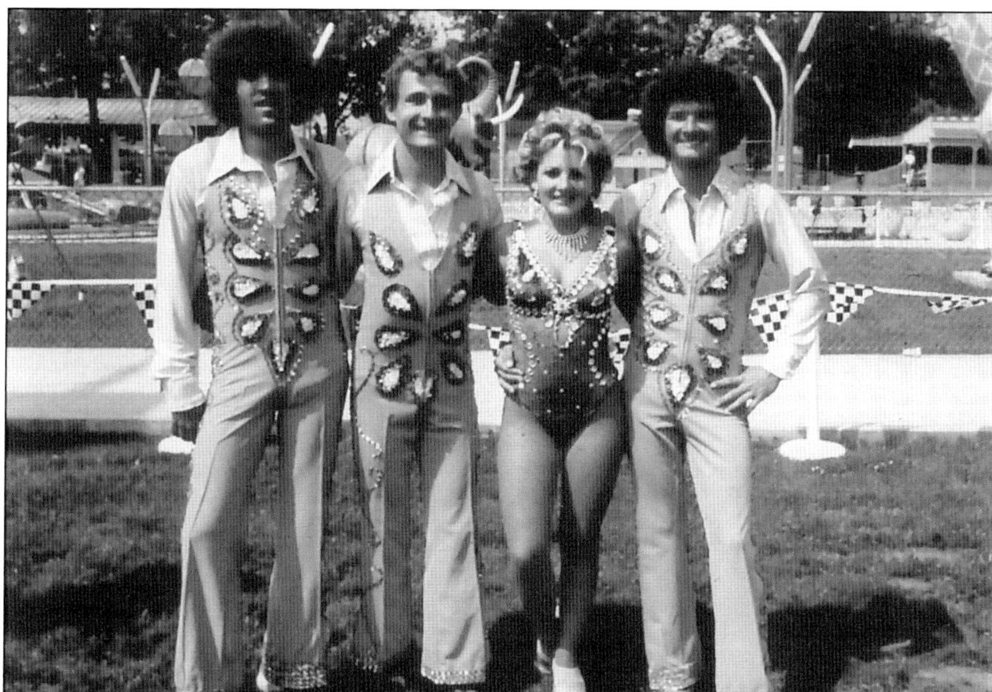

The Great Wallendas made their first appearance at the park in the late 1970s. The family was part of the legendary Flying Wallendas troupe that specialized in high-wire acts. (Courtesy of Bill Robinson/WHR Inc.)

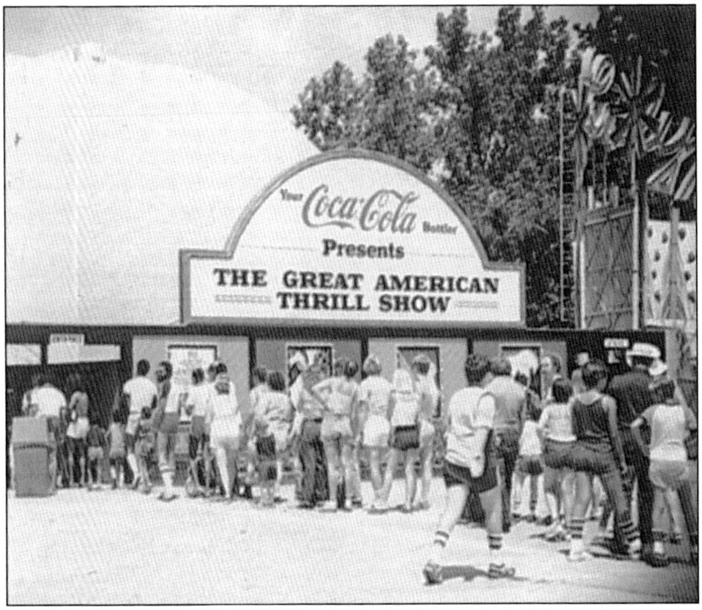

In 1979, a structure to house the Coca-Cola 180-degree movie was constructed. The attraction, produced by Graphics Films, featured a 70-mm picture production filmed aboard stunning airplanes, helicopters, roller coasters, hang gliders, Grand Prix racers, and more.

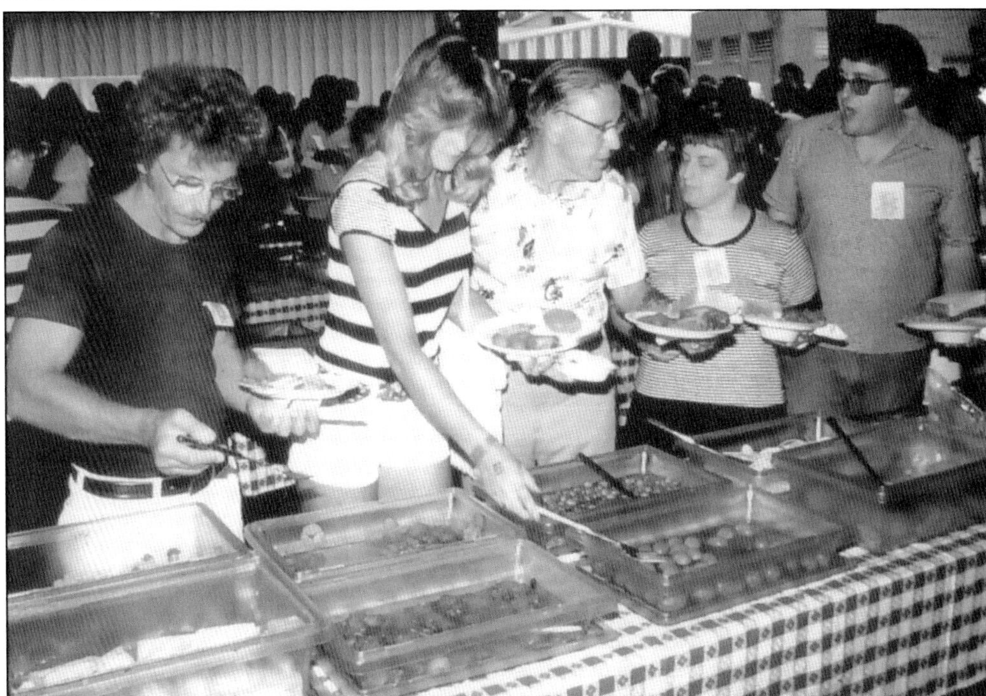

This family utilized one of the covered shelters that were available for corporate and social picnics. In 1979, over $150,000 was spent to enlarge the picnic facilities and add a new restroom facility. That year, the family would have been able to catch a performance of a number of nationally known groups such as Archie Bell and the Drells, Paul Revere and the Raiders, Gary Puckett and the Union Gap, Gary Lewis and the Playboys, Dave and Sugar, the Four Tops, Billy Joe Royal, Joe Frazier and the Knockouts, or Musique. The park estimated their attendance for the year at 500,000 guests.

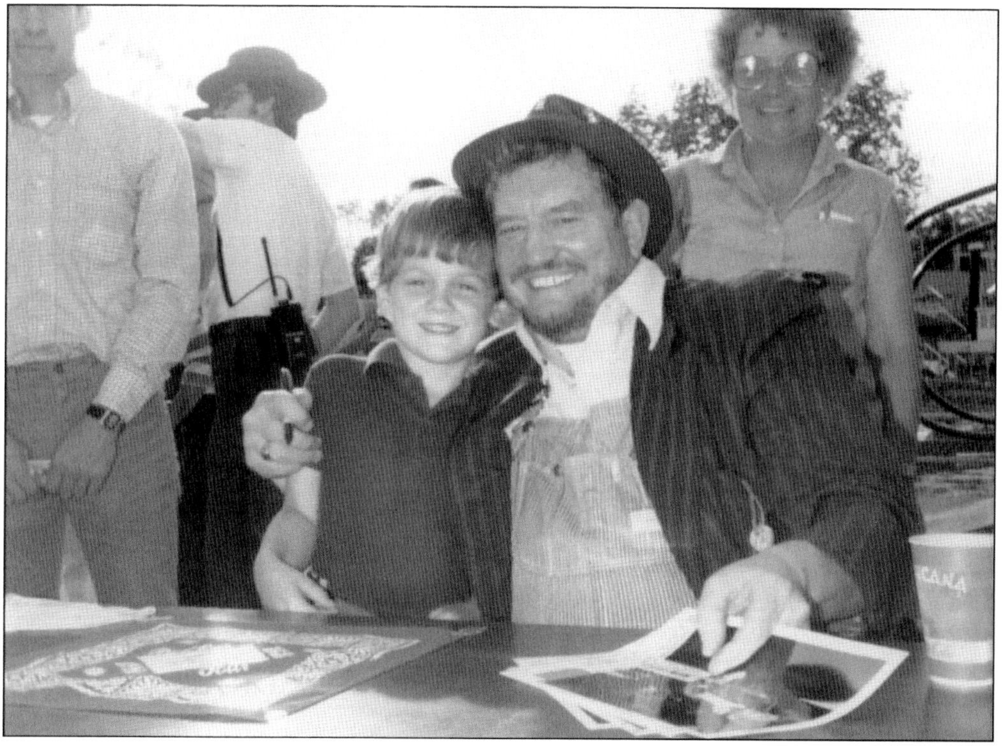

In 1981, Boxcar Willie made an appearance at Americana. Other performers that year included the Sensational Statesmen, Elvis impersonator Glenn Bowles, Earl Thomas Conley, Sylvia, and the Mahoney Brothers. (Courtesy of Bill Robinson/WHR Inc.)

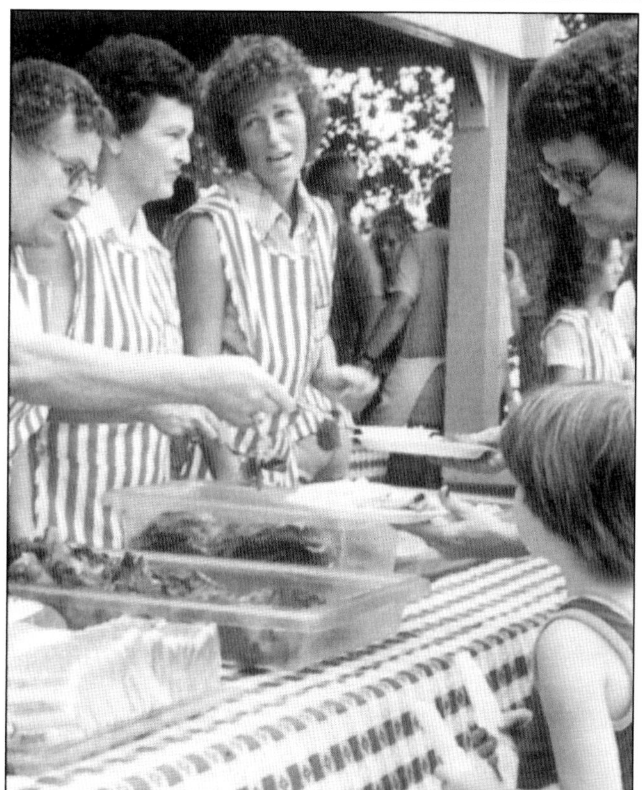

The catering teams were dedicated people who helped serve thousands of guests per year. A typical menu would include fried chicken, mashed potatoes, and baked beans.

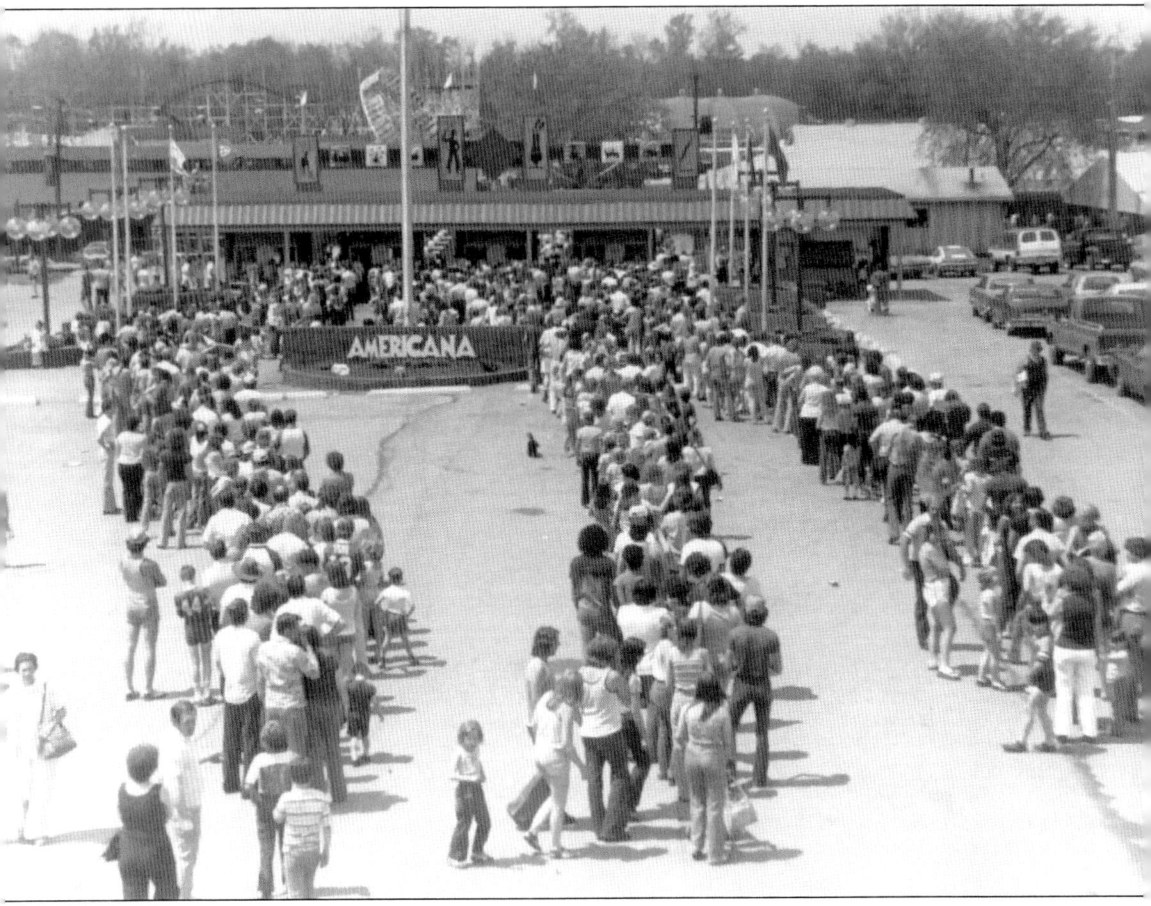

In 1982, a creative marketing idea was attempted to get people into the park during one of its preview weekends. For $1, guests could enter and enjoy over 50 rides and attractions. The plan paid off so much that local police and the State Highway Patrol were called in to try and assist traffic that had come to a dead halt along State Route 4 and nearby State Route 63. "They're parked all over everywhere," said an Ohio State Patrol dispatcher in a *Cincinnati Enquirer* interview. "They're standing in line . . . oh, there must be several thousand people standing in line to get into the park," said an Americana employee. Parking became such a premium that a farmer who lived directly across the street from the park opened up his gate and parked cars on his property. (Courtesy of Bill Robinson/WHR Inc.)

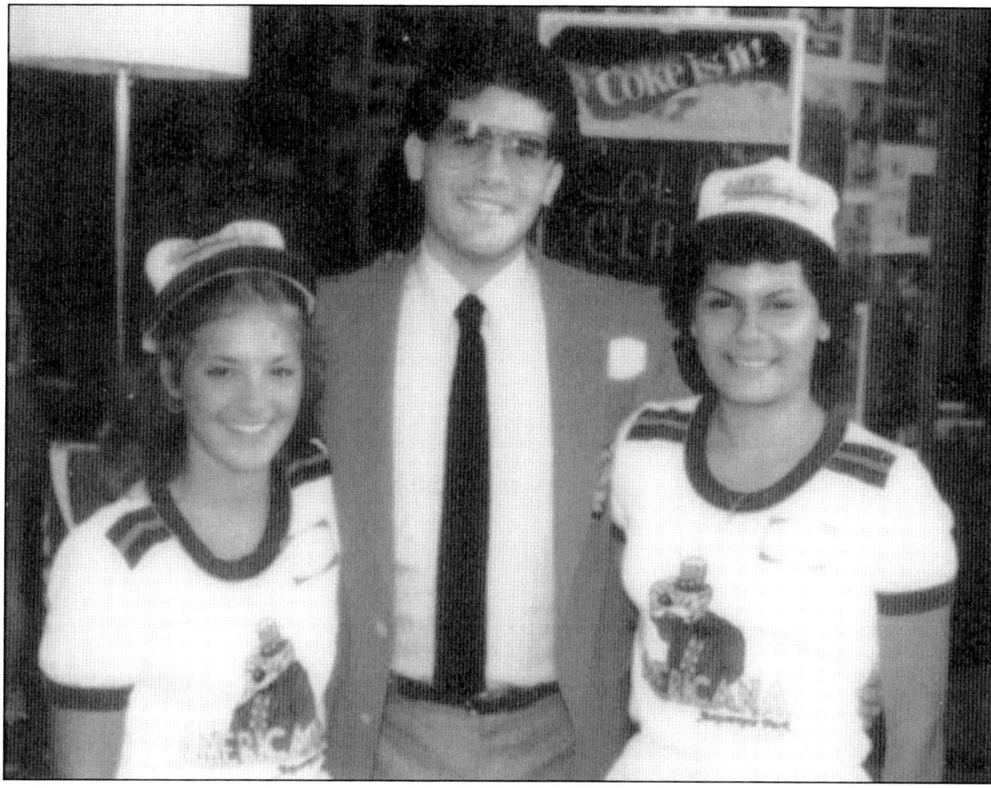

In June 1982, a nationwide tour of the Coca-Cola American Lifestyles Exhibit, a huge display of Coke memorabilia, made a stop at Americana, entertaining thousands of enthusiasts. Other entertainment that year included Elvis impersonator Glenn Bowles, Gale Watson and Kentucky Morning, Bill Gant and the Vigilantes, and Bobby Mackey and the Freedom Express.

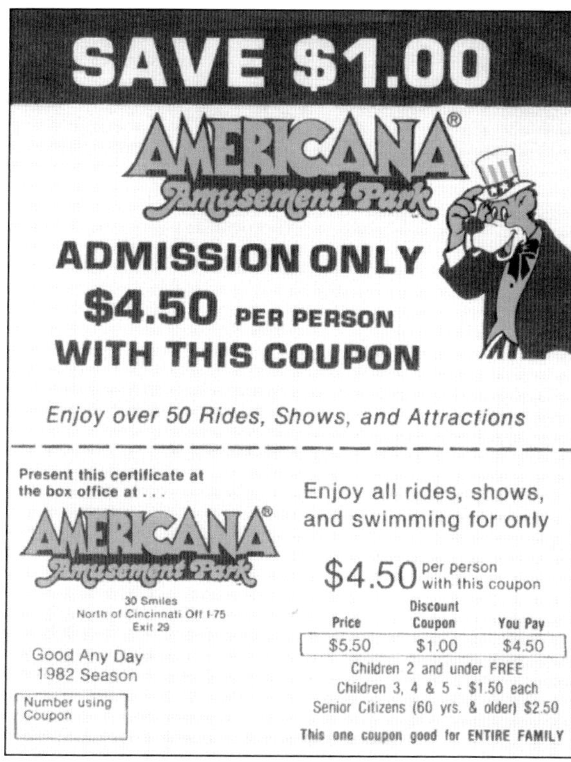

Marketing for the park was heavy after the park changed its name, including radio spots, newspaper ads, and promotional flyers, such as the one pictured. The flyers would be placed on every car in Americana's parking lot throughout the season in an effort to bring guests back to the park. It was estimated by park officials that attendance during this time was around 500,000 annually.

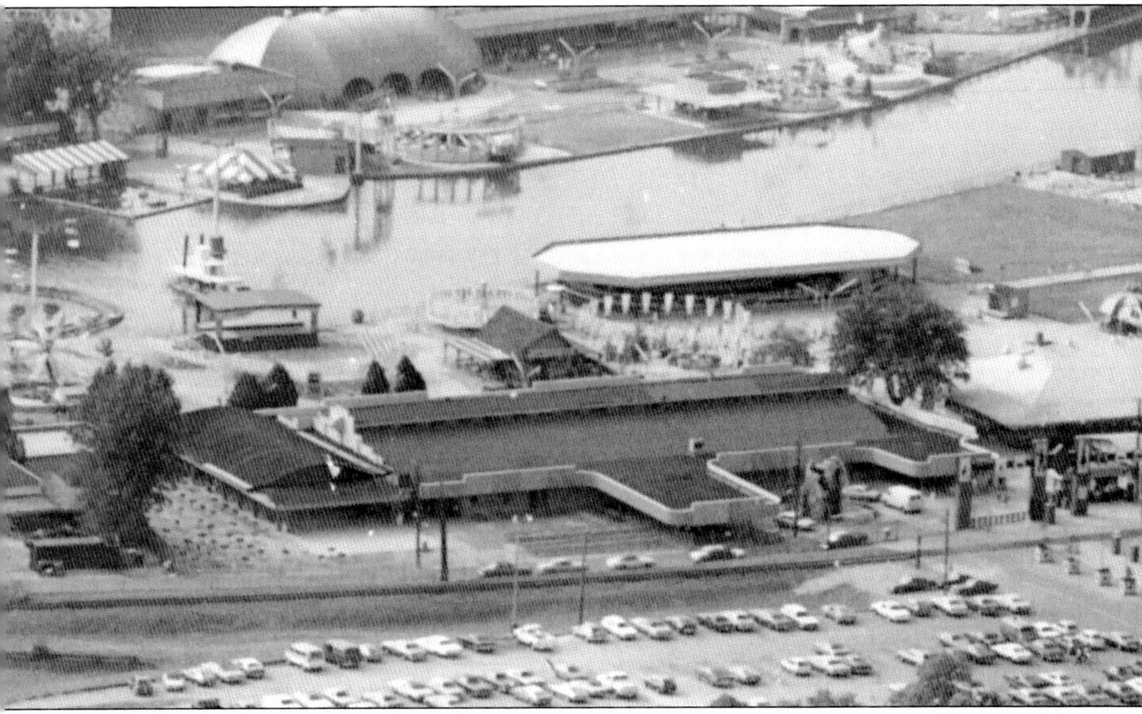

This aerial view of the park in 1982 shows the Screechin' Eagle roller coaster and Super Slide at the top. To the right of the coaster is the midway expansion of 1978. Bumper Buggys, a version of the classic bumper car ride, premiered in the old Hanneford Circus tent next to the turnaround of the coaster. The Stardust Gardens Ballroom is in the center. Americana changed to a six-day-a-week operation and lowered the gate admission to $5.50 due to the recession. The park also offered a season pass (available for $19.95) for the first time in its history.

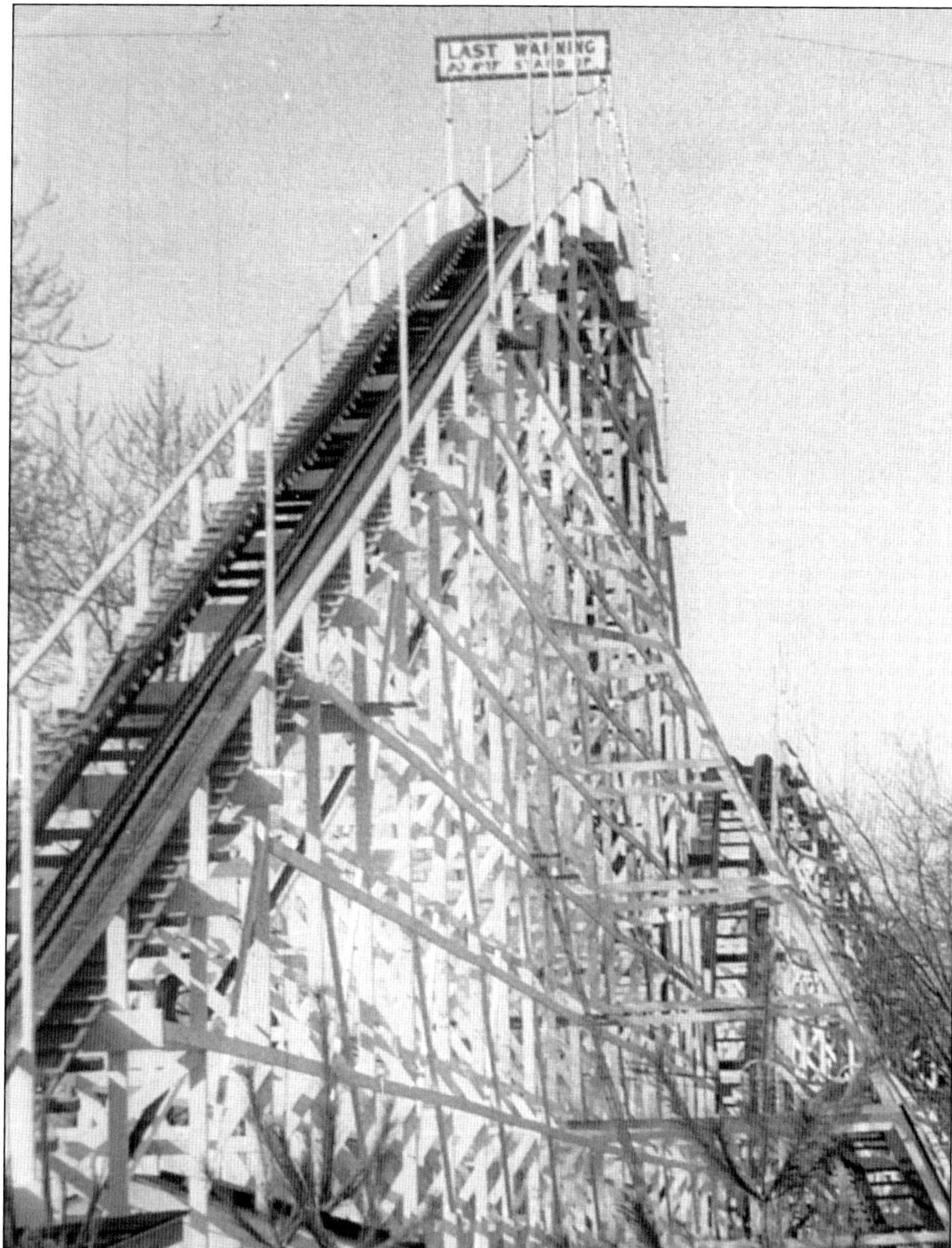

In March 1983, an arson fire destroyed a storage building in Tombstone Territory and caused $40,000 damage. Five months later, a fire broke out in the motor house of the Screechin' Eagle and caused $35,000. In 1985, a small fire destroyed a portion of the first hill of the Screechin' Eagle roller coaster. Needless to say, fire has played a role in how the park has been shaped. (Author's collection.)

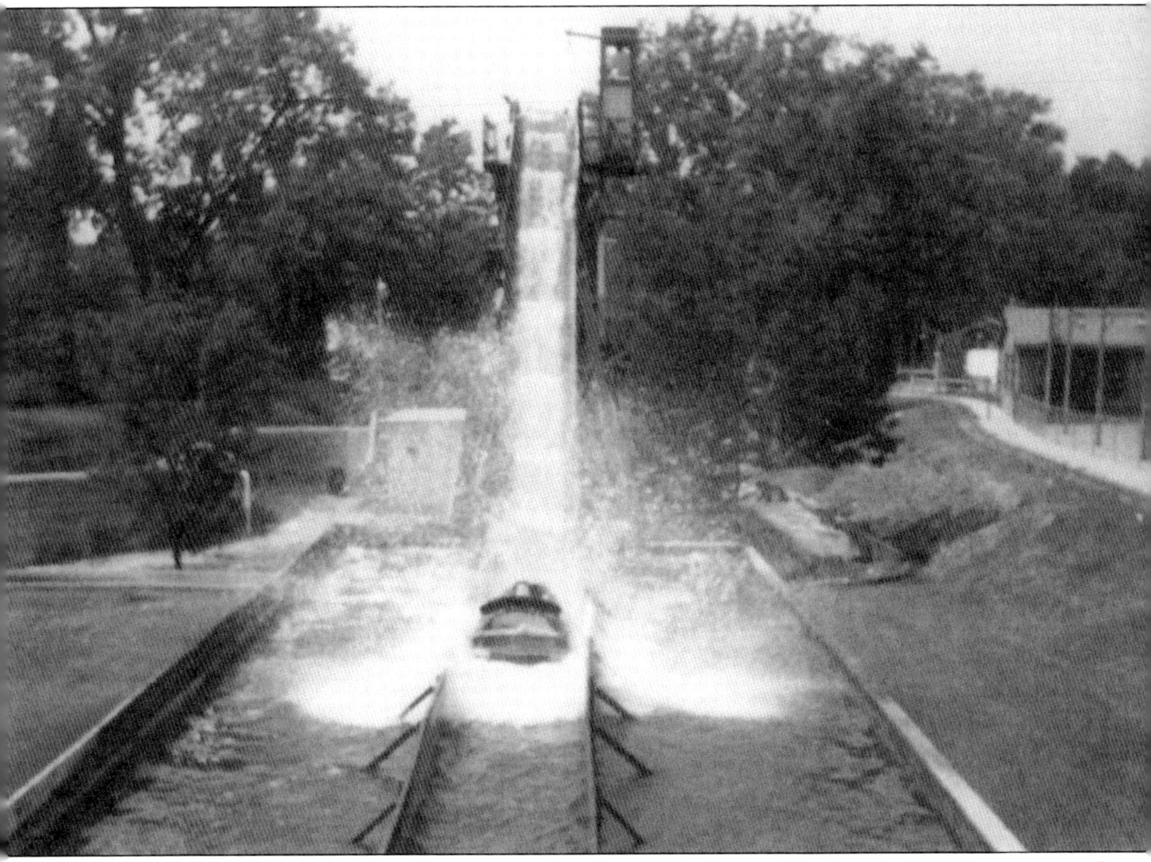

Raging Thunder, a 1,200-foot flume, opened in the old Tombstone Territory in 1984. It represented the largest investment ever in one attraction. The flume, designed by Ron Berni and built by Barr Engineering of Minnesota, was located in a former bird sanctuary. The area was renamed Logger's Run after the flume was added. The total cost for the ride amounted to $900,000 because of construction problems. The 40-foot lift plummeted riders down into a guaranteed wet ride. At the entrance of the ride, two signs were installed to warm riders: the first stated, "You can bet you are going to get wet"; the second ride stated, "No joke you're going to get soaked." The ride also featured a rapids, a waterfall, and one tunnel. Other improvements included a new miniature golf course near the Hanneford Circus tent and the addition of an expanded food complex in Tombstone's old ice cream parlor. (Author's collection.)

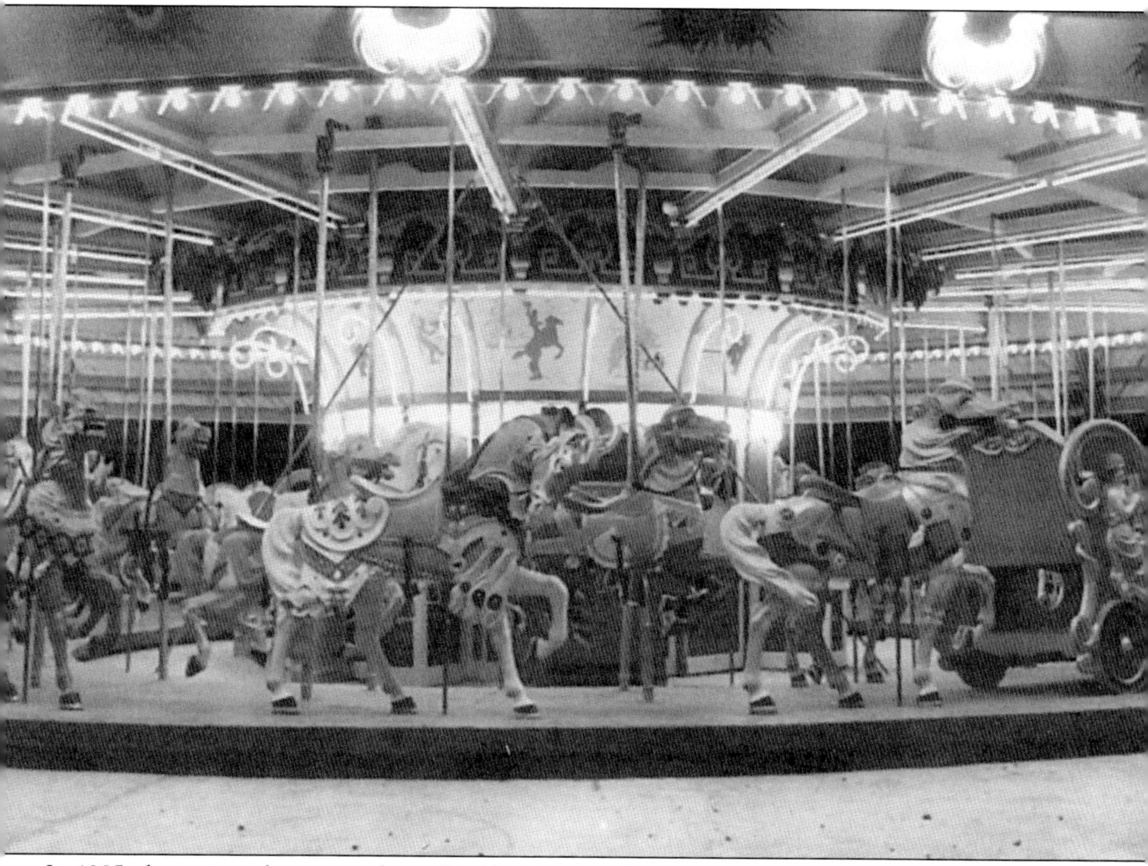

In 1985, the antique horses on the park's 1924 PTC no. 71 carousel were sold at auction. Other items sold included the Old 99 train from Kid's World, a water laser game, the small showboat, the Pretzel ride, a host of late-model arcade games, a Larry Mahon computerized mechanical bull, and a Mangles kiddie fire engine ride from Kid's World.

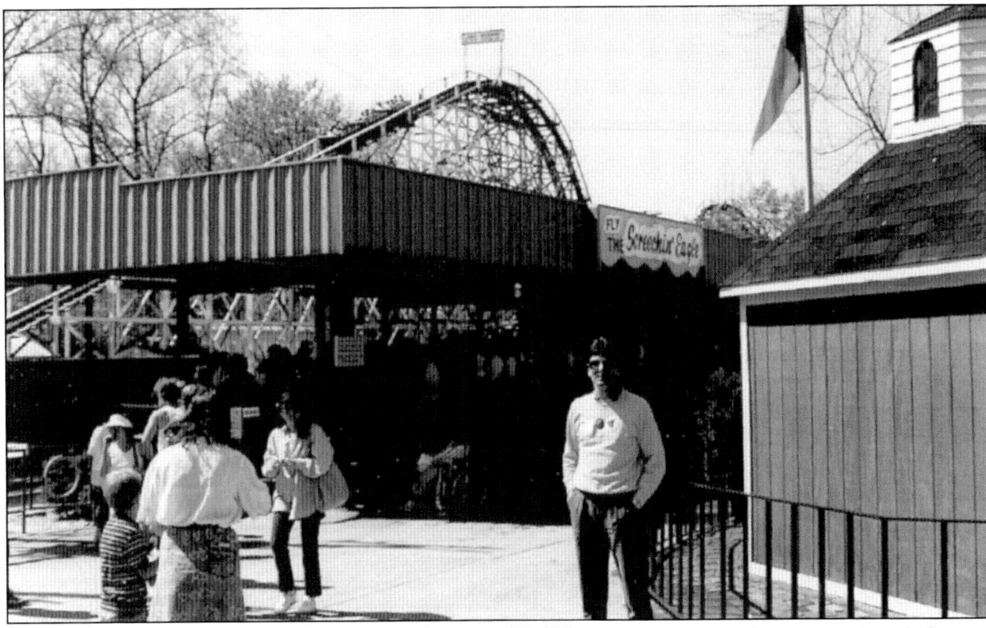

In April 1987, the American Coaster Enthusiasts (ACE), an international organization dedicated to the preservation and enjoyment of roller coasters, held its annual spring conference in southwest Ohio. During that conference, a group came to Americana to welcome the Screechin' Eagle back for another year. ACE Historian Dave Hahner, pictured here, considered himself lucky to ride the Eagle for the first time during that conference. He never got the opportunity to return to the park. ACE members also experienced the new Galleon 60-foot swinging pirate ship in Logger's Run, a renovated Skipper's Wharf that housed the motorboat ride, a new ice cream stand near the roller coaster, a Potato Works concession, and a Rib Pit that served barbecued ribs and chicken. (Courtesy of Dave Hahner.)

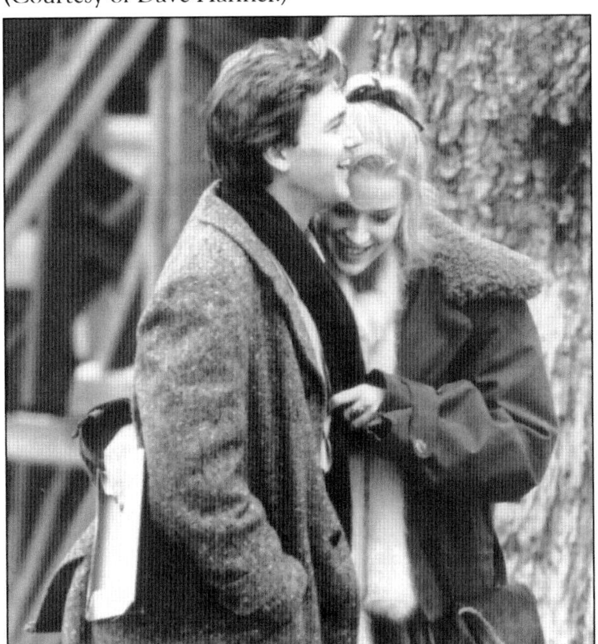

When the park closed after the 1987 season, a movie production crew from Weintraub Entertainment Group in Los Angeles arrived at the park to shoot scenes for the upcoming movie *Fresh Horses*, starring Molly Ringwald and Andrew McCarthy. One scene involved the Screechin' Eagle and part of the Speedway track called "Crazy about the Girl." McCarthy walks up the second hill of the coaster while Ringwald walks parallel on a gravel path. The movie was ultimately released in November 1988. Scenes were also shot at Kings Island, the University of Cincinnati, and the northern Kentucky area. (Courtesy of Sony Pictures, Inc.)

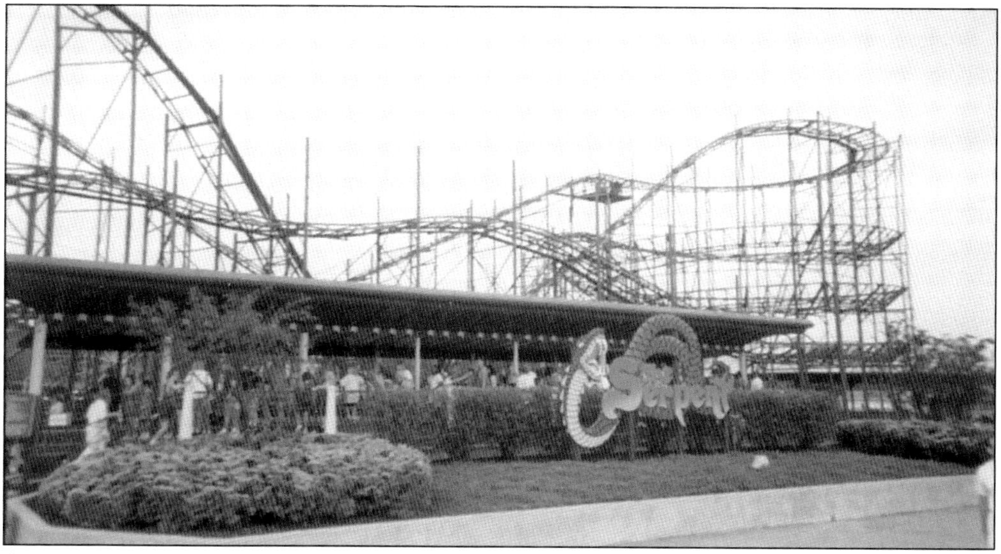

On May 28, a major fire destroyed the carousel and bumper cars, resulting in over $1 million damage and a short evacuation of the park after electricity had to be turned off. One fireman was injured fighting the blaze. The fire was caused by an electrical short in the building housing the carousel. The following October, park personnel purchased a Pinfari Zyklon coaster from Noble Park Funland in Paducah, Kentucky. The coaster was refurbished and renamed the Serpent.

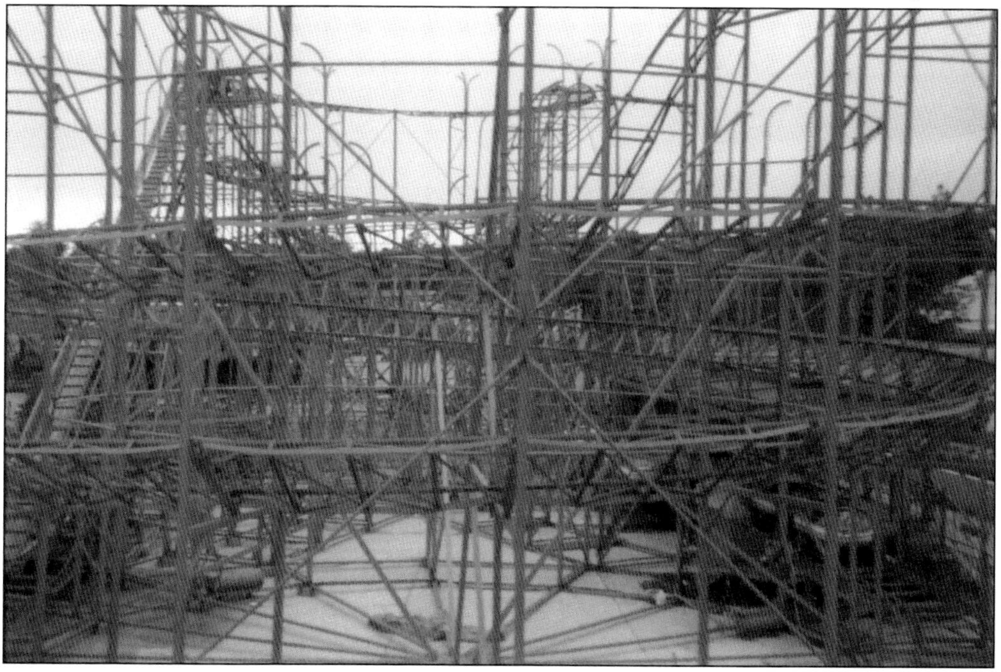

The Serpent cost $170,000 and had a height of only 45 feet; what it lacked in height it did not lack in punch. The track length was 1,919 feet, and a ride typically lasted just under two minutes. The average speed was 35 miles per hour. In 1997, the Serpent was ranked no. 17 among coasters at Six Flags Kentucky Kingdom, Cedar Point, Kings Island, and Stricker's Grove by Jake's Coaster Land. The coaster was also the recipient of the Close Encounter Award for the appearance of smashing into a support.

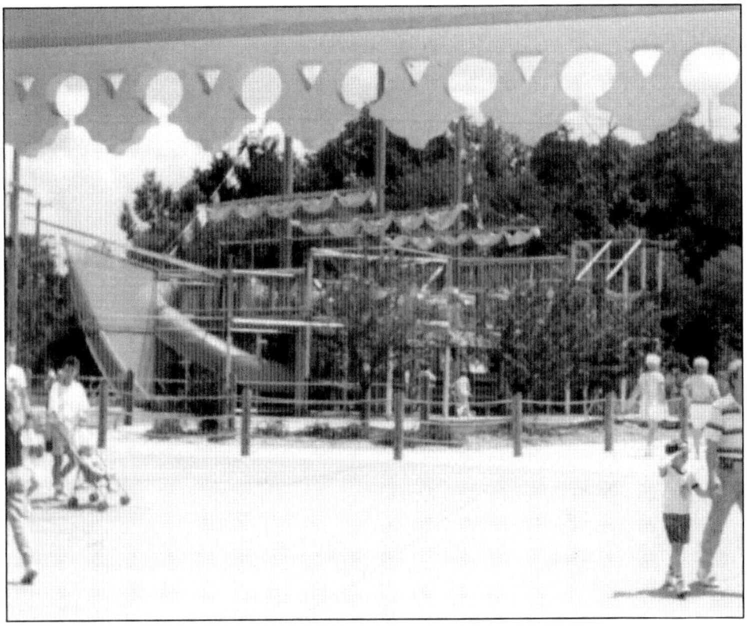

A three-level, 2,220-square-foot pirate ship exclusively for kids was built on the former carousel site. The Jolly Roger Funport included curved and spiral slides, straight and spiral cargo net climbs, web and regular crawl tubes, punching bags, and a ball crawl pit. (Author's collection.)

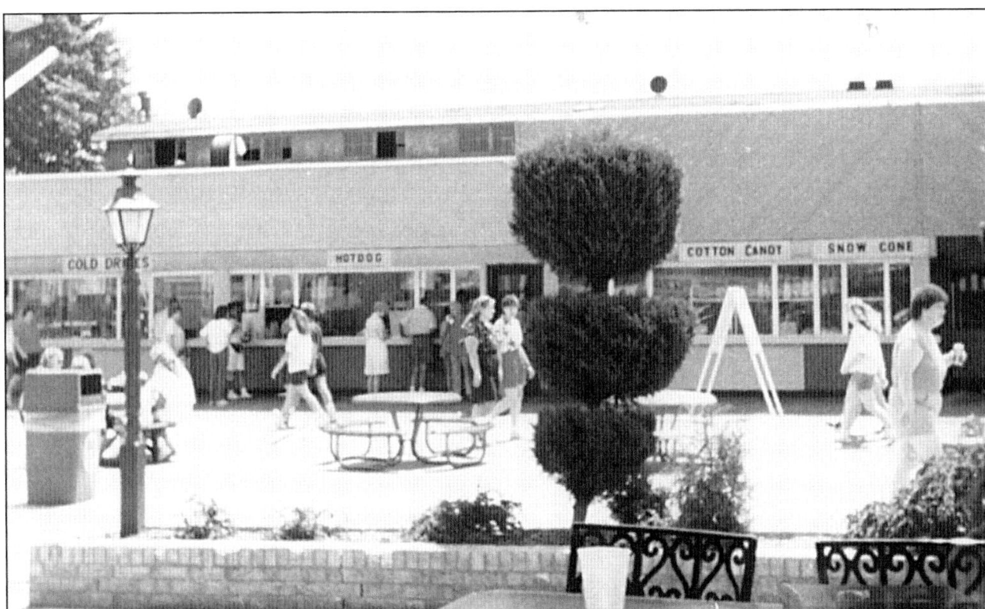

On January 8, 1990, an electrical fire destroyed the bathhouse and the Stardust Gardens Ballroom and resulted in over $5 million in damage. This picture shows the front of the bathhouse as it looked from the midway. The bathhouse served as a locker room with food and games concessions along the perimeter, including a large arcade. During the winter months, the building was used for temporary and permanent storage of parts from rides and surplus equipment. (Author's collection.)

Within hours, the building crumbled to pieces as firefighters focused on keeping the fire from spreading to nearby structures and rides. Ride parts and cars from the Rock-o-Plane, Flying Scooter, Bumper Buggy, and two kiddie rides were also destroyed. Pictured here is a charred car from the Rock-o-Plane ride. (Courtesy of Wade Back.)

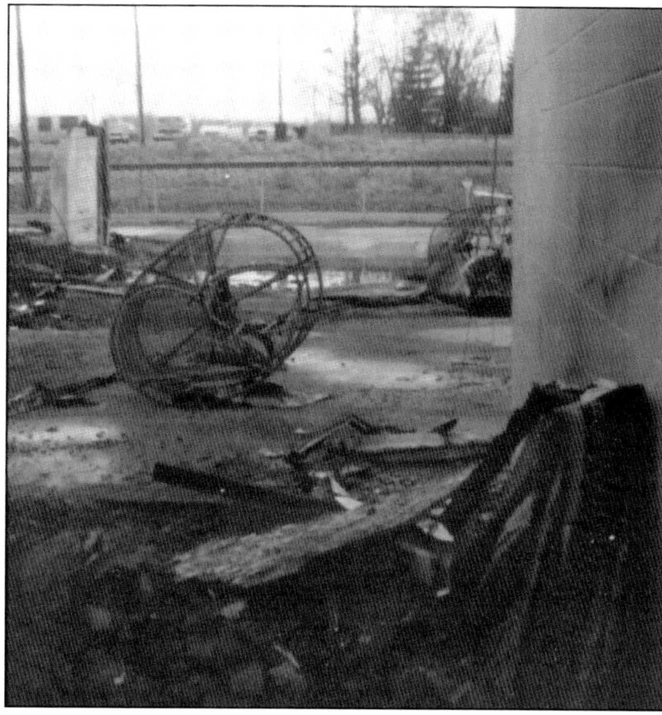

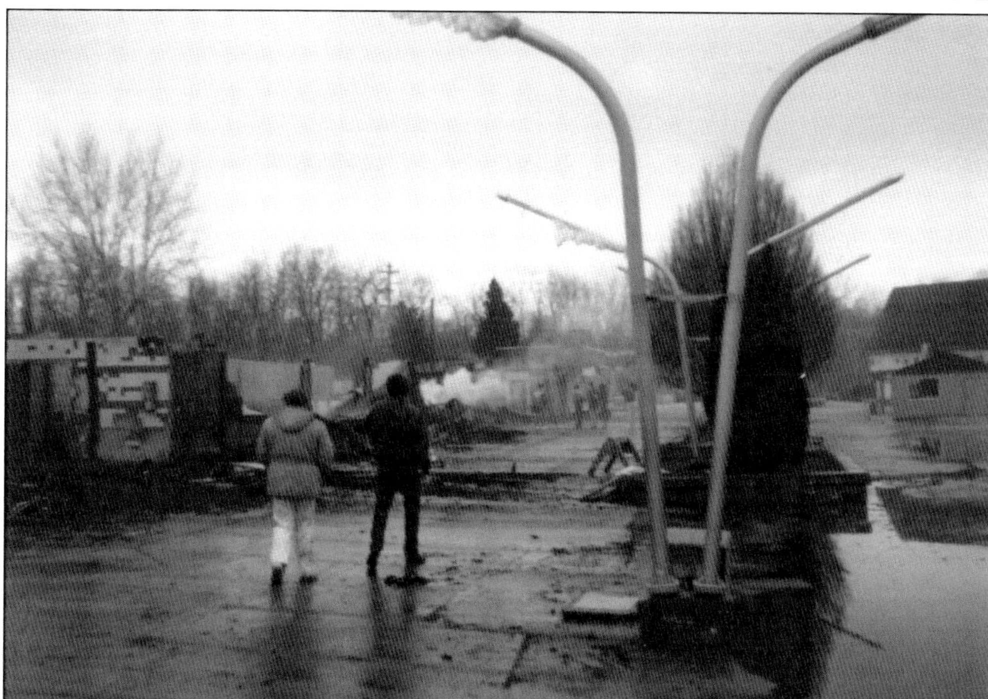

The fire started about 4:45 p.m. and was discovered by park employees. Witnesses at the scene said that smoke could be seen as far away as 15 miles. The fire was brought under control by four departments at 7:30 p.m. Park officials are seen here surveying what is left of the food concessions on the right. (Courtesy of Wade Back.)

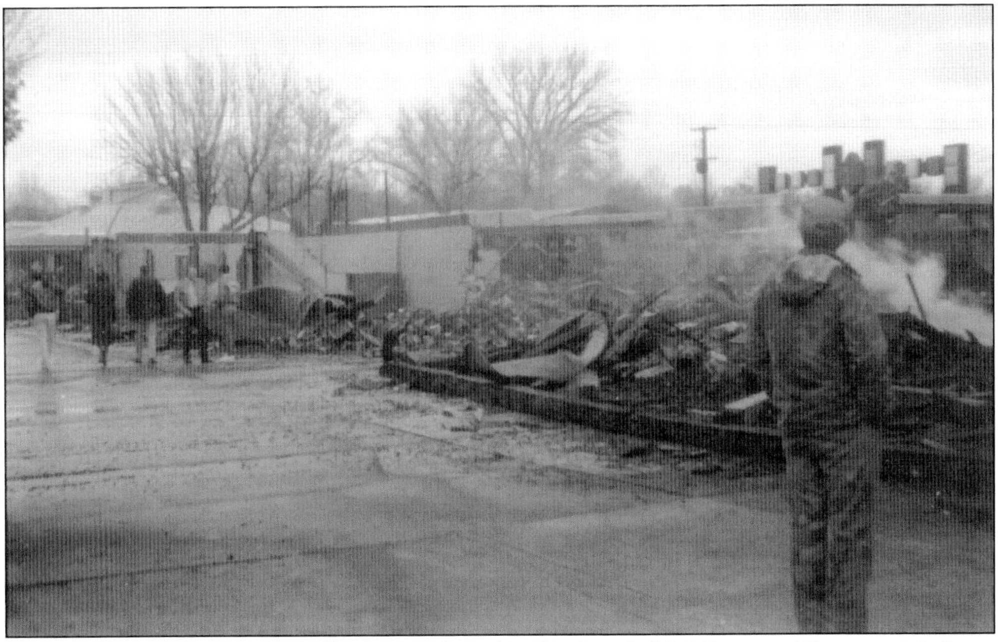

Fire departments from the village of LeSourdsville, South Middletown, Trenton, Madison Township, Liberty Township, Hunter, and Monroe assisted in fighting the blaze. The rear wall of the food concessions can be seen on the left, and an outline of a stairwell can be seen along the wall. (Courtesy of Wade Back.)

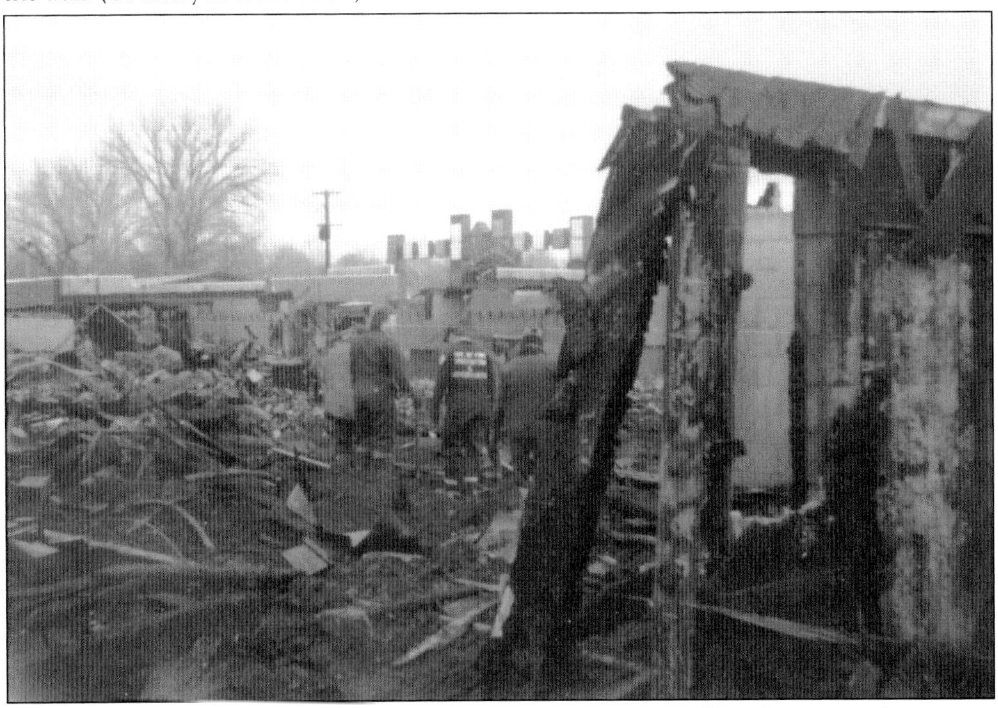

Officials from the Butler County Sheriff's Department Arson Squad, seen in this image, determined that the cause was faulty wiring under the Stardust Gardens Ballroom floor. (Courtesy of Wade Back.)

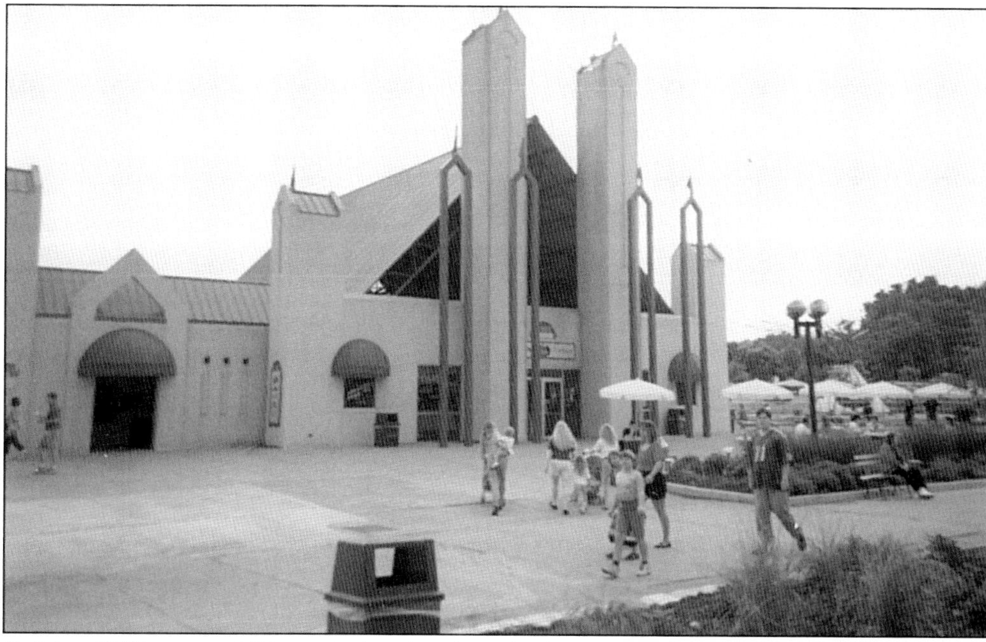

By May 1990, a new 300-seat indoor/outdoor food court, an arcade, a Dodgem ride, and a refurbished Flying Scooter ride reopened on the site of the fire. The park sold the Antique Car ride to Kentucky Kingdom in Louisville, Kentucky. (Courtesy of Alfred Freeman.)

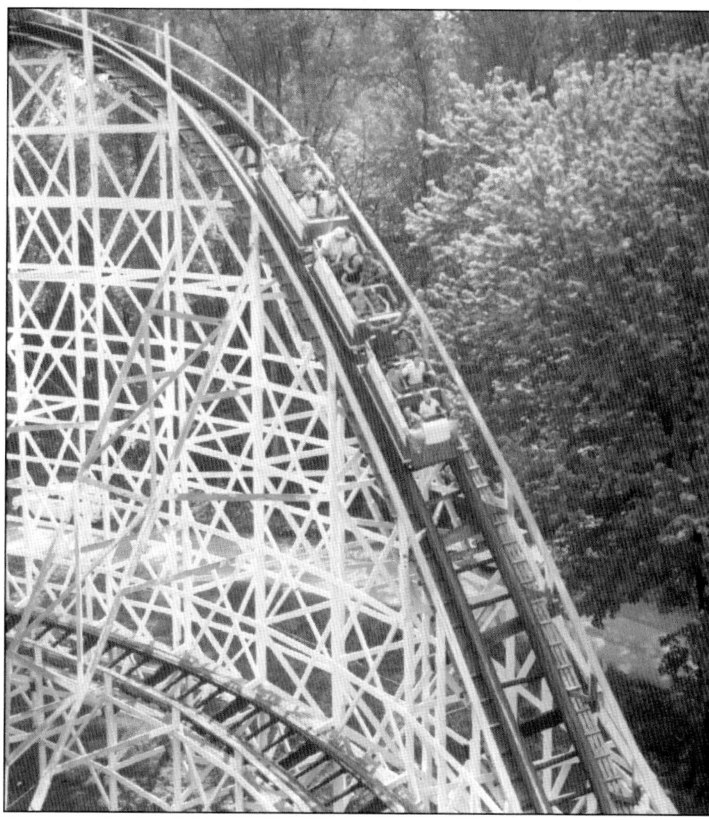

In July 1990, the American Coaster Enthusiasts named the Screechin' Eagle as a Coaster Classic. To be considered as a classic, a coaster car must have a genuine wood frame with padded seats, but it must not have dividers, headrests, or ratcheted lap bars.

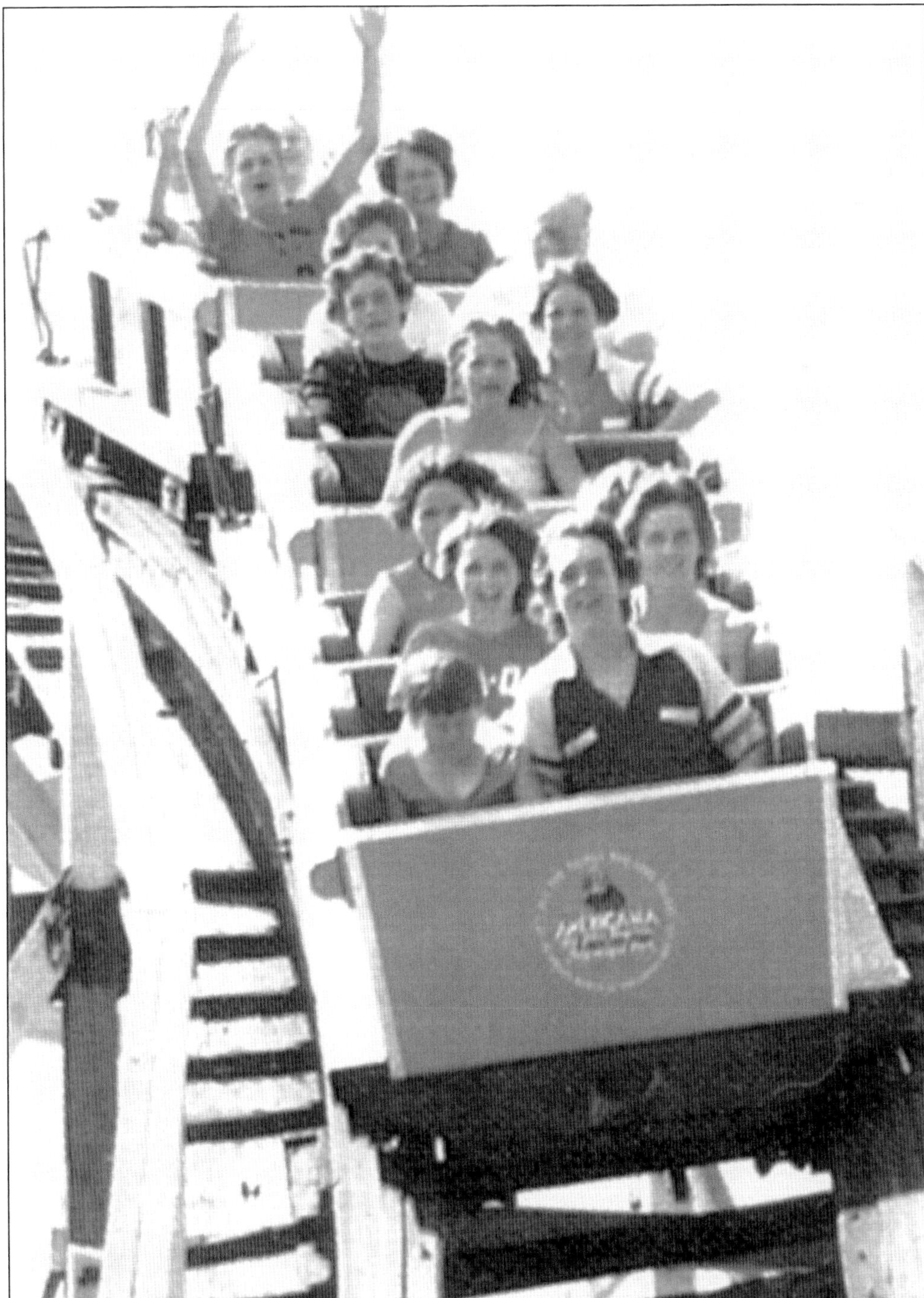

Despite overhauls over the years, the Screechin' Eagle maintained its honor because of its genuine wood frame, well-padded seats, and the lack of seat dividers, headrests, and ratcheted lap bars until 1996, when replacement cars came from the former Wildcat roller coaster at Elitch Gardens in Colorado.

Four

Disasters Take Their Toll

In 1991, the park was purchased by Leisure International, a group of former park managers consisting of Joe Faggionato, Guy Sutton, Lenny Gottstein, and Don Robison. In July, Sutton left to become the operations director at Clementon Lake in New Jersey. New attractions included two volleyball sand courts and an expanded picnic area. Elvis impersonator Rick Saucedo appeared at a Grease Weekend, featuring over 200 street rods and custom cars.

Over $6 million was spent to upgrade landscaping and infrastructure throughout the park. By 1995, it was apparent that a larger company would be needed to continue upgrading the park.

In 1996, Park River Corporation, owners of Cincinnati's Coney Island, purchased Americana for about $3 million. Over $1 million was spent on upgrading the Screechin' Eagle, new merchandising, and rides. In 1997, Park River owner Ronald Walker died unexpectedly and family members put Americana up for sale.

Hamilton camper sales dealer Jerry Couch purchased Americana in May 2000. Plans called for a year-round facility with Halloween and Christmas activities, a campground, and the opening of Couch's Campers Superstore.

In 2002, the LeSourdsville Group, a collection of former carnival operators, was hired to manage the park. The name of the park was changed to the Great American Amusement Park at LeSourdsville Lake.

When the park opened on June 5, the name of the park was changed back to LeSourdsville Lake. A park spokesperson stated that the name change was done because "that's how people remember it." The name was actually changed because of a threat of legal action by the Great American Financial Company.

The park closed a week prior to what was scheduled, and Couch announced that a new company was needed to operate the park. The LeSourdsville Group filed for bankruptcy. Due to the heavy financial loss Couch encountered, he decided to concentrate on expanding his camper sales business.

In 2006, an auction was held and most of the rides were sold. To date, the park remains vacant. In 2010, it was featured in a segment on the short-lived television series *Life After People*, where a detailed description of the neglect of the park was highlighted.

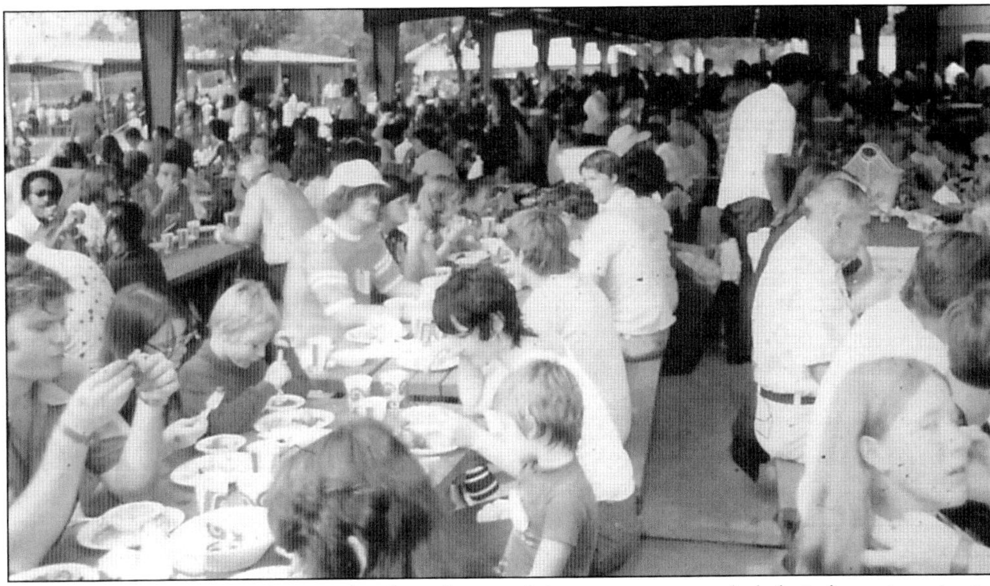

In the midst of serving thousands of meals, area labor unions canceled their lucrative picnics at the park due to media coverage of the park's Mexican student exchange program. Over 25 bilingual students from the Mexican American Institute of Cultural Relations began working at the park to help the void of filling 400 seasonal positions. Within weeks, the workers began complaining about unfair working conditions and poor living accommodations in the park's new dorm building. By the end of the season, attendance reached an all-time low of just under 200,000. The park then learned that its insurance company would only pay $3 million in claims towards the fire damage, leaving the park to pick up the remaining expenses. In December, the park filed for Chapter 11 bankruptcy. (Courtesy of Bill Robinson/WHR Inc.)

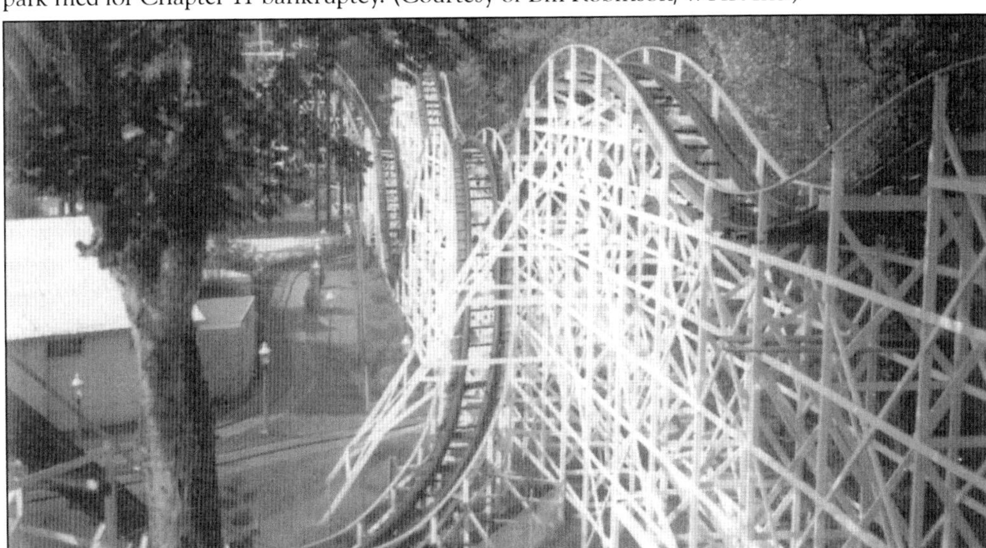

In 1992, the Screechin' Eagle roller coaster was the scene of yet another media event. Jeff Pike, a 14-year-old from Dixie Heights, Kentucky, became a celebrity when he rode the coaster for 70 hours to help raise money for his high school band. Today, Pike is vice president of sales and design for Great Coasters International, a firm dedicated to designing, constructing, and refurbishing roller coasters. (Courtesy of Alfred Freeman.)

A dramatic rescue took place in August 1993 on the Sky Ride after it stopped abruptly and left riders stranded above the lake. Middletown Fire Department rescue specialist Drexel Blevins directed a nighttime rescue of the 14 riders. Mr. Blevins was given a commendation for his efforts by the Butler County Sheriff's Office.

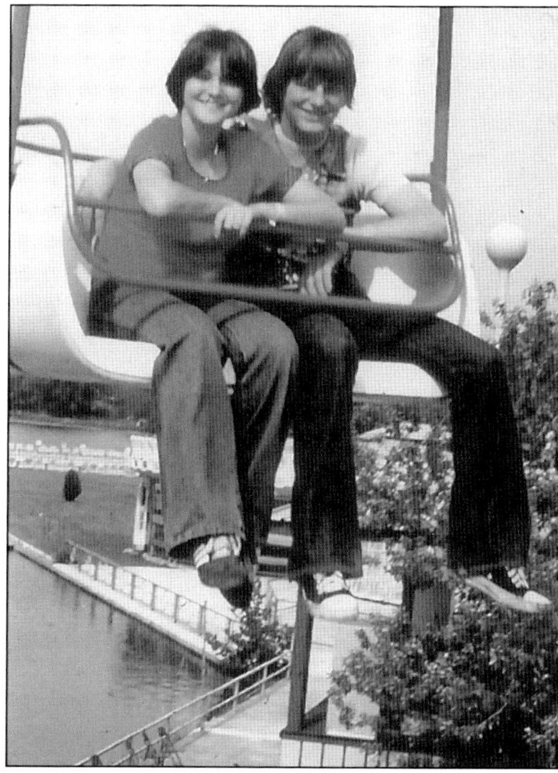

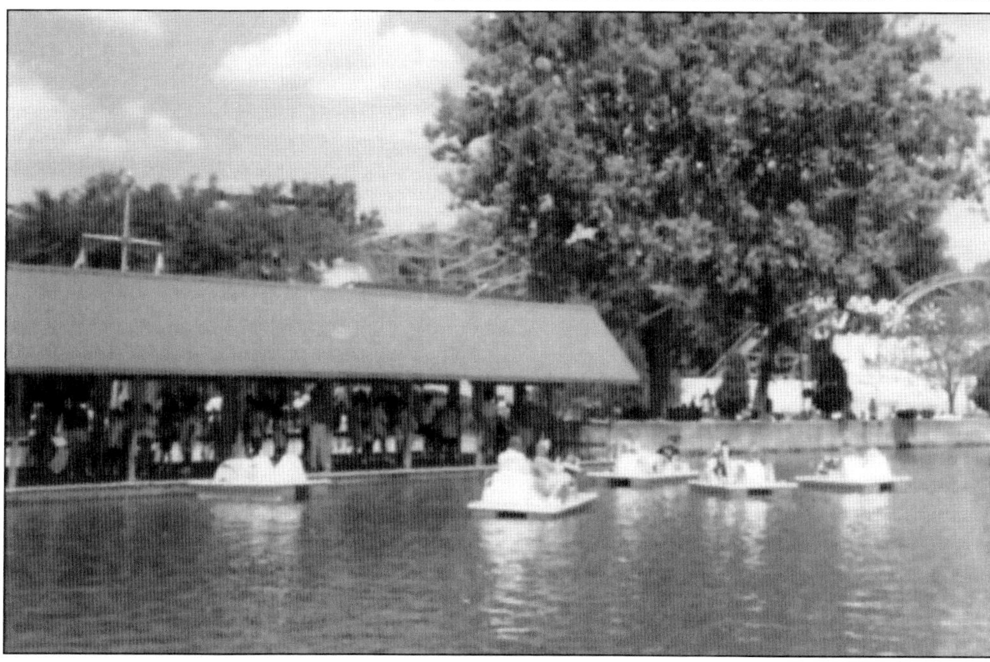

After the park replaced the motorboats with manual pedal boats, enthusiasm in using the lake did not diminish. The motorboats were replaced due to the high gasoline usage and the engine noise, which did not allow for an enjoyable trip. The pedal boats remained in use through the 2002 season. (Author's collection.)

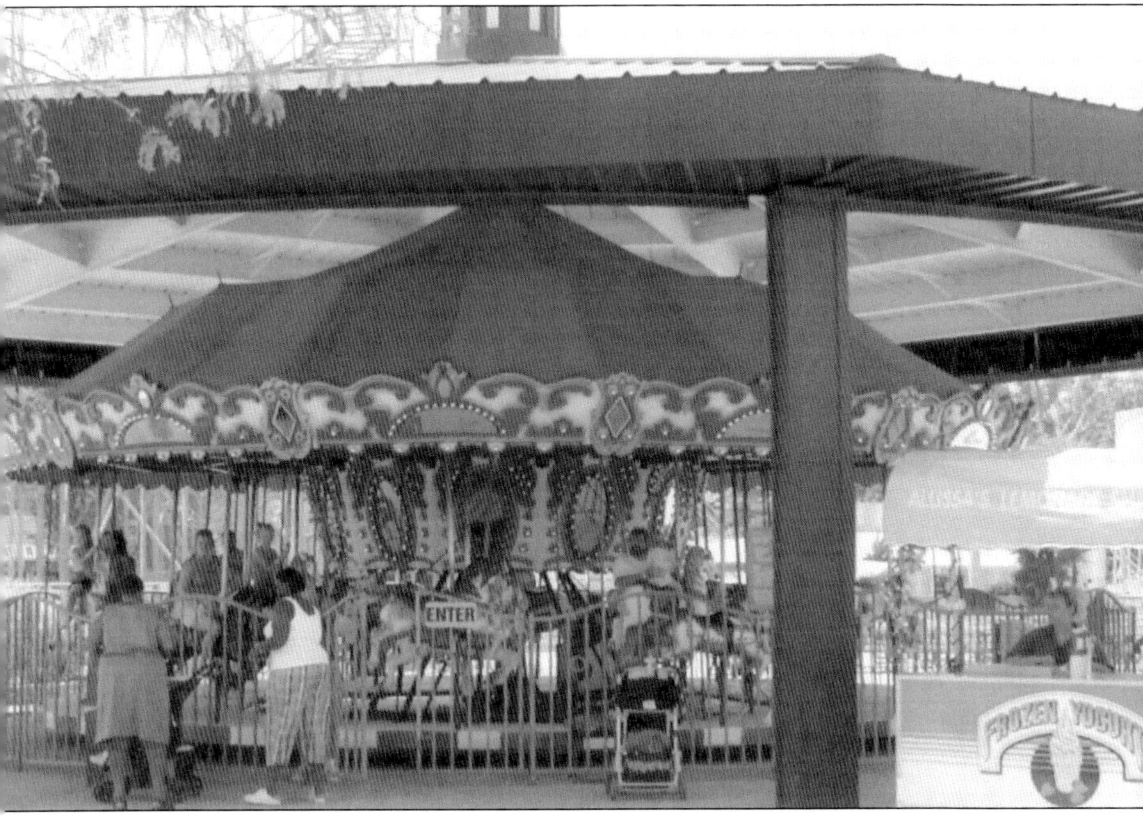

Under new ownership in 1996, the Park River Corporation added entertainment with Broadway and country revues, as well as magic and puppet shows, new food vendors such as LaRosa's Pizza and Skyline Chili, and a new carousel. They also painted walls, poles, and benches with a new color scheme of teal, tan, and magenta. Attendance at the end of the year was approximately just under 200,000, compared to 412,500 in 1994, according to park estimates.

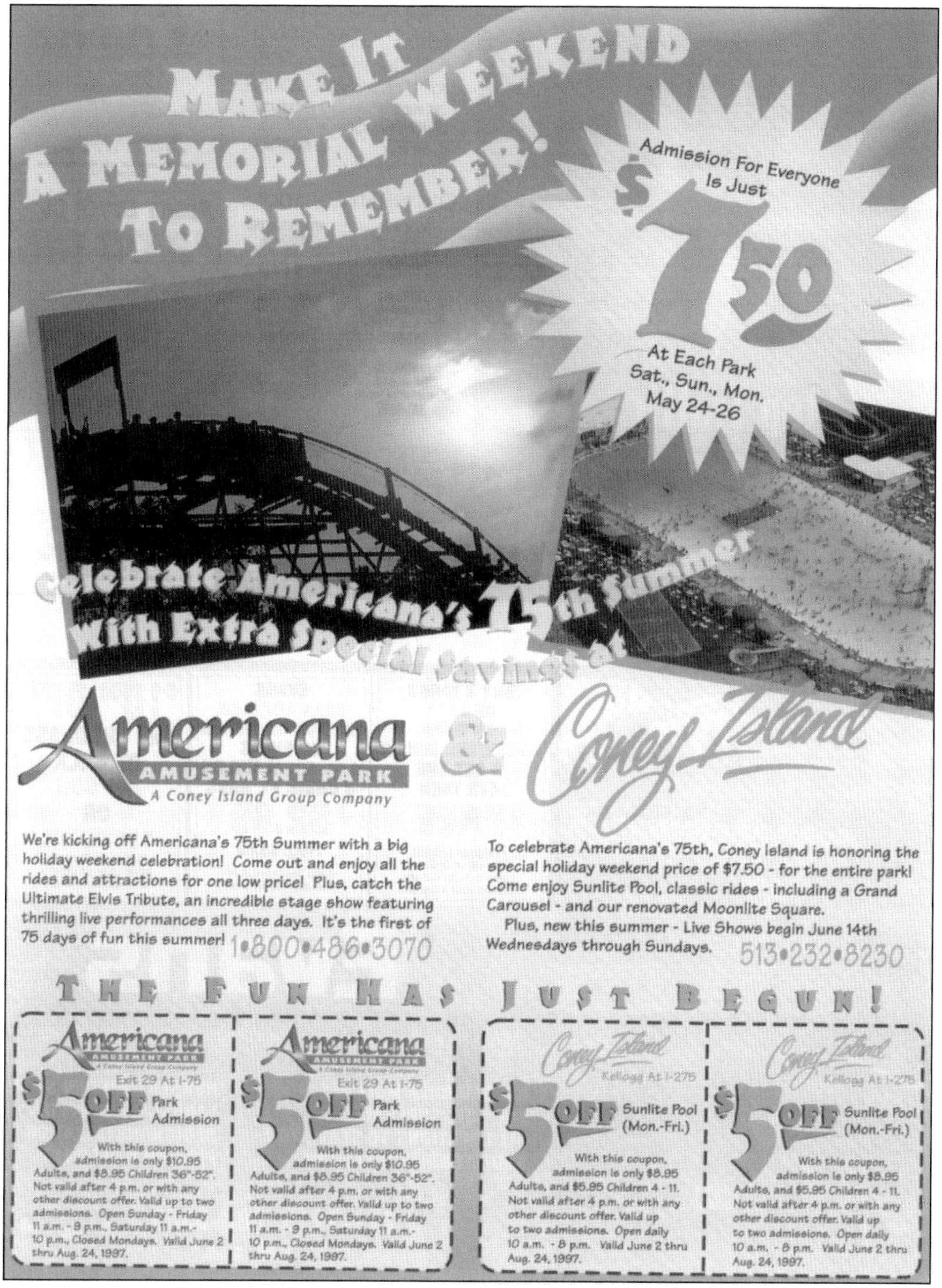

Park River's purchase of Americana permitted the company to promote two parks in one advertisement. This flyer also utilized the park's new paint scheme. The combined marketing effort, however, did not have much effect on either park's attendance record. (Author's collection.)

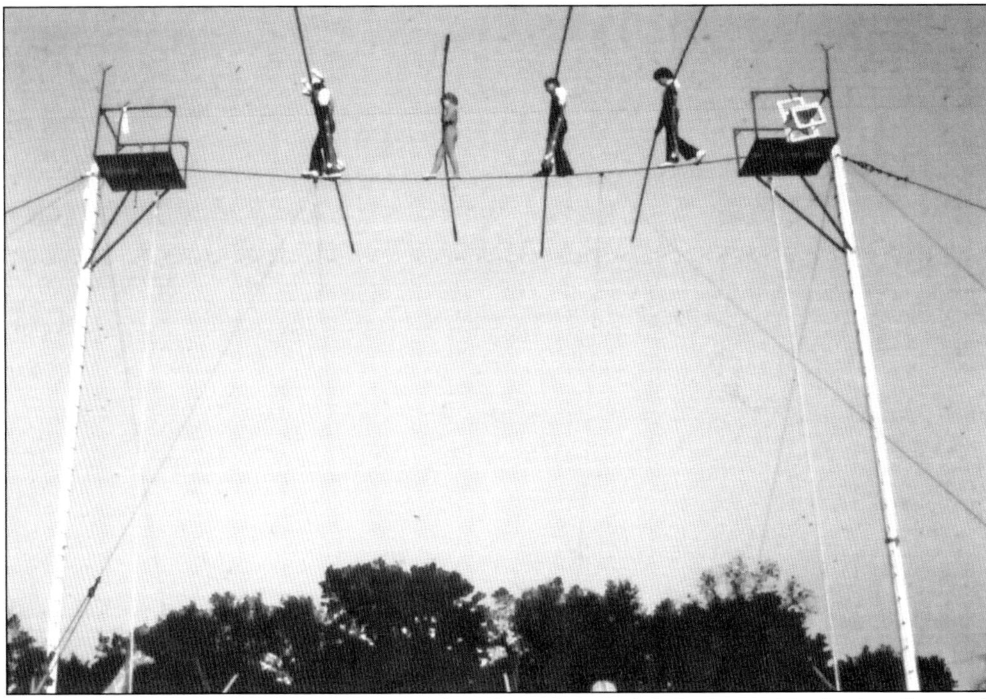

The Great Wallendas returned in 1997 and performed several daily shows. (Author's collection.)

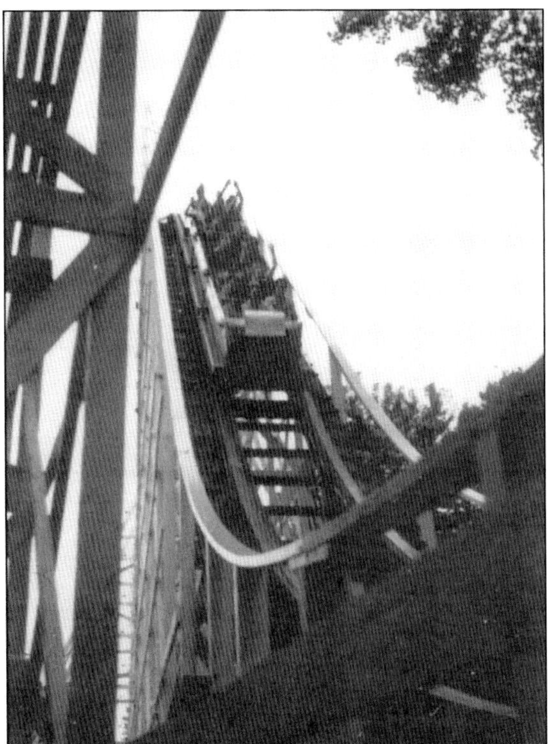

In June 1997, Y96.5 radio personality Wild Bill Cody embarked on a 96-hour roller coaster marathon on the Screechin' Eagle to help raise over $10,000 for the Make-A-Wish Foundation. (Courtesy of Alfred Freeman.)

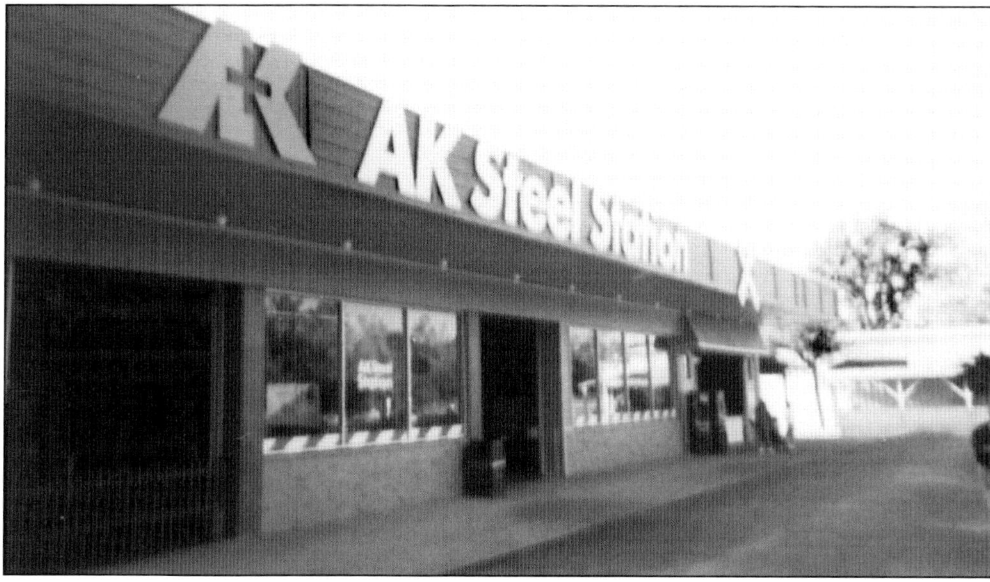

Dayton Dean Perkins brought his special selection of animals with him in 1998 to the AK Steel Building. Named after Middletown's largest employer, the building originally housed games of chance. Later, a miniature train exhibit promoting safety around railroad crossings was featured. The park also opened a new children's section near the pool called the Lagoon Water Play Area during 1998. New rides included a Ferris wheel purchased from Old Indiana (minus from the midway since 1973) and the Tempest. The Americana Museum and Souvenir Shop opened, thanks to contributions from Donna Dazey Switzer and Mike Long. The return of the cowboy fights in Tombstone returned with a show called *Fusin, Fighting and Feuding.*

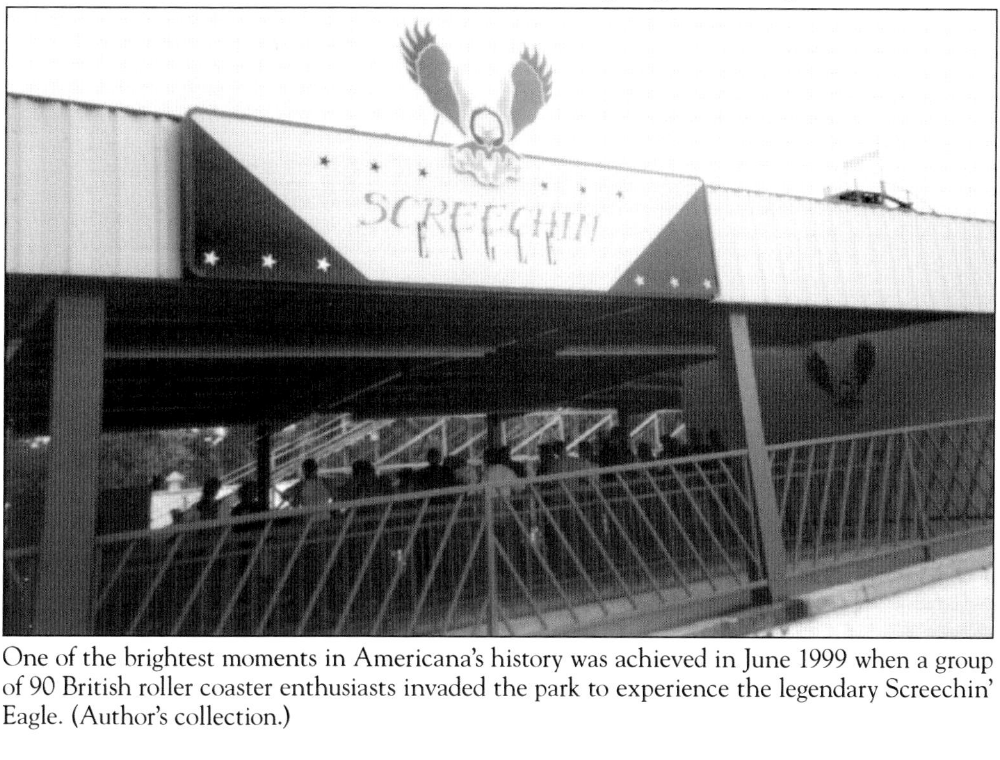

One of the brightest moments in Americana's history was achieved in June 1999 when a group of 90 British roller coaster enthusiasts invaded the park to experience the legendary Screechin' Eagle. (Author's collection.)

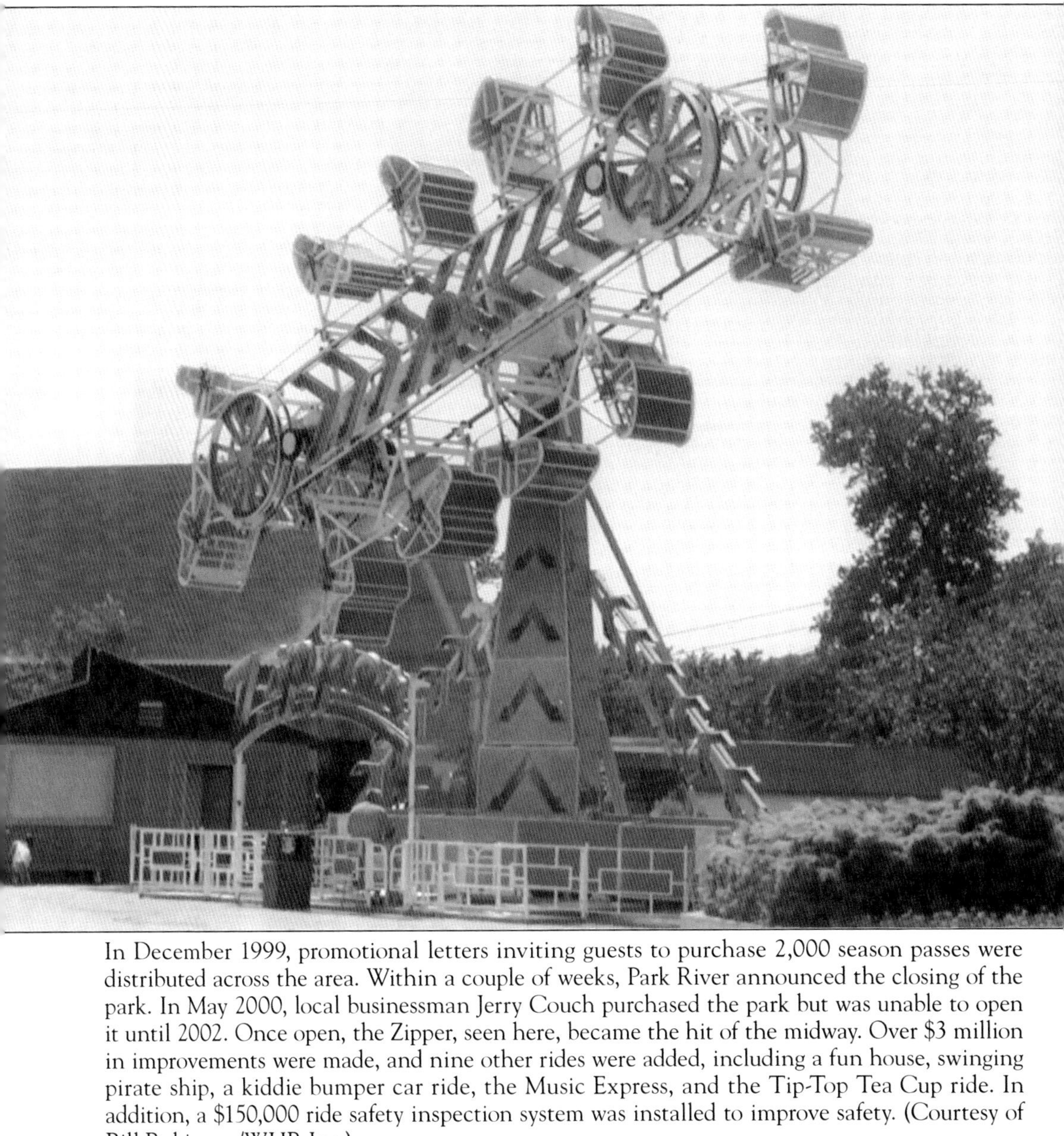

In December 1999, promotional letters inviting guests to purchase 2,000 season passes were distributed across the area. Within a couple of weeks, Park River announced the closing of the park. In May 2000, local businessman Jerry Couch purchased the park but was unable to open it until 2002. Once open, the Zipper, seen here, became the hit of the midway. Over $3 million in improvements were made, and nine other rides were added, including a fun house, swinging pirate ship, a kiddie bumper car ride, the Music Express, and the Tip-Top Tea Cup ride. In addition, a $150,000 ride safety inspection system was installed to improve safety. (Courtesy of Bill Robinson/WHR Inc.)

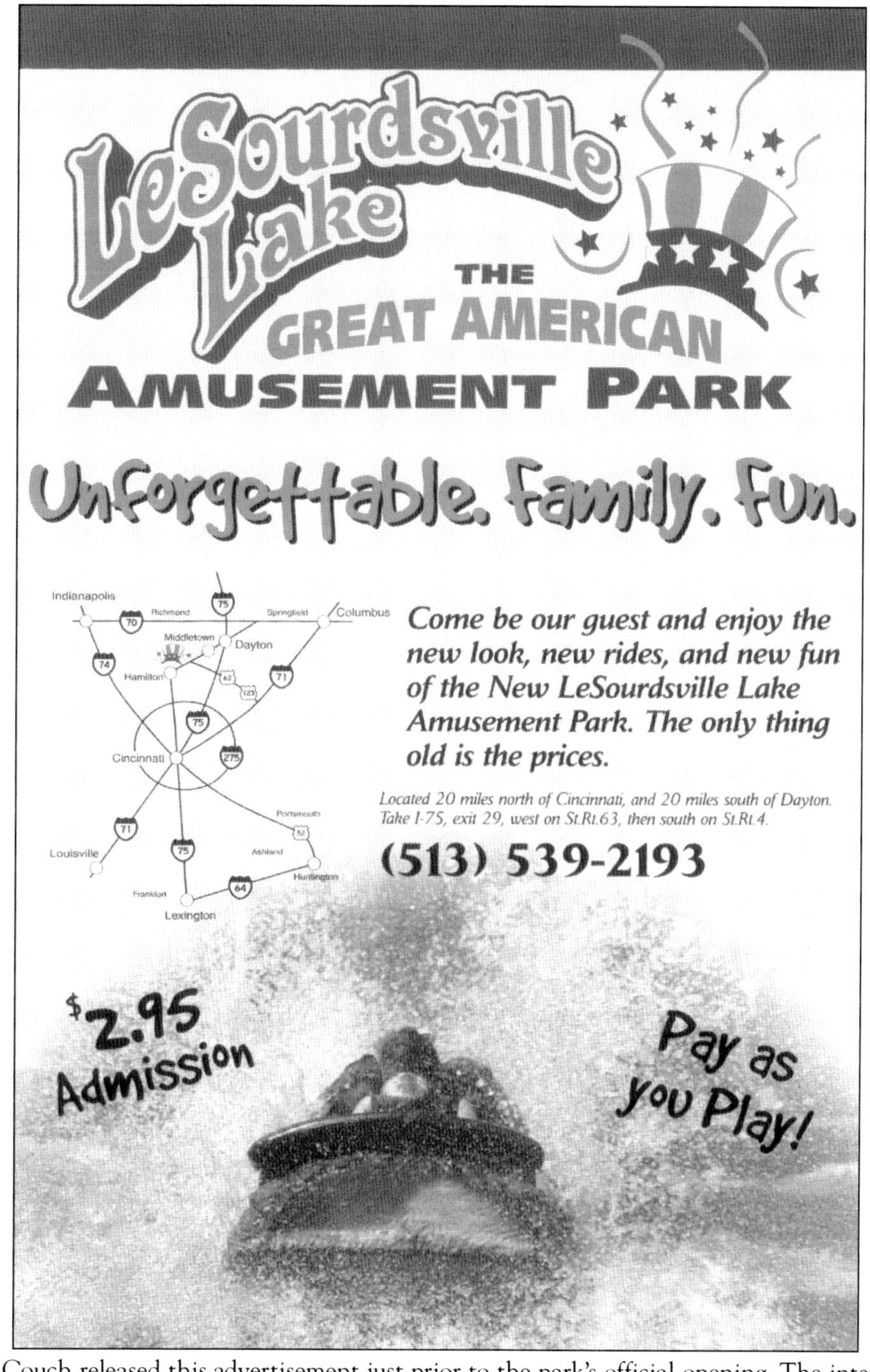

Jerry Couch released this advertisement just prior to the park's official opening. The intention was to use the park's old marketing tag of "the Great American Amusement Park," which had been used in the late 1970s. Unfortunately, the Great American Financial Group (which had part ownership of Cincinnati's Coney Island) took exception to the tag since it made the perception that their organization was affiliated with Americana. Couch quickly dropped the tag and changed the name of park back to LeSourdsville Lake.

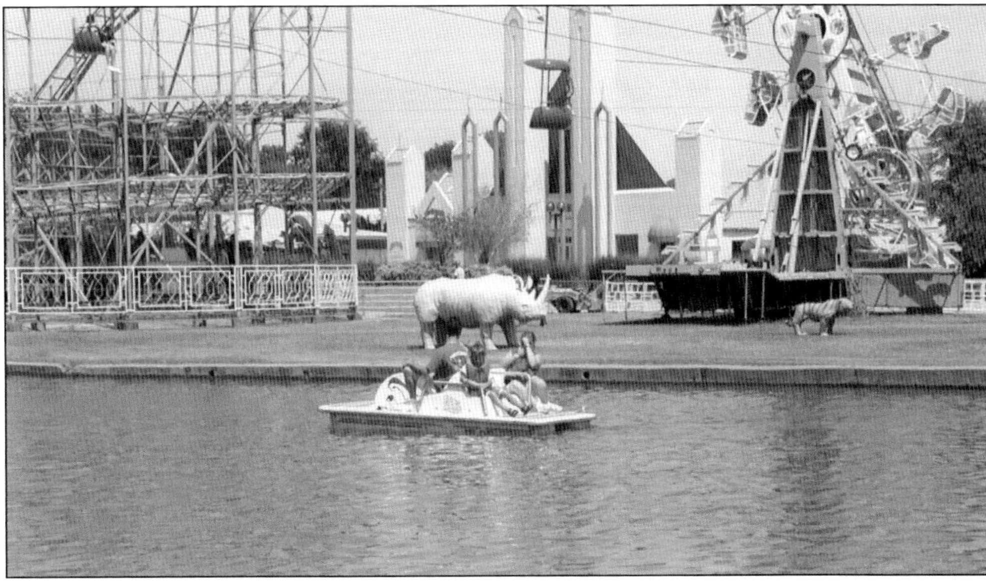

The Kevin Miller family of Springfield, Ohio, is seen taking advantage of the low admission to spend some time on the pedal boats in what would turn out to be the park's final season. Miller has maintained a connection with LeSourdsville Lake and Fantasy Farm; he restored several Streifthau turnpike cars over the years and has established his own memorial to both parks on his farm. (Courtesy of Kevin Miller.)

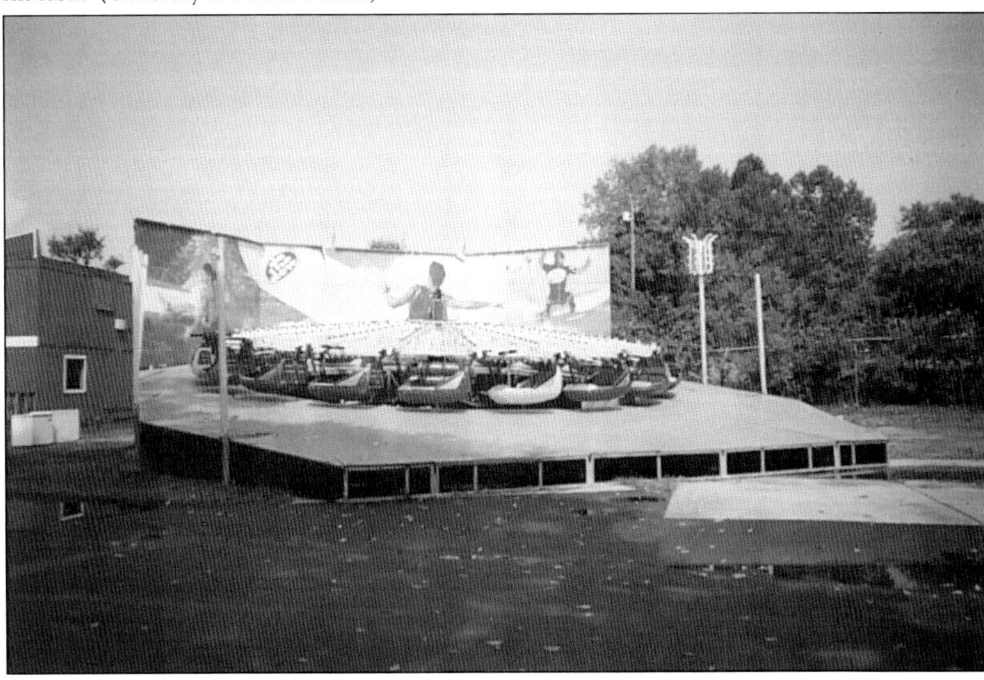

The Sky Surfer was purchased in August and partially installed. The ride was crowned with the distinction that it was the only ride in the park that never operated. Due to the abrupt closing toward the end of the 2002 season, plans for the upcoming "LeScaresville Lake—a Halloween fright event" were cancelled. Although Couch searched for a compatible company, the park was never opened back up to the public. (Author's collection.)

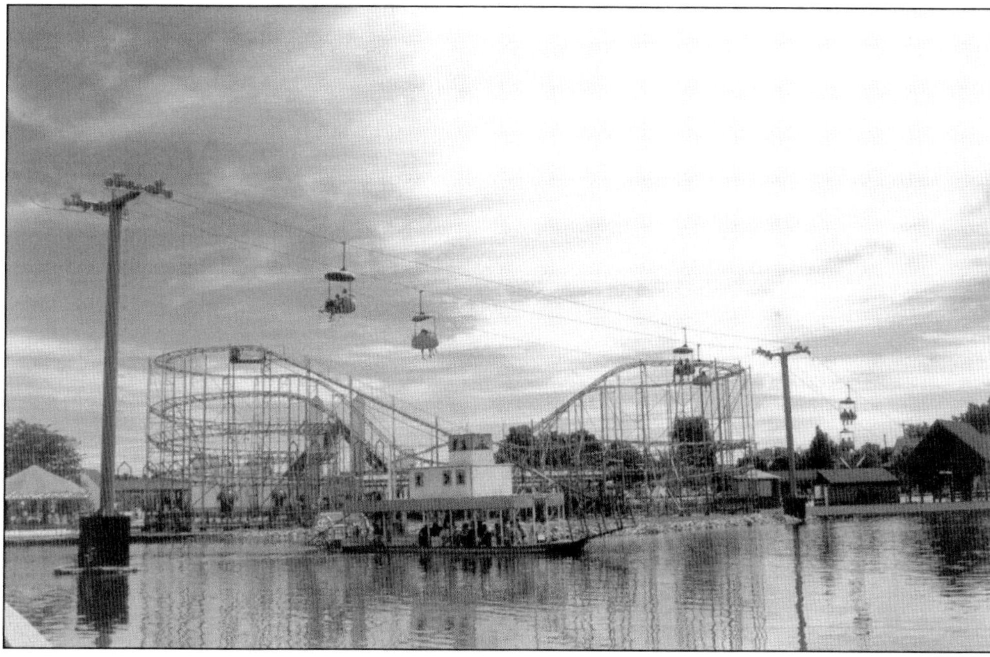

In 2007, the Serpent roller coaster was sold to Kokomo's Family Fun Center, located in Saginaw, Michigan. In 2006, almost all of the rides were advertised for sale.

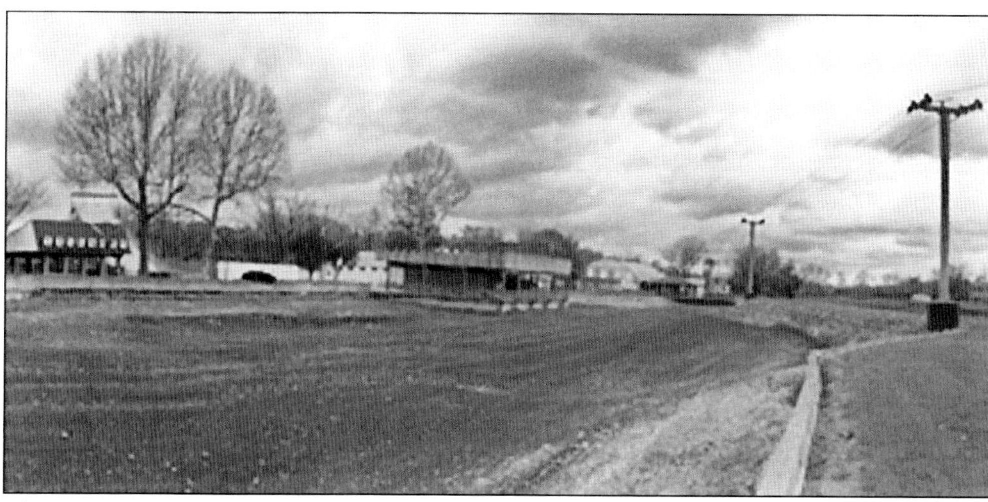

The lake was drained permanently in 2007, much like it was in the late 1800s when the ice manufacturing business closed and the land became a farm. (Courtesy of Ronny Salerno.)

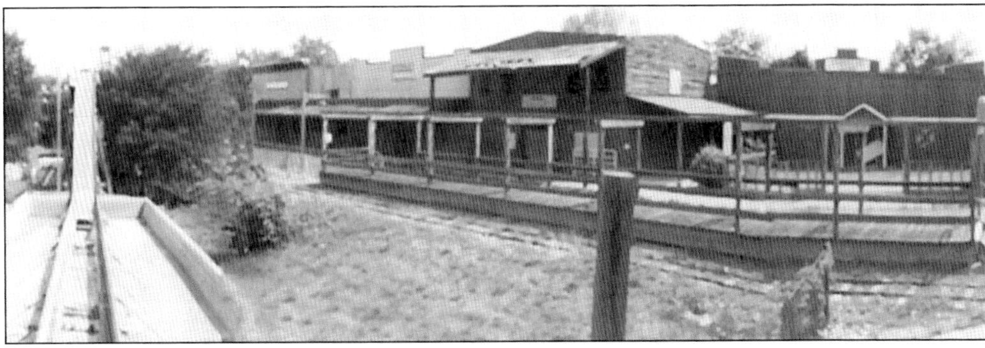

Some of buildings across the park have deteriorated thanks to Mother Nature and neglect. Pictured here are the buildings in the Tombstone Territory and Logger's Run midway with padlocks on the doors and the windows boarded up. A portion of the log flume is shown on the left. (Courtesy of Ronny Salerno.)

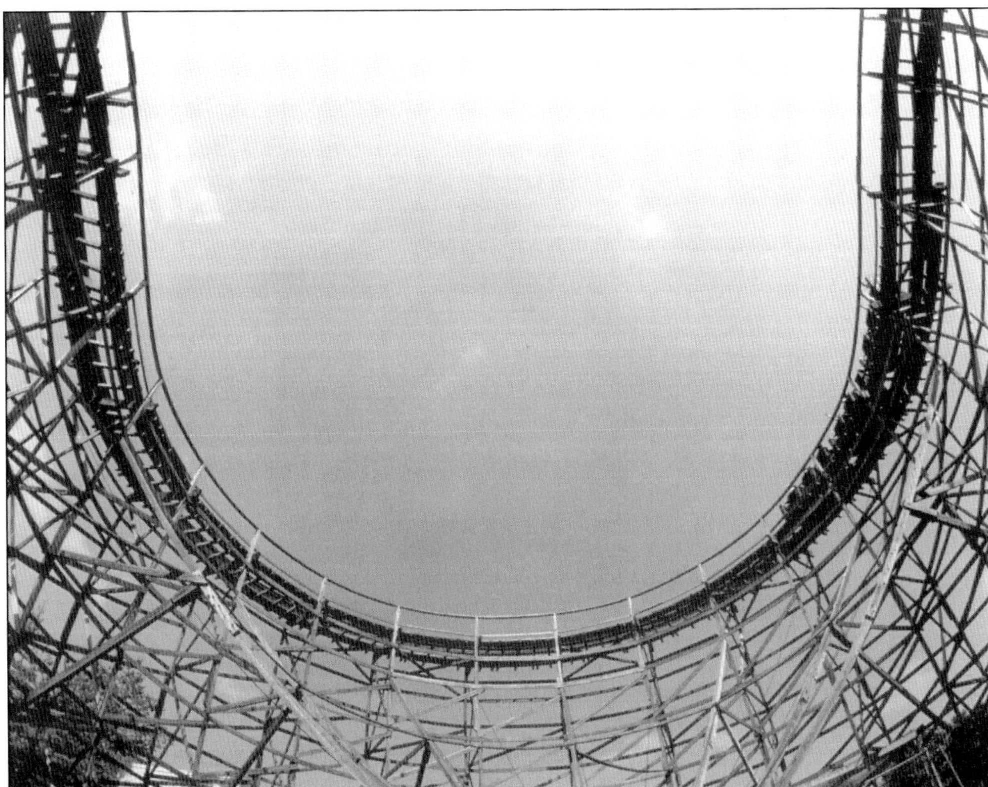

The Screechin' Eagle still awaits a brave new owner willing to rebuild this classic coaster somewhere else. Like the buildings that surround the coaster, it too is slowly deteriorating but still standing as of 2011. (Courtesy of Tom Rhein.)

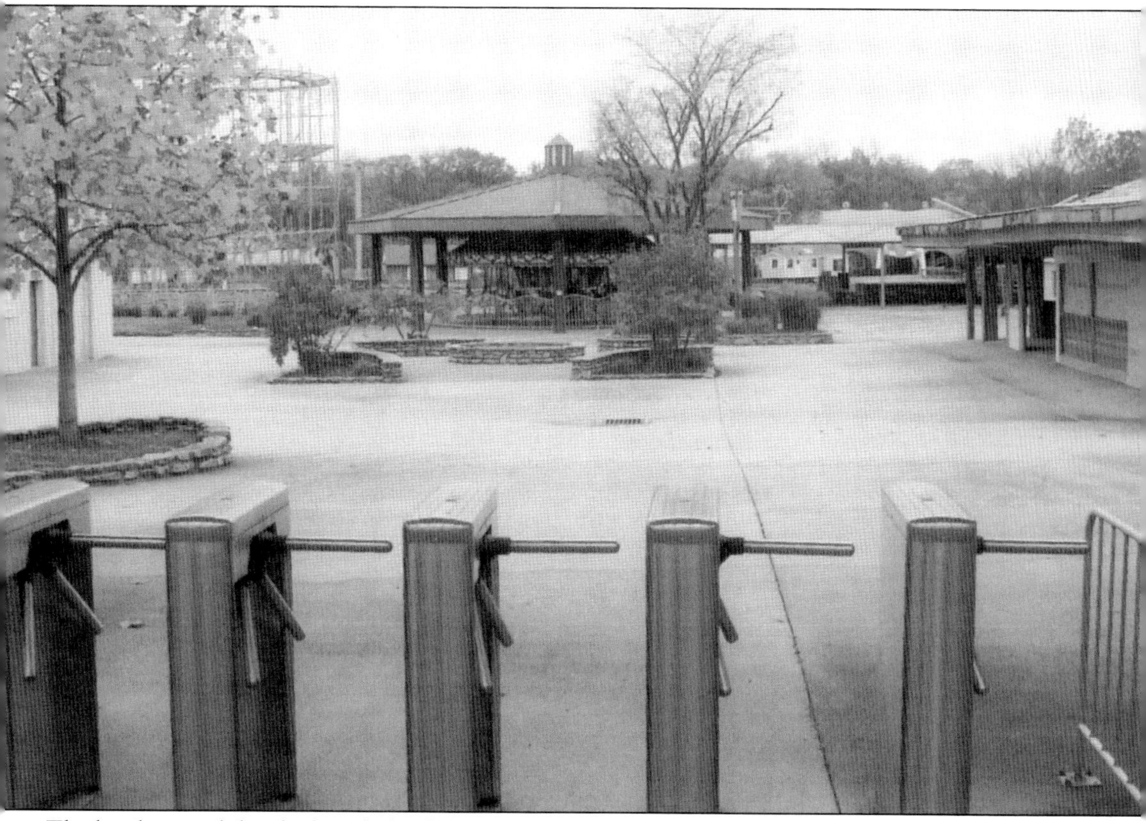

The laughter and shrieks from kids of all ages are gone now. Buildings stand lonely and no longer embrace the laughter from old and young alike. The aroma of fried chicken and cotton candy is lost. The quiet turnstiles yearn for yet another click of someone coming through to enjoy a sunny day at LeSourdsville Lake. Some people claim that if you walk the midway today, you can sometimes see an image resembling Edgar Streifthau picking up items from the ground, hear the call of "all rides closed" from the deep, distinctive voice of Howard Berni, or find a piece of memorabilia on a counter that was undoubtedly left by Bill Barr. That piece of wood that was hanging loose from one of the buildings and flapping in the wind—it was somehow magically fixed and Don Dazey probably had something to do with it. We will always have our favorite memories of the people, attractions, and events that left LeSourdsville Lake with a place in our heart. Now, go share a story about the park with the family. (Courtesy of Kevin Miller.)